Homes of the Presidents

Text and captions by Bill Harris
Designed by Philip Clucas
Photography by Ric Pattison
Produced by David Gibbon and Gerald Hughes

1494 Homes of the Presidents
This edition published in 1997 by CLB
Distributed in the U.S.A. by BHB International, Inc.
30 Edison Drive, Wayne, New Jersey 07470

ISBN 1-85833-756-9
Printed and bound in China

The Publishers wish to record their appreciation of and thanks for the kind and ready assistance given to them in the preparation of this book by the following people, their colleagues and staff, and the authorities they represent: Mr John Kinnaird and Ms. Jula J. Kinnaird of the Mount Vernon Ladies Association; Ms. Wilhelmina Harris, Superintendent, and Ms. Marianne Peak, Management Assistant, at the Adams National Historic Site, Quincy, Mass.; Mr. Matthew V. Gaffney, Director of Public Affairs at Monticello, and its owners, the Thomas Jefferson Memorial Foundation, Inc.; Mr. Carl Melson of the National Trust for Historic Preservation, and Ms. Dorothy Twitchell at Montpelier; Ms. Carolyn Holmes, Director, and Ms. Kay Batey Brown, Administrative Assistant, at Ash Lawn; Mrs. Edith Thornton of the Ladies' Hermitage Association; Mr. Bruce Stewart and Mr. George D. Berndt, Chief of Interpretation at the Martin Van Buren National Historic Site; Mrs. Charles Hamke, Curator, and the Francis Vigo Chapter of the Daughters of the Revolution, owners, of Grouseland; Mrs. Harrison Ruffin Tyler, owner of Sherwood Forest Plantation; Mr. John Holtzapple, Director of the James K. Polk Memorial Association; Dr. and Mrs. William C. Gist, owners of Springfields; the Aurora Historical Society and Mr. Edward Godfrey at the Millard Fillmore House Museum: the President of the Hillsboro Trust, and staff at the Pierce Homestead; Ms. Sally Smith Cahalan, Director of the James Buchanan Foundation for the Preservation of Wheatland; Mr. Jim Kretschmann and Mr. Gary V. Talley, Chief of Interpretation at the Abraham Lincoln Birthplace; Mr. Norman D. Hellmers, Superintendent, and Mr. Jerry Sanders, Chief of Interpretation, at the Lincoln Boyhood National Memorial; Mr. Richard Lusardi at the Lincoln Home National Historic Site; Mr. David A. McCormack, Chief Ranger at the Andrew Johnson Historic Site; Mr. Daniel Ellison, Executive Director at the Mordecai Historic Park; Mr. Thomas A. Campbell Jr., Superintendent of the Ulysses S. Grant Home Historic Site; Mr. Leslie H. Fishel Jr., Director of the Rutherford B. Hayes Presidential Center, and its owners, the Hayes Foundation; Ms. Dale Maughans, Curator, and the Western Reserve Historical Society, owners, of Lawnfield; Mr. John Dumville, Director of the Vermont Division for Historic Preservation, owners of the Chester A. Arthur Birthplace and the Plymouth Notch Historic District; Ms. Sharon Sarrell, Caretaker of the Grover Cleveland Birthplace; Ms. Dorothy Sallee, Director, and her assistant Miss Sue Small, for the Arthur Jordan Foundation, owners of the Benjamin Harrison House; Dr. Richard E. Werstler, Executive Director of the McKinley Museum of History, Science and Industry; Ms. Loretta L. Schmidt, Superintendent of Sagamore Hill; Ms. Ella S. Rayburn, Historian and acting Superintendent of the Taft Birthplace; Ms. Katharine L. Brown, Executive Director, and her administrative assistant Ms. Janet Campbell, at the Woodrow Wilson Birthplace Foundation; Mr. Herbert S. Gary, Curator, and the Ohio Historical Society, owners, of the Harding Home; Mr. Kurt Topham and Mr. Malcom J. Berg, Superintendent, at the Herbert Hoover National Historic Site; Mr. Duane Pearson, Superintendent of Springwood; Ms. Rita Embry, Administrator, and the Missouri Department of Natural Resources Division of Parks and Historic Preservation, owners, of the Harry S. Truman Birthplace State Historic Site; Mr. John E. Wickman, Director, and the National Archives and Records Administration, owners, of the Eisenhower Center; Mr. Stephen Whitesell, Superintendent, and Laurie Joslin, Site Supervisor, of the John F. Kennedy National Historic Site; Mr. Harry O'Bryant, Superintendent of the birthplace and boyhood home of Lyndon Baines Johnson; Mrs. Lady Bird Johnson, owner of the Texas White House, and her assistant Ms. Betty Tilson; Ms. Ardie Halverson at the Chamber of Commerce, and the Nixon Birthplace Foundation at Yorba Linda, and Mr. David McAdam of the Yorba Linda Star, and the Nixon Museum and Library; Mr. James Paxon, President of the Ford Birthplace Garden, and Mr. Kenneth G. Hafeli, Audiovisual Archives Technician with the Gerald R. Ford Library at Ann Arbor, Michigan; Mr. and Mrs. T.R. Downer, owners of the Carter Boyhood Home; Ms. Helen Cruse, Director of the Ronald Reagan Home Preservation Foundation; Mr and Mrs Mark Particelli, owners of 15 Grove Lane, Greenwich, Connecticut; The White House, the Arkansas Department of Parks and Tourism.

Special thanks to the United States Department of the Interior, National Park Service for permissions and co-operation as owners of the following sites: Adams National Historic Site, John Quincy Adams Birthplace, Martin Van Buren National Historic Site, Abraham Lincoln Birthplace, Andrew Johnson Historic Site, Mordecai Historic Park, Sagamore Hill, the Taft Birthplace in Cincinnati, the Herbert Hoover National Historic Site, Springwood, the J.F.K. National Historic Site, the Lyndon Baines Johnson Birthplace and Boyhood Home. Also to the Library of Congress, and the National Portrait Gallery, Smithsonian Institution, for permission to reproduce presidential portraits.

Homes of the Presidents

Text by

Bill Harris

Designed by Philip Clucas

CLB

Contents

Page 1: the Woodrow Wilson Birthplace, The Manse, at Staunton, VA.
Page 3: Thomas Jefferson's Monticello at Charlottesville, VA. The home shown on these pages is the Franklin Roosevelt Home, Springwood, in Hyde Park, NY.

INTRODUCTION

Long before he had any thoughts in that direction, someone told Warren G. Harding that he'd make a "dandy-looking president." Every four years, and it sometimes seems during all the years between, we read in our newspapers about men, and occasionally women, who are looking very "presidential."

But what does it take? Is there some common denominator shared by all the men who have taken the oath of office as president of the United States? The answer is, simply, no!

President Harding did, indeed, have a certain air about him. His voice was inspiring, his appearance made matinee idols jealous. His successor, Calvin Coolidge, was famous for never saying anything, and his personality inspired Dorothy Parker to say, when told that he had died, "How can they tell?"

According to a belief many Americans hold dear, most of the early presidents rose to greatness from humble, log-cabin births. The fact is, only seven first saw the light of day through the chinks in a log wall. Many more than that were born in mansions, including William Henry Harrison, who ran his campaign on the story that he had been born in a log cabin, in spite of the fact it was really a 16-room plantation house in Tidewater, Virginia.

Harrison notwithstanding, it was Lincoln who gave us our fondness for presidents born in houses with dirt floors. Lincoln himself mentioned it many times, but it wasn't until he had been dead for 30 years that anyone went looking for the original structure. A New Yorker bought the original Lincoln farm in 1894 with the idea of making a shrine, and possibly a little profit, from it. But when he went down to Kentucky to see what he had bought, there was no log cabin. Some people in the neighborhood found one for him in the woods nearby and told him it had been made from logs that were in the original cabin Thomas Lincoln had abandoned when he moved his family to a new farm. The story was plausible, and the entrepreneur had already invested all that money in a piece of land he considered useless except as a tourist attraction. So he had the cabin dismantled and moved to what could have been its original site.

Automobiles hadn't been invented and the world didn't exactly beat a path to the Lincoln Birthplace, so the cabin was dismantled and taken to Nashville for the city's centennial celebration. When the party was over, it was taken apart again and shipped off to New York for storage. In 1901, it was reassembled at the Pan-American Exposition in Buffalo. Then it was knocked down and put back into storage. It stayed out of sight, and out of mind, until 1906 when the Lincoln farm was sold and the cabin went along as part of the deal. The new owners built a marble structure to house the once again reassembled cabin on what everyone agrees is its original site. But is it really the original? Even Lincoln himself couldn't tell you.

It wasn't the first presidential home to be restored and open to the public. That honor, appropriately, belongs to Mount Vernon, the home of the first president, George Washington, which became a shrine in 1858.

Some presidents have more than one home open for viewing. John Adams and his son, John Quincy Adams, each have a birthplace still standing, but they share a common adult home. Lincoln, in addition to the log cabin birthplace, has two boyhood homes on display as well as his family home in Springfield, Illinois. Andrew Johnson has two homes in Tennessee and a birthplace in Raleigh, North Carolina. Theodore Roosevelt is another with a restored birthplace and a separate home, as are Woodrow Wilson, Harry Truman, Lyndon Johnson and Ronald Reagan.

On the other hand, three of the presidents have no home at all. William McKinley's Niles, Ohio, birthplace burned down several years ago and his boyhood home, ironically, was torn down to make way for a fire house. Gerald Ford's birthplace in Omaha, Nebraska, was also destroyed in a fire, but the Ford family home in Grand Rapids, Michigan, will eventually be restored. Richard Nixon's birthplace in Yorba Linda, California, will also eventually be restored and open to the public.

Some presidents considered themselves lucky to have homes to go to after they left the White House. Both Thomas Jefferson and his neighbor James Monroe left the presidency deep in debt. The same thing happened to William Henry Harrison and Ulysses S. Grant. In Jefferson's case, a public lottery was suggested, though never instituted, to bail him out. It wasn't until 1958 that any provision was made for pensions for ex-presidents. Up until that time they were cut adrift and on their own.

Compensation these days makes the job seem almost worth it. The president's annual salary is $200,000, subject to tax, plus a $50,000 nontaxable expense allowance and up to $100,000 for travel, and an additional $20,000 for entertainment. The lifetime pension of a former president is $69,630 a year plus free postage and office space, and $96,000 for office help. Their widows are entitled to a $20,000 annual pension. George Bush and Gerald Ford earn more in retirement than Jimmy Carter or Ronal Reagan because they had accumulated points towards retirement benefits during their previous service in the Federal Government.

But before you begin cultivating your own presidential look, consider what some of the previous occupants of the White House had to say about the job.

After he retired and became Chief Justice of the Supreme Court, William Howard Taft said, "In my present life I don't remember that I ever was president." Benjamin Harrison said, "There has never been an hour since I left the White House that I have felt a wish to return to it." Harry Truman said, "Being president is like riding a tiger. A man has to keep riding or be swallowed." Thomas Jefferson who wrote the inscription for his own tombstone and purposely neglected to mention that he had ever been president, once said, "Never did a prisoner released from his chains ever feel such relief as I shall on shaking off the shackles of power." William McKinley said, "I have had all the honor that there is in this place, and have responsibilities enough to kill any man." And on the subject of honor, Abraham Lincoln had this to say: "I'm like the man who was tarred and feathered and ridden out of town on a rail. When they asked him how he felt about it, he said that if it weren't for the honor of the thing he would rather have walked."

And, finally, think of the Civil War General William Tecumseh Sherman. When he was asked to run for the presidency, he said, "If forced to choose between the penitentiary and the White House, I would say, 'The penitentiary, thank you!'." He later formalized his resolve by telling them, "If nominated, I will not accept. If elected, I will not serve." And he looked as presidential as anybody.

The North Room in Theodore Roosevelt's Sagamore Hill at Oyster Bay, NY, is filled with memories of his adventures.

James A. Garfield conducted his presidential campaign from the porch of his house in Mentor, OH.

On the other hand, looking at the office from the other side of the Atlantic, an English statesman once characterized the American presidency as "the greatest object of ambition in the whole world." And he was absolutely right. Except for the occasional Sherman, there isn't an American in public life who hasn't somewhere, some time, said, "I can do that!" There is hardly a parent who hasn't looked at a newborn baby and said, "Some day, president of the United States."

And why not? It's possible. The only qualifications are spelled out in Article II of the Constitution, which says: "No person except a natural born citizen, or a citizen of the United States at the time of the adoption of this Constitution, shall be eligible to the office of President; neither shall any person be eligible to that office who shall not have attained to the age of thirty-five years, and been fourteen years a resident of the United States." It doesn't even say the president has to be a man.

The 41 men who have held the office add up to a fascinating cross-section of the American people. Four of the first six presidents were born in Virginia, the other two in Massachusetts. Both states have kept on contributing presidents. Massachusetts has produced three, but Virginia kept up the pace and has the largest number of presidential birthplaces with eight. Ohio, whose first native son in the presidency was the 18th, Ulysses S. Grant, has produced seven presidents. The homes associated with them run the gamut from simple farmhouses to lavish country estates, from Southern plantations to log cabins. But the one house all but one of them have in common is that at 1600 Pennsylvania Avenue in Washington, D.C., which was known as "President's House," from the day John and Abigail Adams moved there in 1800 until Theodore Roosevelt had the name "White House" engraved on his official stationery in 1901.

When the Adamses moved there, the house was far from finished, but Abigail managed to get it into shape for the first formal reception on New Year's Day in 1801. Thomas Jefferson followed the custom, but instituted a couple of new ones. For one thing, he began shaking hands with his guests rather than bowing to them as his two predecessors had done. He also began inviting ordinary citizens to mingle with the diplomats and other officials.

Midway through James Madison's term, British troops burned the White House, forcing him to move out. But he and Dolley were there long enough to be first to serve ice cream at their dinner parties. James Monroe moved back into the house in time to see his daughter married in the first President's House wedding.

The building was first considered complete during Andrew Jackson's administration, but his successor, Martin Van Buren, was faced with a redecorating job after the rough-and-tumble Jackson days. Jackson had kept his thoroughbred horses on the lawn, but Van Buren had stables built and began to formalize the landscaping. He earned the gratitude of his successors by also having central heating installed.

Millard Fillmore added a library and a few years later Franklin Pierce gave the house its first real bathroom, tub and all. Every president, including the only bachelor, James Buchanan, had the place redecorated to suit his own, or his wife's, tastes. But the most extensive redecoration was done during the Grant administration, in a style his supporters called "elegant," and his detractors called "gaudy."

Rutherford Hayes was the first president to have a telephone in the Executive Office. His successor, James Garfield, took modernity a step further by giving the house its first elevator.

But modern or not, when Chester A. Arthur became president in 1881, he refused to move into the President's House until it was completely redecorated. In the process he had what amounted to a garage sale, disposing of 24 wagon-loads of furnishings and knick-knacks left behind by his predecessors. Eight years later, Caroline Harrison, wife of Benjamin Harrison, had plans drawn up to enlarge the house, but Congress wouldn't give her the money. She used money they would give her to have electric lights installed and to exterminate the rats, which even Congress had to admit had become a problem.

It took a man like Theodore Roosevelt to get the White House enlarged. His redecoration resulted in the sale of 28 wagon-loads of left-over furniture and knick-knacks. He also added a press room and strengthened the building by adding steel beams.

William Howard Taft, though most often remembered for adding an oversized bathtub to the White House collection, was the man who doubled the West Wing and created the Oval Office. As the first president to use an automobile, he changed the stables into garages. Calvin Coolidge, a man who really did enjoy his privacy, added a third floor to the house to make the living areas more private from the public sections of the mansion.

Franklin Roosevelt added a swimming pool, a bomb shelter and an office area for the First Lady. He also rebuilt both the East and West Wings.

And after all that, when Harry Truman moved in and asked for a second floor porch over the portico, workmen discovered that the whole building was structurally unsound. The entire building was gutted and rebuilt from the inside out, following as much as possible the original designer's intentions. In the 1960s, the Kennedys renovated the house again, following the advice of a special Fine Arts Commission, whose responsibility was to redecorate the interior to reflect the lives and personalities of the presidents who had lived there before.

The personalities of the individual presidents and their families are preserved in their own houses. In addition there are ten presidential libraries, and the Bush Library at College Station, Texas, will be added soon. The list includes the Hoover Library at West Branch, Iowa, the Roosevelt Library at Hyde Park, New York, The Truman Library at Independence, Missouri, the Eisenhower Library at Abilene, Kansas, the Kennedy Library at Boston, Massachusetts, the Johnson Library at Austin, Texas, the Nixon Library at Yorba Linda, California, the Ford Library at Ann Arbor, Michigan, the Carter Library at Atlanta, Georgia, and the Reagan Library at Simi Valley, California.

The libraries and their homes are testimony that of the 41 men we have chosen to lead us, there is no one thing, except the office itself, that they have in common. Each has been a man of his time. George Washington's heart was in the land at Mount Vernon, Bill Clinton's is in the mountains of Arkansas. But both men are first in the hearts of their countrymen. It goes with the territory when you are President of the United States.

1

GEORGE WASHINGTON

(1732-1799)

Through his long career, George Washington was a great many things, but the role he himself enjoyed most was that of a farmer. "I think the life of a husbandman, of all others, is the most delectable," he wrote. "It is honorable, it is amusing, and with judicious management, it is profitable."

His major effort after the Revolutionary War was to get the new country moving by encouraging better land management, and as president he toured the country to spread the gospel of scientific farming. It was because of his tour that there are hundreds of places up and down the Eastern Seaboard that still boast: "George Washington slept here." But the place he slept his most contented sleep was his beloved Mount Vernon, on the bank of the Potomac River eight miles south of Alexandria, Virginia. "No estate in United America is more pleasantly situated than this," he wrote. And today the more than a million Americans who visit there each year share his enthusiasm.

Washington was born in a brick plantation house further down the river in Westmoreland County, but by then the place that would become Mount Vernon had already been owned by the Washington family for more than 40 years. By the time the future president was born, in fact, his father had bought the acreage up the river from his sister and moved his family there when the boy was three years old. They moved again four years later and the elder Washington deeded the property to his son Lawrence, who changed its name from Hunting Creek Plantation to Mount Vernon in honor of his friend Admiral Edward Vernon.

The National Portrait Gallery, Smithsonian Institution

Mount Vernon, on the banks of the Potomac River in Virginia, was enlarged by George Washington from a simple farmhouse, built by his father, over a period of 30 years. The Mansion is one of more than a dozen buildings on the estate. The portrait of the first president is by Rembrandt Peale.

The dining room, one of 14 rooms in the Mansion that are open to the public, contains authentic furnishings and color schemes of the period when George Washington and his family lived there. All the furniture and art objects in the Mansion have been collected through gifts, loans and purchases since preservation of the estate began in 1858.

Young George moved back to the plantation after his father died, and became its owner 11 years later, at the age of 22, when he bought the property from his half-brother's widow. At the time Washington was commander of the Virginia Militia and didn't become a full-time resident of Mount Vernon until his first "retirement" and his marriage to Martha Dandridge Custis in 1759.

The house he welcomed his bride into was almost double the size of the original that had been built by his father. He had literally raised the roof and inserted a second floor under it. The number of rooms was increased from four to eight, and all of them were redecorated with the finest materials imported from England.

Less than 15 years later, he began an even more ambitious expansion program, adding rooms on both sides and expanding the size of the outbuildings and gardens. In that era of architect-builders, much of the inspiration seems to have come from nearby Williamsburg, but there are touches of originality, particularly the loggia, which extends the full length of the mansion. It still ranks as one of the most wonderful front porches in all America.

But Washington didn't have much time to sit there and watch the construction going on around him. While the expansion was going on, he was made Commander-in-Chief of the Continental Army. Though work continued during the eight years he was away, it wasn't finished until 1787, when a weathervane in the form of a dove of peace was hoisted to the top of the cupola.

Two years later he answered his country's call again and went to New York to become its first president. For the next year the Washingtons lived on Manhattan's Cherry Street, in a Georgian-style building that eventually vanished to make way for the Brooklyn Bridge. They also lived in New York in a house on lower Broadway that was demolished in the name of progress not long after they moved to Philadelphia. During the half-dozen years they were there, they lived in a house, now destroyed, in the area that has become Independence Park. They also spent some of that time in a house that is now open to the public in Germantown, Pennsylvania.

But through it all, their hearts never left Mount Vernon. When he was asked to accept a third term as president in 1796, Washington instead chose to retire, and he and Martha went home again.

The house appears today exactly as it did when the first president died there on December 14, 1799. The original plantation covered more than 8000 acres, slightly less than half of which was under cultivation, and was divided into five farms. The 500-acre Mansion Farm is what remains today as part of our heritage.

It was bought from the Washington family by an organization known as the Mount Vernon Ladies' Association, founded in 1853 by Ann Pamela Cunningham. Miss Cunningham's group, America's first national historic association, first raised the funds to buy the mansion and 200 surrounding acres and then went right to work to restore the buildings to their 1799 appearance and to find the original furnishings, which had been scattered. They opened the plantation to the public in 1860, and since that time more than 50 million people have benefited from their efforts.

Over those years they were able to buy the additional 300 acres that make up the restored plantation, and thanks to the foresight of one of the Association's members the land on the Maryland shore across the Potomac has been preserved in its natural state. All of the restoration and research has been funded over the years by private donations, entrance fees and museum shop sales.

Everyone who visits there agrees that their work was well worth it. Most find it difficult to say which is their favorite among the 14 rooms in the mansion. All of them contain original furnishings, all offer an unequalled look at

life in 18th-century Virginia.

But the mansion is only part of the experience. There are more than a dozen outbuildings, including a kitchen and an office building connected to the mansion by covered walkways. There is also a museum that looks like the original buildings, but was added in 1928 to house a still-growing collection of memorabilia. Also on the grounds is the tomb containing the remains of General Washington and his wife and other members of the Washington family.

Mount Vernon was a working farm in every sense of the word in the 18th century. But traditionally, the land adjoining the mansion house was never used for field crops. Washington, like his neighbors, used that acreage for landscaping in the manner of English country houses. "Reclaiming and laying the grounds down handsomely to grass and in woods...is among my first objects and wishes," he said.

What he accomplished makes Mount Vernon a delight at any time of the year. The gardens and lawns are separated from the fields by low brick walls. The bowling green, extending from the mansion's west front, is framed with large trees, some of which were planted by Washington himself. Though the vista of the river and the opposite shore was left open, Washington was careful to enhance the prospect with trees, as he did on the north and south sides. There is a flower garden and a kitchen garden on each side of the bowling green. Each is filled with the same types of plantings Washington saw there, and the upper garden is a blaze of color from early spring, with annuals and perennials and with ornamental and flowering trees.

A European visitor said of it: "The whole plantation, the garden and the rest prove well that a man born with natural taste may guess a beauty without having ever seen its model. The General has never left America; but when one sees his house and home and his garden it seems as if he had copied the best samples of the grand old homesteads of England."

But for all that, Mount Vernon is indisputably American. And that is as it should be. It was the handiwork and the delight of the man they called the Father of His Country.

Mount Vernon is 16 miles south of Washington, D.C. and eight miles down the Potomac from Alexandria, Virginia, at the end of Mount Vernon Memorial Highway. It is open every day of the year, and from April through September it is the destination of some Washington Boat Line cruises.

Though a small admission charge is made to tour the plantation grounds and buildings, parking is free and plentiful. The spring and summer months are most popular with visitors, but fall and winter have their special charms, not least of which is the absence of crowds.

There are two other interesting homes in the area, both operated by the National Trust for Historic Preservation. The Pope-Leighy House is an example of a dream for the 20th century by Frank Lloyd Wright, and Woodlawn Plantation, built by George Washington's foster daughter and his nephew, who were given the land by the first president as a wedding present. The Frank Lloyd Wright house is open only on weekends from March through October, but the 19th-century mansion nearby is, like Mount Vernon, open all year.

Visitors to Mount Vernon should also plan to spend at least a day touring nearby Alexandria, which includes many memories of George Washington's day. It was also the hometown of George Mason and Robert E. Lee.

The Classic Elegance of the home of the first president was the result of his own planning, and is one of the best Georgian buildings anywhere in America. The estate, which once contained some 8,000 acres, is now 30 acres of walks, gardens and inspiring views across the Potomac River.

2

JOHN ADAMS
(1735-1826)

The Old House is what John Adams called this home in Quincy, MA, when he and Abigail moved there in 1788. It had been built in 1730 as the country home of a wealthy sugar planter from the Island of Jamaica. It was later formally named Peacefield, but to the Adams family it was always a comfortable old house. The second president eventually retired to the Quincy estate he once described as "but the farm of a patriot." He died, at age 90, in the wing chair in the corner of the study (facing page bottom) on July 4, 1826.

The John Adams portrait on this page is by Gilbert and Jane Stuart.

When John Adams was born on October 30, 1735, the town that welcomed him into the world was called Braintree, Massachusetts. By the time its name was changed to Quincy, in 1792, he was living in a suburb of New York City called Greenwich Village and he was the country's first vice president. He had married Abigail Smith of Weymouth 28 years before and had become the father of one daughter and three sons, one of whom, John Quincy Adams, would one day become the sixth president of the United States.

John Adams himself would move to Philadelphia five years later to become the nation's second president.

But his roots never left Braintree. By the time he married Abigail he had inherited the house next door to the one where he was born, and it was there that his second child, John Quincy Adams, was born. The family home, at 141 Franklin Street, didn't see much of John Adams in the years that followed. The young Harvard graduate established a law practice in Boston and over the next several years he lived in at least three different houses there. During the American Revolution he served on no less than 90 different committees of the Continental Congress, and when the war was over he was sent to Paris to help negotiate the peace treaty. With that accomplished, he was made American Minister to Britain and established a legation in London's Grosvenor Square. But, before taking on that assignment, he drafted the Massachusetts Constitution in an office in the house at 141 Franklin Street.

After nearly ten years abroad, both he and Abigail were thoroughly homesick and he negotiated from London to buy a two-bedroom house in Braintree that was known all over town as "the Borland place," for its owner, Leonard Vassall Borland, whose grandfather had built it in 1730.

Adams had a plan to become a Massachusetts farmer and to spend his days enjoying his neighbors and his family. He named his new home "Peacefield," partly in recognition of the dream but, just as importantly, in recognition of his own accomplishments at the peace table in Paris. Abigail completely approved of his plan and their trip back from England may well have provided the happiest moments of their lives. But dreams, even when they come true, often don't quite match the expectations of the dreamer.

The house they bought was a lot smaller than either of them had pictured in their minds. The ground floor had a paneled living room, an entry hall and a dining room. Though the previously-detached kitchen had been joined to the house, it gave small pleasure to poor Abigail, who took a look at the low ceilings and the tiny rooms and realized that the second floor, with just two bedrooms, wasn't much roomier. "It feels like a wren's house," she wrote to her daughter, who fortunately was married by then and wasn't likely to claim one of the rooms for herself. But she still had three sons at home, and the small rooms in the attic didn't seem nearly enough.

But 18th-century New Englanders like the Adamses never went in much for hand-wringing, and Abigail's hands over the next dozen years were busy making the house a home to be proud of. John Adams, meanwhile, found his dream of life as a country squire shattered when he became the first vice president a year after buying the Borland place. He had already begun calling the house "the Old House;" it was, after all, five years older than he was, but it was beginning to look very much like he wasn't going to have a chance to grow old there himself. As Washington's vice president for two terms, he was chosen by the electors, 71 to 68, over Thomas Jefferson to become president in 1797.

It would be four more years before John Adams could go back home to the Old House. Abigail had, meanwhile, taken charge of making it into something new and

The National Portrait Gallery, Smithsonian Institution

improved. She took on general repairs first, but quickly moved on to the expansion and remodeling of the farm building behind the house, which she converted into a library to house the huge number of books her husband had collected in their years abroad. Then she went to work on the house itself, adding a whole new wing with a new entry, a spacious "long room" and a wide hallway. The rooms above were just as spacious and the size of the house was about double what it had been when they bought it. It all came as a surprise to John Adams when he finally did go home in 1801 after having been defeated in his bid for a second term as president.

The surprise was made even greater by the fact that Abigail was at his side through all those years in New York, Philadelphia and, finally, the District of Columbia. She had been the first First Lady to move into the new White House in Washington and had won everyone's admiration for being able to cope with a building that had only six habitable, though unfinished, rooms. And every housewife in America agreed she did the right thing when she hung the family laundry in the East Room. Very few, in fact, didn't understand what it had been like to have to carry water in buckets a mile and a half to do the laundry in the first place. But what nobody understood, her husband included, was that Abigail Adams was an old hand at such things. She had been hard at work on the house in Quincy for a dozen years.

As soon as she went home from Washington, the Adamses seemed able to settle down in the Old House in exactly the same way they had dreamed life was going to be after they left London all those years before. But the former president didn't become a farmer as he had planned. And the life of an elder statesman didn't seem like enough of a challenge, either.

Eventually he did return to Quincy and the Old House, where he lived to the fine old age of 90. In his last years he entertained old friends, patched up broken friendships and enjoyed the well-deserved admiration of his neighbors.

The stone library (facing page) at Peacefield was built by Charles Francis Adams, the grandson of John Adams and son of John Quincy Adams, the sixth president, to house the books and papers (right) of the Adams family. Arranging them to be useful to scholars occupied him for more than 40 years.

He was probably the most brilliant of all the Founding Fathers, certainly the one with the best sense of the future. But, once in a while, his predictions about what was ahead for a united America went slightly off the mark. He was in Philadelphia with the Continental Congress when it voted to become independent from England. The evening after passage of the resolution, he wrote to his wife that: "The second day of July, 1776 will be the most memorable epoch in the history of America. I am apt to believe that it will be celebrated by succeeding generations as the great anniversary festival. It ought to be solemnized with pomp and parade, with shows, games, sports, bells, bonfires and illuminations from one end of this continent to the other, from this time forward forevermore."

He was off by two days, of course. The date we devote to pomp and parade and the rest is the date Congress adopted the Declaration of Independence rather than the date it accepted the idea.

July Fourth became a significant date for John Adams exactly 50 years after that momentous day in Philadelphia. On July 4, 1826, the former president was asked if he knew what day it was. "Oh yes," he said. "It is the glorious Fourth of July. God bless it!" With that, he lapsed into a coma and by the end of the day he was dead. Ironically, the man who had defeated him for a second term, Thomas Jefferson, had died in his own beloved home a few hours earlier.

The Adams family lived at Peacefield, at least part of each year, until 1927, during which time the study (above) was always an active place and the master bedroom (right) a quiet retreat through four generations.

The Adams National Historic Site is at 135 Adams Street in Quincy, Massachusetts, a few miles south of Boston at the Furnace Brook Parkway exit (8) on Route 93. Peacefield is open to visitors for a small admission charge between mid-April and mid-November. The house contains original furnishings and has been faithfully restored.

The John and John Quincy Adams birthplaces at 133 and 141 Franklin Street are open, with guided tours, between mid-April and mid-October. There is no admission charge.

All three buildings are administered by the National Park Service, U.S. Department of the Interior.

In the same area, the Quincy Homestead, at Hancock Street and Butler Road, features period furnishings from four generations of the Quincy family, beginning in 1686. The house is open April through October, daily except Monday.

Both John Adams and John Quincy Adams and their wives are interred in a crypt at the United First Parish Church on Hancock Street.

3

THOMAS JEFFERSON
(1743-1826)

Monticello (facing page), a gem from every angle, was the pride of its architect, Thomas Jefferson. He worked in his study (bottom left) in a reclining position to ease the pain of his rheumatism. The entrance hall (bottom right) was his museum, the country's largest private natural history collection.

Jefferson's portrait on this page is by Gilbert Stuart.

When Thomas Jefferson was 27 years old, his birthplace, a house called Shadwell in Goochland County, Virginia, was burned to the ground. When he was told of it, his first question was whether any of his books had been saved. The answer was no, but he was consoled by the fact that the only survivor of the fire was his equally beloved fiddle.

Over the rest of his life he rebuilt his collection of books, and in 1815 he was able to sell more than 6000 volumes to the federal government to become a new institution called the Library of Congress. He never parted with the fiddle.

By the time Shadwell burned down in 1770, Jefferson was already well along in building Monticello, near Charlottesville, Virginia. It was a labor of love that began at the age of 14, when he inherited a 500-acre estate from his father and picked a mountain at the center of it to crown with a dream house that says more about the dreams and ideals of Thomas Jefferson than all the biographies that will ever be written.

In 1768 construction had already begun, and the young Jefferson was supervising the cutting of trees, quarrying of stone, manufacture of bricks, even the forging of nails. He had long-since named the mansion Monticello, from the Italian for "little mountain," when it finally became his home. The use of Italian was no idle affectation. The design seems to demand it. It was influenced by the great 16th-century Italian architect, Andrea Palladio. Jefferson wasn't as influenced by any specific Palladian design as by the architect's "bible," *The Four Books of Architecture*. In

The National Portrait Gallery, Smithsonian Institution

The entrance hall at Monticello (facing page, top left and right, and bottom left) contains items collected by the Lewis and Clark Expedition, which Jefferson authorized. It also has five sculptures and a collection of religious paintings as well as his famous seven-day calendar clock. Jefferson did most of his work in the study (facing page bottom right), the only part of the house where guests were not welcome.

it, Palladio describes a temple in Rome designed by Numa Pompilius and dedicated to the goddess Vesta. The book tells us it was built in a round form "in resemblance of the element of earth, by which human generation is subsisted." Words like that were music to Thomas Jefferson's ears.

It would be hard to say whether Jefferson was more interested in the natural world around him or the human condition. He had an incredible passion for both. "I know nothing so charming as our own country," he wrote. And he seems to have done everything in his power to make it more charming. He selected the site of the house to give him a sweeping view of the nearby Piedmont where he had been born. He said the gentle, rolling farm country was his sea view. For his nearby view, he followed the lead of other Virginia planters to combine a working farm with an ornamental landscape. He planted shade trees and flowering trees and planned walks and roadways winding under them. And no one strolling even a considerable distance from the house was ever out of sight of fragrant flower gardens, many of which contained plants not seen anywhere else in Virginia. Some were European imports, but at least one bed contained a variety of lily from the Pacific Northwest, brought back from there by Lewis and Clark.

The mansion itself was built on the flat top of a mountain, which gave Jefferson an opportunity to surround himself with the necessary buildings for running a plantation without having them as part of his view. He terraced the hillside with a series of 27 gardens, where he grew more than 250 varieties of vegetables and herbs, including tomatoes, an almost unknown vegetable in Colonial America, and an amazing 20 varieties of English pea, his favorite. At the foot of the hill, along a street shaded with mulberry trees, was the working center of the farm where there were 19 buildings, including housing for the slaves Mr. Jefferson preferred to call "servants." The servants who worked in the house lived and worked in an ingenious pair of wings built under the hillside and connected to the house itself through passageways leading to the cellar. The tops of the wings are terraces leading outward from the main floor of the house. There are pavilions at the end of each terrace, one of which Jefferson used as his office; the other was where he and his bride lived while the main house was being finished.

The classical dome (above) was the first ever placed on an American house. Though Monticello is three stories high, its exterior makes it look like a single story structure. At the front entrance (above right), other structures were concealed from view by the master

Actually, if you were to ask Mr. Jefferson about it, he'd probably tell you the house never was finished. There was never a period in his adult life that he wasn't either changing it or planning to. When his wife died in 1782, the original eight-room house still wasn't finished. He had been away from Monticello as a member of the Virginia House of Delegates and the Continental Congress. He served as Governor of Virginia for three years and, in 1774, he was sent to Paris with John Adams and Benjamin Franklin to negotiate the treaty that ended the war that had begun when Jefferson's own Declaration of Independence had been sent to London. The following year he was made minister to France, a critical event in the history of Monticello.

Though he came home to more public service, as the first secretary of state, as vice president and then as president, his head was fairly bursting with ideas for improving his house. Its eight rooms would be expanded to 21 and the interior would be adapted to a style that had fascinated him in Paris.

The French were building elegant, one-story houses that appeared to be dedicated entirely to sumptuous entertainment. The sleeping rooms were hidden away in two-story wings that fitted the low lines of the buildings and were reached by narrow stairways that gave a new kind of privacy and comfort. The style up until that time had been to build multi-storied palaces with grand staircases.

Jefferson like what he saw and saw immediately how such a design would suit his Monticello. The original concept had been for a low, domed structure that would crown the hilltop but seem to embrace rather than dominate it. He realized that great central staircases took up too much space, not to mention too much money, and knew that the French had given him the perfect answer to breaking with tradition.

His new plan allowed him to change Monticello into a three-story house that would still look like the one-story temple Palladio had written about. The second and third floors are reached by steep, narrow stairs and are tucked under the eaves. Light in the rooms comes through windows at floor level or through skylights.

But if Jefferson borrowed ideas from the French and the Italians for his great house, the things that delight visitors today are all inventive touches of his own. The huge clock over the entrance door is possibly the most delightful of all. It is connected by ropes and pulleys to heavy weights that drop past markers to tell you what day of the week it is. If it's Saturday, though, you have to go down to the basement to find out. Because of a miscalculation, the weights go through a hole in the floor.

The room that contains the clock also contains artifacts brought back by the Lewis and Clark expedition, which had been Jefferson's brainchild. It is the largest private collection of American Indian and natural history objects in the United States.

To save heat, he installed double doors between the dining room and the tea room. But to save effort, he designed them so they opened and closed together. He also built revolving serving doors between the kitchen and dining room so the servants didn't have to enter the room.

"My own sea view" were the words Jefferson used to describe his vista of the Virginia Piedmont (right). His neighbors' views were enhanced by his Monticello (top center), built on the 867-foot crest of a "little mountain." Jefferson's parlor (above) was familiar to all of them.

The president's bedroom (top right) included an alcove bed, open on both sides. The space above it was a closet he reached with a stepladder concealed at the head of the bed.

And he designed tiered tables in the dining room so guests could serve themselves without interrupting their conversations.

In his study, he designed a revolving table and revolving chair that allowed him to read and write comfortably in spite of his rheumatism. The lighting is improved by a skylight, one of 14 he built in the house.

Though a lot of people in the history of the world have been called "renaissance men," because of their ability to do anything well, few have earned the name better than Thomas Jefferson. He was adept at mechanics, probably more than most engineers. He was an accomplished farmer, an expert lawyer, and knew medicine better than the average physician. His interest in religion was legendary and his skill as a writer changed the course of American history. But one visit to Monticello, or anywhere in the Charlottesville area for that matter, would convince anyone that he was one of the greatest architects America ever produced. He even improved the design of the White House when he lived there. In fact, every house Thomas Jefferson ever lived in was made better for it. The same could be said of America itself.

Monticello, located on Route 53, two miles southeast of Charlottesville, is open every day of the year except Christmas Day. The small entrance fee includes admission to the house and grounds. The upper floors are closed because of fire regulations.

The Charlottesville Visitors Center is a clearing house of local information, from restaurants and hotels to other sites to see in the area, not the least of which is the landmark University of Virginia, designed and founded by Jefferson.

Very near to Monticello is Ash Lawn, a 19th-century working plantation that was once the home of President James Monroe.

Jefferson and Monroe and James Madision often met at the Michie Tavern, now a museum, and still operating as a restaurant in a 200-year-old log building. Court Square, two blocks from the Main Street business area, was another likely place to have seen the three presidents meeting each other and to find memories of all three today.

You'll also find their memory preserved at Castle Hill, built in 1765 by Jefferson's friend, Dr. Thomas Walker. It is open for a small admission fee from early spring to late fall.

Not far from Charlottesville, more than a half-dozen caverns as well as Civil War historic sites are in the beautiful Shenandoah Valley less than a day's drive away.

4

JAMES MADISON
(1751-1836)

Of all the treasures of James Madison's Montpelier, the ornamental temple (above), patterned after one at Versailles, is among the best in the country.

The portrait of Madison is attributed to Chester Harding.

James Madison was, of all the presidents, possibly the most even-tempered and fair-minded. But he could get a little testy if you were to call him the "Father of the Constitution," as many did in his lifetime. "You give me credit to which I have no claim," he protested. "This was not, like the fabled Goddess of Wisdom, the offspring of a single brain." Yet no other brain involved in the framing of the Constitution had accumulated as much information about other states and nations, and few were as eloquent about what should be done to make this nation a beneficiary of the best ideas in the collected history of mankind. The debate that resulted in the document lasted non-stop for 86 days, and "the great little Madison" made important speeches on all but 15 of them.

Much of the reading that resulted in his prodigious knowledge was done in the shadow of the Blue Ridge Mountains in the Virginia Piedmont, at Montpelier, the family estate built by his father in 1760.

The fourth president inherited the house in 1809, but he and his wife, Dolley, went to live there with his parents in 1797 after having been away at school and then at Philadelphia at work on the business of government. By the time of his marriage, he had decided to give up politics and follow in his father's footsteps as a Virginia planter. The brick mansion, though large, had only four rooms arranged on two floors with a wide, transverse hall. Though two families could probably have lived comfortably there, the young bridegroom decided to expand the building and make it even more comfortable. He turned for help to his friend Thomas Jefferson, who lived just 20 miles away and was well-known for many more miles around as one of the country's great architects. Jefferson's first touch was a front portico with widely-spaced Doric columns. Jefferson also loaned him the services of workmen from Monticello to make sure the job was done right.

When the renovated house was ready for occupancy at the end of 1798, the Madisons moved in. But as often happens, "ready for occupancy" is a long, long way from "finished." In her book, *Dolley And The "Great Little Madison,"* Conover Hunt Jones reported that "Madison's handsome front portico in the Tuscan order was added during this period, but its brick pillars were still naked until April, 1800, when he again turned to Jefferson to see 'whether there be known in Philadelphia any composition for encrusting brick that will effectively withstand the weather.' He admitted he was considering 'common plaister thickly painted with white lead and overspread with sand' and thought that some inquiries in Philadelphia might lessen 'the risk of experiment.' Structural evidence in foundations at Montpelier shows that Madison's renovation in the late 1790s transformed the Georgian building into a neoclassical Federal style. ...He constructed the portico with the full complement of Palladian elements: podium, plinths, proportioned columns, full entablature and pediment. In addition to the portico, Madison added about 30 feet to the south end of the house, then painted the exterior to hide the seams."

He added another wing in 1809, his first year as president. The renovation was necessary partly to accomodate his library, which was nearly as large as Jefferson's. The books had spilled out of the room designated for them and began to crowd the living room, which distressed poor Dolley, who needed the space for her famous entertaining. It was entirely appropriate for them to add also an icebox, the first in Virginia. After all, Dolley was first to serve ice cream at the White House.

Madison's second expansion was even more the result of an anticipation that his home would eventually become a tourist attraction as the homes of Washington and Jefferson already had. But he himself wasn't there to supervise the work until he retired from the presidency in 1817. The work was done by men from Monticello, who were considered the best in the area, if not the whole country. Among the changes they made was the addition of a circular structure over the ice house modelled after the temple of Venus at Versailles. It ranks as one of the best examples of garden architecture in America, and was surely the envy of Mr. Jefferson, who had designed, but not built, several such structures.

Like so many early buildings in America, Montpelier has been in an almost constant state of change. After the former president died in 1836, his widow sold the property, and in the next half century the building had six different owners, each of whom left his mark on it. In 1901 it was sold again to William du Pont, Sr., who began the most ambitious alteration program of all. He added a second floor to the wings, bringing the space up to some 35,000 square feet, compared to about 13,000 in Madison's day.

The original brick exterior is now covered with beige stucco, and a very modern exercise room was added in the basement by William du Pont's daughter for her husband, the actor Randolph Scott. Mrs. Scott lived in the house until her death in 1983, at which time the National Trust for Historic Preservation acquired it.

The National Trust's restoration program concentrated on restoring Montpelier to the Madison era, but has not neglected the historical and architectural period that influenced the du Ponts. It is a continuing program that may take as long as twenty years to get the building into perfect shape. It has fifty-five rooms, compared to the original four.

The house was reopened to the public, even though work was still continuing, on Madison's birthday, March 16, 1987, with a celebration marking the 200th anniversary of the Constitution. Meanwhile, the National Trust for Historic Preservation is working to acquire as many of the original furnishings as possible. They were scattered after Dolley Madison sold the house. And because the du Pont furnishings were divided among family members, the house was empty when it was acquired by the National Trust. Teams of restorers went over it with a fine-tooth comb, photographing every detail, and measuring and documenting every inch of it.

The hunt country of Virginia is the setting for the Georgian mansion built in 1760 by James Madison's father. It has been altered repeatedly by the six different families who have owned it since the former president died. But though it has grown to more than three times its 1836 size, it has never lost its original charm.

The finished product will be a rare combination of 18th and 19th-century architecture and decoration. The 2700-acre estate will still be home to Mr. Madison's little temple over the icehouse, but it will also include the race track and steeplechase course that provided diversion for the du Ponts.

Until he retired, Madison spent very little time at Montpelier, but after 1817 it seemed wild horses couldn't drag him away. In their last days together, he and Dolley continued the round of entertainment of friends and associates that made them as famous as his work with the Constitution. According to one story, one of their parties went ahead at his insistence, even though he was ill and bed-ridden. He simply left the door to his bedroom open so he could hear what was going on, and helped keep the party going by adding suggestions through the open door.

He lived there until 1836, at which time he was 86 years old and the last living survivor of the Continental Congress. He was also the last remaining signer of the Constitution, which was entirely appropriate since so many people thought he had written it himself. "Having outlived so many of my contemporaries," he said, "I shouldn't forget that I may be thought to have outlived myself."

No one thought such a thing. And no one who visited him at Montpelier thought that he could possibly have found a better place to be if he should happen to decide to live forever.

An air of charm, that special brand of Southern charm, abounds at the rear of Montpelier. The original house, inherited by Madison in 1801, was the four-room, two-story portion at the center. He added one-story wings and, to the delight of his wife, Dolley, installed the first ice box in Virginia.

Montpelier, on Route 20 at Montpelier Station, VA, four miles southwest of Orange, VA, is open every day, 10 a.m.—4 p.m., March through December. It is open on weekends during January and February. There is a small admission fee. Annual special events include Hunt Races on the first weekend in November; President Madison's Birthday, May 20; Virginia Garden Week in late April, and Constitution Day, September 17. For information on this and other sites owned by the National Trust for Historic Preservation, call 1-800-944-NTHP.

5

JAMES MONROE
(1756-1831)

His "cabin-castle" was officially called Highland in James Monroe's day. Now called Ash Lawn, the dining room (below), the study (far right) and other rooms have been restored to the house's appearance when it was Monroe's tobacco plantation.

The Monroe portrait is by John Vanderlyn.

The National Portrait Gallery, Smithsonian Institution

James Monroe is often called "the last of the founding fathers," but he was only 18 years old when Thomas Jefferson's Declaration of Independence stirred the country to action. He was a student at the College of William and Mary in Williamsburg at the time and did what any student would do: he joined up.

He served under General Washington as a lieutenant, experienced the long, hard winter at Valley Forge and was wounded at the Battle of Trenton, across the Delaware. He won a battlefield commission to captain that day and was later promoted to lieutenant-colonel by the Virginia legislature.

Four years later he was back in Williamsburg, where he studied law under Thomas Jefferson and began a lifelong friendship with the man who would eventually become his next-door neighbor.

In 1789, after having served two different terms in the Virginia House of Delegates and one as a delegate to the Confederation Congress, he moved to Charlottesville with his wife of three years, the former Elizbeth Kortwright of New York, to be near his friend Jefferson. The site of his first house, which became incorporated into the University of Virginia, is within the town itself. His second house, which he called a "Cabin-Castle," is a country retreat about two and a half miles past Jefferson's Monticello, on a thousand-acre estate. A very short time after he bought it, President Washington named him minister to France and he was away from the country for the next three years.

Rather than let any grass grow under his feet, he asked Jefferson to find a good spot for the house and to begin planting orchards for the plantation he had named "Highland" - partly because of his Scottish ancestry and partly because of its location on higher ground than its neighbors.

Like Jefferson, Monroe was quite impressed by Paris and by the French. In fact, he was so friendly to his hosts that he was recalled by President Washington, who became worried that his minister might give the European community the wrong idea about American neutrality. But in 1803, President Jefferson saw an advantage in Monroe's admiration of the French and sent him to Paris again to negotiate with Napoleon to buy the territory the French called "Louisiana." In later years, Monroe considered the purchase his greatest diplomatic achievement. But Napoleon was smiling, all the way to the bank, as they say, over the thought that he had been able to extract $15 million from those foolish Americans for enough territory to double the size of their country.

The past still lives at Ash Lawn, where spinning and weaving demonstrations (below) and other aspects of early 19th century plantation life are an important part of a visitor's experience.

That same year, Monroe was sent abroad again, this time as minister to England. Once again, his American ways got him into trouble when he remained tight-lipped as a toast was drunk to the King. But they let him stay anyway, possibly because he was also minister to Spain and had work to do in Madrid negotiating for the purchase of Florida. The British also knew that, in spite of what he may have said in Paris, James Monroe had but one love and it was the United States.

And of all the places in the United States, he loved Highland best. His only son, who died before his second birthday, spent his short life there; his second daughter, who would eventually be married in the White House, was born there the year he went off to deal with Napoleon, and his oldest daughter would soon be married there.

Even though he was away, he kept in touch with the latest ideas for making the land more productive, and with the help of his neighbors he was able to make it modestly profitable. But the expense of serving his country and the State of Virginia meant that most of the profit went toward paying off his debts.

During his eight years in the White House he added more rooms to Highland, to make it more comfortable when he eventually could retire. But in 1825, the year he did retire from the presidency, his debts totaled $75,000 and he was forced to sell his farm.

The new owner renamed it "Ash Lawn." It passed through several hands and in 1863 was bought by a retired Baptist minister named John Massey, who built a two-story Victorian Wing which he used as a school to educate newly-freed slaves. The house stayed in the Massey family until 1930 and then was sold to Jay Winston Johns, a Pennsylvania businessman who began restoring it and collecting the Monroe furnishings which had been scattered. When he died in 1974, Johns willed the house and its furnishings to the College of William and Mary, who began an even more extensive restoration program and reopened the house to the public in the spring of 1975.

Though the restoration is far from complete, the College is well on its way to bringing back the working farm of Monroe's day, and the house itself would be quite familiar to James Monroe and his wife if they were to return there today.

They would recognize the 1825 dropleaf table that was a gift to the president from the people of Santo Domingo, and they would also be fascinated by the print in the entry hall of the famous painting *Washington Crossing the*

The 550-acre estate includes the plantation house (above), gardens, picnic spots and a statue of Monroe (right) by Piccirilli. The site was selected by Thomas Jefferson, whose home at Monticello is less than three miles away. Jefferson, who said he wanted to create a "society to our taste" in the Charlottesville area, helped the Madisons become established after they moved to the house in November, 1799.

Delaware, which shows young lieutenant Monroe holding the American flag. Monroe's French-made sofa and chairs in the sitting room would make them feel at home, and the wallpaper, with its scenes of rural France, would help him remember his meeting with Napoleon. And if he needed another reminder, the Canova bust of the Consul in the window would do the job.

In the dining room, they could sit at the huge dining table, one of the first pieces of furniture they owned, and recall the reflection of candle light in the mirror that added a festive touch to their dinner parties. Upstairs, they would see their own four-poster bed and next to it a writing desk that had been owned by James Madison, the best man at their wedding.

They would recognize the grounds around the house, too, except for one striking detail. In 1976, in honor of the country's Bicentennial, the National Zoo gave 13 peafowl to Ash Lawn. Today there are more than two dozen roaming the grounds, the peacocks adding touches of color to the scene with their fanned tails.

The birds especially love the gardens, where they find flowers and plants they consider quite tasty. Visitors find the gardens quite beautiful, and so did the Monroes, who relied on the kitchen garden to feed their family, their guests and some 30 servants.

The staff that keeps Ash Lawn running today goes

The French touch in the sitting room at Ash Lawn (facing page) is a legacy of Monroe's service as Minister to France, a post that seems to have impressed him more than similar assignments in England and Spain. James and Elizabeth's two daughters, Eliza and Maria Hester, used the crib that is still in the children's room (right).

home at night, but in the early 19th century, ironworkers and weavers, lumberjacks and farmers all lived on the plantation and were supported by it.

Unfortunately, it wasn't able to support Monroe in his retirement. After selling Highland in 1826, he lived at Oak Hill, in Leesburg, Virginia. It was designed by Thomas Jefferson in the Classical style with Doric columns and a huge portico overlooking the garden and on south toward Bull Run. In 1831 he moved again, this time to New York City, where he lived for a few months with his daughter in a row house on Prince Street, where he died, as had two of the four presidents who preceded him, on the Fourth of July.

A wall of boxwood frames a garden walk where visitors find the sculpted image of the president giving a silent welcome (below).

Ash Lawn, which is owned and operated by the College of William and Mary, is open every day except New Year's Day, Thanksgiving and Christmas. For a small admission fee, visitors can see the restored and furnished house, stroll the gardens, see demonstrations of spinning and weaving, even have a quiet picnic.

There is a gift shop and a garden shop and ample parking on the grounds. The estate is located two and a half miles beyond Monticello, near Charlottesville, Virginia.

Charlottesville itself, with the University of Virginia and the homes of two presidents, is a treasure in American history. It also offers easy access to the beautiful Skyline Drive over the Blue Ridge Mountains and the Shenandoah Valley. Lovers of the outdoors can find hiking, fishing, boating and camping here and, in winter, downhill skiing.

In the spring, the Dogwood Festival adds another beautiful dimension, and in the fall the leaves turn the area into a wonderland. As Christmastime, Ash Lawn joins the rest of Charlottesville in celebrating a Colonial Christmas, and in the spring it joins the whole State of Virginia in celebrating Historic Garden Week.

The James Monroe Museum and Memorial Library in nearby Fredericksburg is the president's former law office containing memorabilia of the fifth president and his family. The library contains thousands of books and manuscripts.

6

JOHN QUINCY ADAMS (1764-1848)

His own appearance didn't impress John Quincy Adams, but this portrait by George C. Bingham makes you wonder why.

The National Portrait Gallery, Smithsonian Institution

As a young man, John Quincy Adams spent a great deal of time in Europe with his father. In 1794, President Washington made him a world traveller in his own right by appointing him minister to the Netherlands. He also had a mission in London, where he met his wife. When his father became president, he changed his son's appointment and made him minister to Prussia. The young man protested because it seemed wrong to him for a president to give an important job to his son. The elder Adams refused to change his mind, though he did consult with George Washington on the ethical question. Together the president and former president were able to convince him that he was the best man for the job, and in 1797 John Quincy Adams arrived in Berlin ready to go to work. But the captain of the guard hadn't been warned he was coming. He took one look at the young man, who later admitted "I am a man of cold, reserved, austere and forbidding manners," and thought he was too cold and austere even for a Prussian. He carefully checked his papers and returned them with a click of his heels and a suspicious look. "Who are the United States of America?" he asked.

Fortunately, though reserved and forbidding, John Quincy Adams was a natural diplomat and was able to avoid an international incident. He went on, in fact, to win an international reputation that earned him an appointment, in 1817, to secretary of state, not by his father, but by President James Monroe, who himself had been secretary of state in the Madison administration.

John Quincy Adams was born in 1767 at 141 Franklin Street in Braintree, Massachusetts, right next door to the similar house at 133 Franklin Street where his father had been born in 1735. Both houses were built in the second half of the 17th century and are typical of the style of house that nearly everyone in New England lived in at the time.

Braintree, which changed its name to Quincy in 1792, is what people are thinking of when they talk about "typical" New England towns. They weren't planned towns in the modern sense, and the plan, such as it was, didn't find much acceptance in the other English colonies in North America. It isn't an easily expandable town design, for one thing, and folks who came in late came out with less than wonderful building lots. But every town in Colonial Massachusetts followed the same pattern. It began with a big square in the center, sometimes as big as six or seven acres, which they called a "common." It was a public park, a parade ground, the center of activity. At the most commanding spot along the common, they built a church and, right next door, a house for the minister. Another nearby building lot was earmarked for a school, and all the remaining land around the perimeter of the common was divided into building lots, with the best of them going to the leaders of the new community and the rest divided among the original settlers. Some land was held for expansion just beyond the common, but clearly the best homesites in any town were right on it. Though all the lots were generous in size, each resident also got a patch of farmland just outside of town. And every town included a large tract of land for common pasture and a section of woodland free to all for the cutting of firewood.

They usually named their towns after places they had left behind in England. In the case of Braintree, this was a town in Essex. The name Quincy came from Colonel Josiah Quincy, whose house is still standing.

The two houses on Franklin Street where the Presidents Adams were born are of a style that is as much a part of New England history as the Adams family itself. It is a steep-roofed house that is based on the homes the Puritans had lived in back in England. In New England, they call it a salt box.

Both houses began, as all salt boxes do, as four-room, two story affairs. Both houses, as all salt boxes have, have been altered extensively in the years since. As settlers became more prosperous, and as their families grew, their houses were easily expandable.

Modernization usually began by adding a room onto each floor by building a second identical house against the existing one. Then, when they needed more room, they added one-story, lean-to extensions to the back of the house and lowered the roof line to cover it. The overall impression was that the house looked like a salt box, and that's where the name comes from.

The houses were built around a fieldstone fireplace, in some cases as big as 12-feet square. Oak timbers were cut by hand, and wooden pegs made to hold them together. When it came time to raise the center beam and construct the frame, everyone in town came to help. After the party was over a man was well on his way to having his house finished, and all he had to do was close it in with cedar shingles and finish the inside rooms.

Of the two houses on Franklin Street, the John Quincy Adams birthplace is the older, probably dating back to 1663, which makes it the oldest surviving home of any president. John Adams inherited it from his father and was responsible for the two-room addition in the back, which was used as a kitchen. He converted the original kitchen into a law office library.

After having bought his own birthplace from his brother in 1774, the elder Adams sold both houses to John Quincy Adams, who lived at 141 Franklin Street with his English-born wife and two of their children for three years, until he was assigned as minister to Russia and England and they moved to a small country house at Ealing, near London.

During his eight years as secretary of state, and his four years as president, he was away from Massachusetts, and when he returned in 1829 it was to his father's house, "Peacefield." His parents were dead by then, and the house neglected. Though he had a mind to live out his days "in deepest retirement," his heart wasn't in it and the following year he accepted a challenge to run for Congress as the representative of the Plymouth district. He was

A classic saltbox house in Quincy, MA, similar to the one next door where his father, the second president, was born, is the restored birthplace of John Quincy Adams.

elected, of course, and served the district, and the country, for the next 17 years.

Meanwhile, he had given some attention to Peacefield. He planted some trees and built a passageway on the second floor, but he really preferred his new career to such things and turned the responsibilities of the house over to his son Charles Francis, who spent seven years of his life as minister to England. The former president's youngest son gradually converted his grandfather's farm into a Victorian mansion. He removed many of the outbuildings and improved the condition of the ones he left, and built a library building to house the books and papers of his father and grandfather. He also built a new carriage house that blocks the view of a street that had been cut along the eastern boundary of the property. The house remained in the Adams family until 1927, when it was taken over by the Adams Memorial Society, which had been established to care for the homestead.

In 1946, the Society gave the property to the Federal Government, which designated it a national historic site. Both Peacefield and the two houses in town are administered by the National Park Service.

Because the house was occupied by four generations of the Adams family, none of the furnishings have had to be replaced. Because it was occupied, it was altered over time, and because of that represents a span of history from 1788 to 1927 with all parts intact. From the first Adams to the last, a sense of history has made Peacefield one of the most unusual, and fascinating, houses in America.

The "Old House," Peacefield, is open every day from mid-April through mid-November; the two birthplace houses are open every day from mid-April though mid-October.

Other sites worth visiting in Quincy are the United First Parish Church, the Quincy Homestead on Hancock Street, the Colonel Josiah Quincy Homestead on Muirhead Street and the Quincy Historical Society.

Quincy is a short drive southeast of Boston in an area rich in Colonial American history. It is also the birthplace of John Hancock.

7

ANDREW JACKSON

(1767-1845)

The Hermitage (facing page top), Andrew Jackson's mansion at Nashville, TN, replaced a simple log cabin he had shared on the same site with his beloved Rachel for nearly 15 years. The double parlors (this page top right) were after-dinner gathering-places, the men using the one in front for weighty discussions and fine cigars, the women the back for reading aloud, catching up on their sewing, and possibly a little gossip. Jackson's bedroom (facing page bottom) is furnished exactly as it was when he died there in 1845. The drapes on the windows and over the bed were used to give warmth in the winter months.

The Jackson portrait on this page is by Ralph E.W. Earl.

The day Andrew Jackson moved into the White House, one of the wildest mobs the Capital had ever seen moved in with him. It was like a scene from a 1920s slapstick movie. People carrying jugs of whiskey and picnic lunches swarmed into the building through windows as well as doors. Waiters carrying trays of food were swept off their feet. Trinkets were swept off mantles and tables and either broken or stolen. They spat tobacco juice on the rugs and tossed chicken bones into the corners. They stood on chairs and knocked over furniture and, before the new president

The National Portrait Gallery, Smithsonian Institution

managed to escape through a back door, they managed to make the entire house a shambles. Even though their hero had made his escape, the mob seemed bent on staying a spell, and the only way to get them out was to take all the punch outdoors to the lawn. The lure of a free drink did the trick, but not before they had made their point that the seventh president of the United States was the first president of "the people."

They said Jackson had been born in a log cabin. But even he himself wasn't sure. No one is quite sure what state he was born in. Both North Carolina and South Carolina claim him and both have plaques and restorations to prove it. His father died a short time before Jackson was born and his mother went to stay with her sister in Waxham Creek, South Carolina, which is where he spent much of his boyhood. But North Carolinians say that on the day the future president was born, in 1767, she was visiting her other sister in their state.

Either way, log cabin or not, Jackson was of as much a patrician background as any of the men who preceded him, and that is nowhere more clear than in his beautiful Hermitage, near Nashville, Tennessee.

Old Hickory's father was the son of a wealthy Irish merchant, and when he arrived in America he was able to settle on a 200-acre farm. The home in South Carolina where Jackson spent his youth was owned by James Crawford, his uncle, who was known around those parts as a man of "substance." His plantation included a gristmill and a still and dozens of slaves. He was considered a member of the aristocracy and young Jackson grew up in the company of horse breeders and local politicians. When he was a teenager, his grandfather left him £400, some of which was used to educate him in a private school.

He became a lawyer in North Carolina and within a short time was made a public prosecutor and district attorney, which required that he divide his living between Jonesboro, which was in North Carolina then but is now in Eastern Tennessee, and Nashville. He managed to acquire a lot of land as fees in civil cases, but lived in boarding houses in the two towns. In the latter, he lived with his future mother-in-law.

Her daughter, Rachel, who was married at the time, was a frequent visitor and, as often happens, romance bloomed between them. It flowered when her husband left town, telling her he was off to get a divorce. When he didn't come back, Rachel and Andy were married. Two years later, though, her husband did come back and took her to court on charges of bigamy and adultery. Jackson spent the rest of his life defending her honor, even to the point of challenging several men to duels when he didn't think they had the proper attitude. It was said that he kept loaded pistols cleaned and ready for such occasions for nearly 40 years.

At the time of the real divorce, the Jacksons were living on a 330-acre farm on the banks of the Columbia River. It even had a frame house, something very few could afford out on the frontier.

In 1801 he bought 600 acres just outside Nashville and three years later built a log cabin there. In 1819, after he had risen to prominence as Tennessee's first representative in Congress and had served the first of two terms in the United States Senate, he began building a house worthy of a man of such stature. It would be his Hermitage.

He had also served as a Major General and Brigadier General in the U.S. Army and became a national hero by defeating the British at Chalmette, near New Orleans, in one of the decisive battles of the War of 1812. The soldiers he commanded were all backwoods fighters, which helped brighten his own backwoods image. It led, in 1818, to an assignment to do something about the Seminole in Florida. Though he wasn't completely successful in handling that particular Indian problem, as he had been against the Creeks in 1814, it all added up to valuable P.R., and when he ran for president in 1824, he got an easy majority of popular votes, though not enough electoral votes to claim the office. The election was decided in favor of John Quincy Adams by the House of Representatives. Jackson was in the senate at the time, and work on his Hermitage moved slowly. But he and Rachel had been living in the new house, which was built of brick made on the property, for three years by then. Four years later, Jackson challenged Adams for the presidency again, this time winning more than twice the number of electoral votes he had gathered in '24. He turned the trick again in 1832.

As the first president of the people, he managed to drive a monopolistic bank out of business by withholding government deposits. He also took a tough stand against foreign countries that didn't seem to understand that the United States was not to be trifled with. In 1835, when the French government seemed too slow in repaying a debt to the United States, General Jackson put the navy on alert and announced that France was in danger of imminent attack if the money wasn't forthcoming. The French didn't know quite what to do. Paying back the debt under such a threat didn't seem like the right answer, but neither did gearing for war. Finally, the British agreed to negotiate

Flickering candles and the glow of whale-oil lamps made the crystal sparkle in the Hermitage parlors when the Jacksons were at home and entertaining their guests. The lamps and chandeliers are electrified these days, but nothing else has changed since the days the president and his family danced the Virginia reel from room to room and made the dangling crystal dance along with them.

between the two countries, the debt was paid and the navy sailed back home.

Home for Andy and Rachel at that time was the White House, of course. In spite of the debacle on the first day there, Jackson ordered that the White House, now considered finished after 40 years of building, was to be open to all the people who, after all, really were its owners. He had to add two or three dozen spittoons to accomodate his visitors, and at one point in his administration there was a cheese weighing three-quarters of a ton ripening in the basement to provide them with snacks. He also kept thoroughbred horses on the White House lawn.

But if he loved showing off his house in Washington, he loved his estate in Nashville even more. During his White House years he added a brick portico with white Corinthian columns, as well as new wings, a new kitchen and a gallery in front of the second floor. After it was badly damaged by a fire in 1834, he rebuilt the mansion and painted it white to hide the smoke damage.

The house is little changed today. Run by the Ladies' Hermitage Association, it contains original furniture and mementoes of Jackson and his family. The president, in spite of his rough and ready style, had quite fine taste in decoration and furniture. But in keeping with his egalitarian image, he left much of the choice up to other family members. He had only one rule, and it was easy to follow: "Keep the bedposts plain or you won't be able to keep them clean."

The house is surrounded by natural woodlands of cedar, maple and poplar, and includes Rachel's formal garden, established the same year the house was built,1819. The garden is the last resting place of President and Mrs. Jackson, and other members of their family.

The Hermitage is a short distance from downtown Nashville, Tennessee, on Rachel's Lane off Old Hickory Boulevard. It is open, for a small admission fee, every day of the year except Thanksgiving and Christmas. Guided tours are conducted by hostesses in period costume. It is the only presidential home completely furnished with original pieces. Also on the grounds is Tulip Grove, an 1836 Greek Revival house built for Mrs. Jackson's nephew, Andrew Jackson Donelson. The Hermitage Church, built in 1823, is also part of the estate.

Though there is usually a small admission charge, visits to the house are free on January 8, the anniversary of the Battle of New Orleans, and on March 15, President Jackson's birthday.

Also in the Nashville area, Belle Meade is the mansion house of one of the great horse breeding farms of Jackson's day.

And, of course, Nashville is the country music capital of the world and home to the entertainment complex known as Opryland, and the Country Music Hall of Fame.

8

MARTIN VAN BUREN

(1782-1862)

The "red fox" lived in a setting (below) worthy of a Dutch patroon, which Martin Van Buren's great grandfather had been, in the Hudson Valley town of Kinderhook, NY. Almost from the day he was born he was one of its leading citizens, but it was obvious early in his life that his influence would extend far from the town line.

Library of Congress

If Andrew Jackson really was the first president born in a log cabin, as is often claimed, his second vice president, and the man he backed to follow him into the White House, has the distinction of being the first president to be born in a tavern.

Martin Van Buren's father was a landowner and wealthy farmer in the community of Kinderhook, New York, on the east side of the Hudson River south of Albany, the state capital, where he would, in 1829, serve as governor for six weeks. His great grandfather was one of the area's original settlers, having come from Holland in 1633. His father expanded the family holdings and by 1782, when the future president was born, he also owned the tavern in the village, which was in those days a mark of real prosperity. His mother was also a representative of one of the original patentee families, her father having paid the largest taxes in the county.

Van Buren was a master politician who had a knack of making anyone who listened to what he had to say think he agreed completely with the listener's point of view. Actually, what he did was confuse his listeners so they never knew what his point of view was. In his own autobiography he tells the story of an encounter with a congressman who was determined to get him to take a stand. "It has been rumored that the sun rises in the East," said the congressman. "Do you think it's true?" "Well," responded the president, "I've heard that too. But I never get up until after dawn, so I really can't say."

But of course, the man they called "The Red Fox of Kinderhook" was up before the sun most mornings. There was work to do, especially when Andrew Jackson made him his secretary of state in 1829. He had already served two terms as a United States senator and knew his way around the political maze of Washington. The house he chose to live in, the Stephen Decatur house on Lafayette Square, had a view of the White House and he had a special window cut in one side so he could send signals to the president across the way.

When he became president himself in 1837, he made some alterations in the White House, too. He added central heating for the first time, and put stables, fountains and decorative walls in the gardens.

It was all a warm-up for the main event. Halfway through his single term as president, Van Buren invested $14,000 in an estate near Kinderhook. The land that went with it had formerly belonged to his own ancestors and the house itself had once been owned by his employer. It had been built in 1797 in the Georgian style by Judge Peter Van Ness. It stayed in the Van Ness family until 1824, when it was sold to pay off some debts. Fifteen years later, when Van Buren bought it, the house had been altered from the original simple, square building, and now included a Classical ballroom. But the president had other improvements to make. His first step was to convert the 220 acre estate into a farm with decorative gardens.

Then came the spectacular part. He moved the central stairway, possibly following the example of his friend Thomas Jefferson, and made the rooms on both floors much larger. He installed more than 50 wallpaper murals, imported from France, in the downstairs hall, and he furnished the house with the best rugs and furniture he could find. He even added an indoor bathroom. After ten years of his dabbling in interior decoration and gardening, his son moved into the house and took over the job of running it. His father gave him carte blanche to do what he wanted, and what he wanted most was the services of Richard Upjohn, one of the best architects available. As the designer of Trinity Church in Manhattan, it was probably predictable that Upjohn would transform Lindenwald from a Georgian to a Gothic house. But he changed more than the style. Inside he added central heating, modern kitchens and many more rooms. He added a four-story Italianate tower at the rear and raised the roof in a central gable and a series of dormers. Then, with a flourish, he added "as beautiful a porch as ever you laid your eyes on." It faced east, by the way, just in case the former president might get up early some morning to find out if it were really true that the sun came up where folks said it did.

When his son painted the house yellow, some of his friends wondered aloud if the president would approve. Van Buren, true to his personal style, never said what he thought. But he did say that it amused him to see his son and heir doing things he would surely do anyway after he was gone.

There was only one rule that could not be broken. Van Buren had decided that the front door with its distinctive knocker could not be changed. It reminded him of the day, 35 years before he bought the house, when young Billy Van Ness came back to Kinderhook to his father's house as a fugitive from justice and frantically pounded the doorknocker, the sounds of which fell on deaf ears inside. The young man's crime had been to serve as a second to Aaron Burr in his fatal duel with Alexander Hamilton.

The alterations were largely finished when Van Buren retired and sailed up the Hudson in a steamboat to be welcomed back to Kinderhook with brass bands, cannon fire and the ringing of church bells. "I come to take up residence with you," he told a cheering crowd, "not, I assure you, in the character of repining, but in that of a satisfied and contented man." When he was at home in Lindenwald after that, he rode to the village on horseback every morning exchanging cheery greetings with his neighbors, usually in Dutch. On Sundays he rode to the nearby Dutch Reformed church in a carriage he had built in England, and until his dying day it was said that his voice rose above all the others in the hymn-singing.

He lived alone in Lindenwald for two months after his return, but then his son, Abraham, moved in with his wife and their newborn son. It rejuvenated the former president, who once again became an active politician, traveling around New York and the country, wielding influence in Democratic politics. When he was at home, he entertained politicians and statesmen. He had help with his parties in the form of Margaret Silvester, who was nearly 30 years younger than he, but was nevertheless seriously considered by most people, including her parents, as the likely candidate to become the second Mrs. Van Buren. But when he asked her, she politely told him that she had decided never to marry.

Not long after the rejection, the 68 year-old Van Buren went to Europe, where he retired to a villa in Sorrento and began writing his memoirs. Four years later, the death of one of his sons brought him back to Kinderhook, where he lived most of the time until he died in 1862 at the age of 79.

Not long after he bought Lindenwald, President Van Buren made Kinderhook one of the stops in a campaign tour in behalf of some Democratic congressional candidates. As is customary on such tours, he was expected to make a speech. The speech he made was, in the opinion of the reporter from the *Albany Argus*, "...one of the most beautiful and effective addresses I have ever heard. ...All hearts were melted and he himself was almost overcome."

The actual text of the speech was never published because most of it was extemporaneous. He looked across the square in the direction of the grave of his wife and parents and talked of scenes of his youth that had changed and were no more. He talked of people they all remembered, but were now dead, and he told his neighbors that he was back home among them and that none of those people had died because their spirits were still there.

His own spirit has joined them now and they are all still there, both in the streets of Kinderhook and on the restored, 22-acre estate and mansion that make up the Martin Van Buren National Historic Site.

The Martin Van Buren National Historic Site, administered by the National Park Service, is open for a small admission fee, which includes a guided tour, every day from May through October. It is open Wednesday through Sunday from mid April to May and November 1 to December 5. Lindenwald lies southeast of the village of Kinderhook, N.Y., on Route 9H, the Old Post Road.

Nearby in the village itself is the burial place of the former president and his wife, Hannah, as well as those of his parents and son. The tavern where he was born was destroyed in 1926, and the Dutch Reformed church where his singing was so famous burned down in 1867, but has been replaced. Both sites are marked.

Lindenwald's charm comes directly from the heart of Martin Van Buren. When he bought the house it had already been altered from its original Georgian style, but he took the alteration further afield by making it Victorian Gothic. Then, after modernizing the interior, he disguised the style by adding the Italianate tower at the rear. It was his son's idea to paint it yellow and, true to character, the elder Van Buren never said whether he approved of the choice.

ENTRY
IN REAR
OF MANSION

9

William Henry Harrison

(1773-1841)

It's no coincidence that William Henry Harrison's Indiana home (facing page top) looks like a Virginia plantation. It looks like his birthplace. As the governor's mansion, its parlor (below) was the scene of many official meetings, and the bedroom (facing page bottom) an escape from the problems of Indians and struggling settlers.

The Harrison portrait on this page is by Rembrandt Peale.

Though Andrew Jackson may have been born in a log cabin, the other seven who were elected president before William Henry Harrison were clearly born into comfortable surroundings. And Harrison was no exception. He was born in 1773 in a 16-room brick plantation house in Berkeley, Virginia. The land it stood on had been granted to the Harrison family by England's King James.

Yet he was elected with almost nothing else in his platform except the fact that he was a farmer from North Bend, Ohio, where he had, indeed, lived for two years in a log cabin. But the house had long since been expanded to16 rooms with clapboard siding.

He also had lived at Grouseland, in Vincennes, Indiana, the first brick building in Vincennes, which he built to resemble the house in Virginia where he had been born.

Why the log cabin? When Harrison was nominated by the Whigs to run against Martin Van Buren in the 1840 election, a newspaper editorial said that with a nice pension and a barrel of hard cider, "...he'll spend the rest of his days in a log cabin studying moral philosophy." Somebody connected with the campaign, a man who probably sat at the feet of P.T. Barnum, turned the insult around and presented his candidate as a man of the people and his opponent as a man who wore corsets and eau de Cologne. Harrison himself made very few speeches during the campaign, but the beat was kept going with log cabin headquarters buildings in every major town, with hoe-downs and rallies and song-fests. They provided gallon after gallon of hard cider, which was served in log cabin teacups. They marketed brands of tobacco and whiskey with log cabins on the label. And when they weren't

The National Portrait Gallery, Smithsonian Institution

pushing humble beginnings, they promoted Harrison's impressive war record, especially his defense, as Governor of the Indiana Territory, of the town of Prophetstown in the famous battle of Tippecanoe. It gave rise to the most enduring political campaign slogans in American history, exhorting the voters to cast their ballot for "Tippecanoe and Tyler, too." It also made John Tyler history's most visible vice presidential candidate.

Though Tippecanoe was an important battle, Harrison scored an even more impressive victory at the Battle of The Thames where, as Commander-in-Chief of American forces in the West during the War of 1812, he defeated the British, eliminated the Indian Chief Tecumseh and made the West safe for expansion. But somehow, Tippecanoe had a better ring to it, and campaign literature often referred to Harrison as "Old Tip." The Democrats loved to alter that to "Old Tip-ler," but the voters were more impressed by the Whig outlook on campaigning, and more people turned out to vote in the 1840 election than in any contest up to that point. Nearly double the number of voters participated than had eight years before to re-elect another hero of the War of 1812, Andrew Jackson.

During the campaign, the Whig hierarchy had issued a memo cautioning not to let the candidate say anything. It was an insulting piece of writing that said: "...Let the use of pen and ink be wholly forbidden as though he were a mad poet in Bedlam." But after the election, he was the biggest Whig of all and he retired to the room where he had been born in Virginia, put pen and ink to paper and went to Washington to read it at his inauguration. It took more than two hours on a cold, windy March day, during which time the 68-year-old president stood hatless and coatless. Within days he contracted pneumonia and exactly a month after becoming president he was dead.

During his short time there, he scandalized Washington society by insisting on doing his own grocery shopping and even brought a cow to the White House so he could be guaranteed fresh milk

Harrison's funeral was the first to be held in the White House, and his body was taken to the former log cabin in Ohio, where his widow remained until it burned to the ground 17 years later. Though his birthplace in Berkely, Virginia, is still standing, it is privately-owned and open to the public on a limited basis. His great house in Vincennes has been restored and since 1911 has been maintained by the Francis Vigo Chapter of the Daughters of the American Revolution.

Harrison built the Vincennes home, which he called Grouseland, in 1804 after having been appointed governor of the newly-created Territory of Indiana. Though the appointment meant he had to give up his seat in Congress, he was ideal for the job and both his wife, Anna, and he seemed to enjoy living on the banks of the Wabash River. Five of their ten children were born there, which meant that even though he often called Grouseland "The Great House," it might have been a bit crowded for them with only 13 rooms.

In 1812, after war broke out with Britain, he moved his wife and children back to the house in Ohio which, with 16 rooms, gave them all a little bit more elbow room.

In 1819 Harrison's oldest son moved back to Grouseland with his wife. They lived there for ten years, during which time their six children were born. When their parents died, the house was left to the children, who eventually sold it in 1850. For the next ten years, Grouseland was first a warehouse, then a hotel and in 1860 became a home again, and through it all, each use and each owner brought change to the original structure the Harrisons knew when they lived and entertained there between 1804 and 1812. In 1904 it became the property of the local water company, who announced plans to tear it down. What is there today is the fruit of bake sales and rummage sales and a lot of friendly arm-twisting on the

Grouseland's 13 rooms are all restored. The dining room (top left and bottom right) is ready for a dinner party, and the kitchen (top right) set to prepare it. Later, the master bedroom (bottom left) is welcoming.

Grouseland is big, but the proportions inside are almost cozy. Harrison needed a big, impressive house as governor of an important territory, but he felt that it was just as important to be welcoming as impressive, which he accomplished in this entrance hall.

part of the Daughters of the American Revolution, and though they opened it as a historic house in 1911, they hadn't accumulated enough money to do real justice to the house until 1949. It was a labor of love that is still continuing, but the house today is furnished with pieces dating back further than 1812, many of which were in the house when Governor and Mrs. Harrison lived there. The furniture in the dining room is a set given to the couple by Anna Harrison's father, a judge in the New Jersey State Supreme Court and a former delegate to the Continental Congress. When he told her of the gift, he wrote, "...I don't know when your dining room furniture will be finished as the fellow (who is making it) drinks too much."

Even though he had a rather large family, Harrison built Grouseland as big as it is because, as governor of a large territory, he knew there would be a lot of formal entertaining to be done. Among the people entertained were chiefs of local Indian tribes, who by then were becoming disturbed at the way their lands seemed to be shrinking in the face of the invasion by the white man.

One of the great chiefs who visited there was the Shawnee Tecumseh, who came to Grouseland in an attempt to head off the Battle of Tippecanoe. When he arrived, the governor asked a servant to go inside the house and get a chair for the Indian. The man delivering the chair told the chief that it was a token of hospitality from "the great father, General Harrison." With that the Indian turned on the man and hissed, "My father is the sun, my mother is the earth and it is at her bosom I will sit." With that he sat down on the grass and the meeting continued.

Grouseland, at 3 West Scott Street in Vincennes, Indiana, is open every day except Thanksgiving, Christmas and New Year's Day. There is a small admission charge.

Also in Vincennes is George Rogers Clark National Historic Park, which includes the site of Fort Sackville, captured and re-captured from the British during the Revolution, opening up the Northwest for settlement. The park is also on the site of the Buffalo Trace crossing of the Wabash River.

At Vincennes University is the original capitol building that served the Indiana Territory between 1800 and 1813. The Territory included all of present-day Indiana, Illinois, Michigan, Wisconsin and part of Minnesota.

In late May every year, the Spirit of Vincennes Rendezvous reenacts the battle for Fort Sackville.

10

JOHN TYLER
(1790-1862)

If the name Sherwood Forest conjures up the name of Robin Hood, it was quite intentional on the part of John Tyler, who considered himself the outlaw of the Whig Party.

As the first vice president to become president, Tyler had an opportunity to set the pattern for all who would follow him. Some in Congress thought that a vice president becoming president would be known as an "acting president," and should follow the ideals and policies of the man he replaced. Others thought he should take on their ideals and policies. Tyler himself thought that he was President of the United States just as much as any of the nine men who held the office before him.

The National Portrait Gallery, Smithsonian Institution

The Virginia reel was important to John Tyler when he altered his estate. He needed a 68-foot ballroom. He already had an above-ground wine cellar (right), and space for the only copy (far right) of America's first written law by Virginia's House of Burgesses.

His portrait is by G.P.A. Healey.

His first confrontation was with his cabinet, which had been appointed by President Harrison. When he told them he had some ideas for change, all but one resigned. When he told his own party's leaders in Congress that he didn't agree with their ideas on the power of the states versus the power of the federal government, and then backed it up with vetoes, he soon became known as a president without a party. He preferred to be known as a rebel and an outlaw, and when he bought an estate in Charles City County, Virginia, he was smiling in the direction of Henry Clay and other Whig leaders when he named it Sherwood Forest.

The house was in a run-down condition when Tyler paid $10,000 for it in 1842, but by the time he moved there permanently after retiring from the White House three

Breakfast time at Sherwood Forest could have been a problem. The family breakfast table (below) was indoors. But the front verandah (right) was inviting. So was the back porch (facing page)! The indoor table, where the president's lap desk and record book is displayed, was the usual choice.

years later, he had considerably altered it and doubled its size. Partly because of the 68-foot ballroom he installed, which had to be that big so he could dance the Virginia Reel, the house grew to be 300 feet long, making it the longest frame house in America.

He also needed more space than the average family because, at the time he began expanding the Big House at Sherwood Forest, he had eight children. Over the next 20 years, his second wife would bear him seven more. He had more children than any other president.

Tyler himself was born at Greenway, a 1200-acre plantation not far from Sherwood Forest and Berkeley Plantation, where William Henry Harrison was born 17 years before him. The house, which is still standing, looks very much as it did when the future president was born in 1790. His father, Judge John Tyler, several times Governor of Virginia, was Chancellor of the College of William and Mary in nearby Williamsburg.

William and Mary was young Tyler's alma mater. By the time he was 19 he was practicing law in Charles City County, and when he was 26 he represented the county in the House of Representatives. After a term as Governor of Virginia, he became a United States Senator.

The year he bought Sherwood Forest, his wife of 29 years, the former Letitia Christian, died, and while he was still in the White House he slipped off to New York and married Julia Gardiner, daughter of the owner of Gardiner's Island at the end of Long Island. She was considerably younger than the president, and many in the country were scandalized. The diarist George Templeton Strong wrote: "...Infatuated old John Tyler was married today to one of those large fleshy Miss Gardiners. ...Poor, unfortunate, deluded old jackass!" But anyone visiting Sherwood Forest today and seeing Julia's portrait in the Main Hall must wonder about Mr. Strong's taste in women. The infatuated president obviously knew exactly what he was doing. She bore him seven children, and he told a friend, "I have a houseful of goodly babies budding around me." The babies and Julia kept him happy until the day he died 18 years after his second marriage.

The house they lived in is still full of their memories, including the ghost of a woman they called the Gray Lady, who still enters their family sitting room from a secret staircase and rocks away the night in a phantom rocking chair. There are chairs and other furniture as well as decanters, china and other souvenirs of the former president and his bride inside the house, and directly behind it a birdbath that was sent down from New York for Julia.

All 1600 acres of the plantation John Tyler bought are still owned by the Tyler family, and it is still a working plantation just as it has been since it was built in 1730. All of the furnishings in the Big House are Tyler family heirlooms gathered during the 18th and 19th centuries. The house is surrounded by 12 acres of lawn and accented by 80 varieties of trees, many imported from other parts of the world by the former president.

Though its length is impressive, it seems even longer because of the way it has been lined up with other buildings, such as the smoke house and the tobacco barn Tyler converted into a wine house. There are six separate small buildings stretching out on both sides, and a kitchen

war or poverty, both of which we have known."

According to family tradition, an ancestor of the Tylers was with William the Conqueror when he went to England in 1066. Six hundred years later, one of his descendants, Henry Tyler, moved from England to Virginia, where he acquired an estate and started his family on the road to becoming one of the "First Families of Virginia," as close as anyone in America gets to being what would be the aristocracy in any other country.

Yet, this son of a prominent family got to be President of the United States by running with a man who won the election by claiming to have humble origins, even though he himself had been born right down the road at the beautiful Berkeley plantation.

Except for summers on the beach at Hampton, Virginia, where he owned a home called "Villa Margaret," President Tyler spent the last 17 years of his life at Sherwood Forest, and when not involved in promoting the cause of states rights, he spent his time enjoying his family and improving the landscaping of his plantation. He died in 1862 at the Exchange Hotel in Richmond, where he was serving as a member of the provisional congress of the Confederate States.

Southern comfort is reflected everywhere on the Tyler estate, even in the overseer's cottage (top). From the back porch (above) to the drawing room (above right and facing page top right) to the parlor (facing page top left) and the dining room (facing page bottom) there is elegant comfort everywhere you turn your eye.

and law office connected to the house. In Tidewater, Virginia, where in the 18th century there was plenty of time for such long-winded appellations, the architectural style of the house was called "big house, little house, colonnade and kitchen." Though it is very long, the house is also very narrow and is just one room deep. The center section is three stories tall, the wings that flank it are two, and the dependencies have just one floor.

The current owner is Harrison Ruffin Tyler, a grandson of the president and a great nephew of President Harrison. He and his wife have collected many pieces of furniture used by both presidents including some that was used in the White House. They have dolls and Bibles and books; china, silver and works of art that not only reflect the life of a president, but all plantation life over the course of two centuries. And, as Mrs. Tyler is fond of saying, "the house is pretty much intact since the president's occupancy and fascinating things still continue to pop up in odd drawers of secretaries."

"We are extremely fortunate to have the majority of the original buildings still standing," she says. "It is quite a rarity in Tidewater Virginia as most were destroyed by

Sherwood Forest is just 18 miles west of Colonial Williamsburg on Route 5. It is open to the public, though still a private house, for a small fee. The house is also available for formal balls and receptions.

It is the first of the James River plantations on the north side of the James River, where it is also possible to visit such other historic houses as Berkeley, birthplace of Presidents Benjamin Harrison and William Henry Harrison, and Shirley, birthplace of Anne Hill Carter, mother of Robert E. Lee. The road eventually leads to Richmond, 35 miles away, which in itself, as the capital of modern Virginia and the former capital of the Confederacy, is rich in history.

Tidewater Virginia is beautiful at any time of the year, but during Historic Garden Week, at the end of April, more than 200 historic houses open their gates, many of which are closed at other times.

11

JAMES K. POLK

(1795-1849)

The camera's eye was turned on James K. Polk in 1845, only five years after cameras were invented. The first president to be photographed was also the first president of a coast-to-coast United States. His family home (facing page), in Columbia, TN, was one of the first in town to be built of brick. It has been restored to its original 1816 appearance, a time when the future president was a student at the University of North Carolina.

When the Democrats nominated James K. Polk to run for president in 1844, some people who got the news by telegraph decided the device had made some sort of mistake; it was a new-fangled machine after all. It wasn't as though no one had ever heard of Mr. Polk. He was the Speaker of the House and a veteran of seven terms in Congress. He had been Governor of Tennessee, too. But nobody knew who he was. Henry Clay, the Whig candidate, made one of his campaign slogans, "Who is James K. Polk?" and the more he asked the question, the more people remembered the name. Today it is remembered as that of the 11th president of the United States and Henry Clay's as a three-time also-ran.

Polk is also remembered as the first president of a coast-to-coast United States. While Clay was busy making fun of his name, he was making the names Oregon and Texas fighting words. When he was elected, he managed to negotiate with Britain to settle the old argument about where the Oregon boundary might be, and though his rallying cry had been "54-40 or fight!," he settled on the 49th parallel as the line between Vancouver and Oregon without a fight. The question of who owned California and the Southwest was settled by a war with Mexico. In his administration, more than 800,000 square miles of territory was added to the country.

Polk was born in 1795 near Pineville, in Mecklenburg County, North Carolina. The house was torn down in the 1850s, though a replica has been reconstructed. By the time it was destroyed, Polk was already dead, a victim, many said, of overwork during his four years in the White House. When James was still a teenager, his father moved the Polk family to Tennessee, where he eventually built a simple brick house at 301 West Seventh Street in Columbia. It is the only house associated with Polk that is still standing. During his years in Congress, he and his wife lived in a variety of rented houses, the last of which was torn down to make room for the Supreme Court. During the three months that were left to him after his term as president ended, he lived in a house in Nashville, which was demolished to make room for an apartment house, which the developer named for the former president.

The house in Columbia was built in 1816 when young Polk was at college at the University of North Carolina. He didn't go there to live until 1820 and, when he was married to Sarah Childress four years later, he moved into a log cabin down the road. The following year he was elected to Congress and the house in Columbia became his home base.

When Sarah Polk died in 1891, she had already collected memorabilia from their White House years and from other periods in her husband's life and willed them to the State of Tennessee, to be housed in the new War Memorial Building in Nashville. Eventually, with help from the State of Tennessee, it was possible for the James K. Polk Memorial Association to buy the Polk family home in Columbia and restoration was begun in the mid-1920s.

Over the years, additional land was purchased, including the adjoining house that had been the home of the president's sisters. It was converted into a museum and gift shop.

In recent years the house has been restored again to the way it looked the day James K. Polk first saw it after his graduation from college. The floor plan was returned to the original, the arrangement of the doors and windows restored. The color scheme of 1816 was carefully researched, and the original furnishings of the senior Polks were recovered. Other artifacts and memorabilia in the house and the museum next door are from President and Mrs. Polk's White House years.

The house is one of the few Federal-style homes in the Columbia area and nowhere is the style more pleasing than in the front door with its fan-shaped transom. Inside, the staircase continues the theme and the wide-planked pegged floors on the first floor bring back a feeling of the days when the house was built and this part of Tennessee was the gateway to the frontier that, as president, James Polk would expand.

Most of the furniture in the front parlor was used by Sarah Polk during the more than 40 years she lived at Polk Place in Nashville. Her fan, known as "the national fan," on display in this room, was given to her by her husband for his inaugural ball. It is one of the treasures of the house. On one side are miniatures of himself and of each of the ten presidents who preceded him, and on the other side an oval painting of the signing of the Declaration of Independence. Also in the room is a circular table of Egyptian marble with mosaics of the American eagle and the motto of the United States. It was given to the retiring president by a friend.

The downstairs rooms are accented by portraits of the Polk family, including one of the widowed Sarah dressed in black, as she was every day from the time her husband died in 1849 until her own death in 1891. In the upstairs hall is a huge portrait of Hernando Cortez, the man who made Mexico Spanish. It was presented to the Polks by Major General Worth, who participated in the war that made part of Spanish Mexico American.

One of the upstairs bedrooms contains a bed and chair the president used at the White House as well as many of his books. The other two bedrooms are restored to their original use with four-poster beds and other original furnishings. One of them contains a bust of Andrew Jackson, given to President Polk, complete with a lock of the former president's hair, by Old Hickory himself.

The reconstructed kitchen was brought back in 1945 after its foundations and courtyard were discovered a few inches underground. It contains an open fireplace with ovens on each side. The fireplace and cooking utensils are believed to have belonged to the president's mother. There is another room in the building that may have served as a laundry.

The formal garden with ivy, myrtle and boxwood was created in 1949. The fountain was brought from Polk Place in Nashville.

The so-called Sisters' House next door is almost completely intact, having remained in the Polk family until 1870.

Though President Polk never achieved any fame as a party-giver, he and his wife never shied from the entertaining duties in the White House. They did ban all alcohol from social affairs, which prompted Sam Houston to say that Polk's problem was that he drank too much water. In her years at Nashville as a black-draped widow, Sarah entertained her husband's colleagues on a regular basis, and during the years of the Civil War she enjoyed the distinction of having her home declared neutral territory by troops on both sides, which allowed her modest entertainments to continue.

But if his contemporaries described James K. Polk as small and cheerless, his record denies it. He was a man who knew what he wanted, and was willing to work hard to get it. A friend once wrote that "...In public speeches there was always an earnestness and sincerity of manner which was particularly impressive. He seemed to feel what he said, and to speak with an animation and ardor which flowed from his heart. ...He was persuasive because he spoke from his heart as well as from his head."

It was a talent that earned him the title of Speaker of the House, the only president ever to sit in that chair. Yet Henry Clay, who never really wondered, and certainly

never forgot, kept asking the American people "Who is James K. Polk?"

For the first 43 years after his death, James K. Polk rested in a tomb in front of the Nashville house known as Polk Place. After Sarah's death, both were moved to the State Capitol ground in Nashville.

The family homestead of James K. Polk is in Columbia, Tennessee, a short drive south of Nashville. It is open, for a small entrance fee, every day except Thanksgiving, December 24, Christmas Day and January 1.

Also nearby is the Athenaeum, an 1852 Moorish structure that was once a girl's school.

In early June, the Maury County Fairgrounds is the site of the national Tennessee Walking Horse Jubilee. The County Fair is held during the first week in September.

In April, Mule Day is celebrated in Columbia with a liar's contest, a mule pull, a parade and other events.

12

ZACHARY TAYLOR
(1784-1850)

A tornado hit it in 1974, but Zachary Taylor's Springfield (facing page), in Louisville, KY, has been restored to its original appearance and furnished with 19th-century antiques (below). Taylor was often amused by jokes about his appearance, though this camera image of him makes you wonder what the jokes were all about.

Zachary Taylor was born near Barbourville, Virginia, on his father's estate, Montebello. At the time his father was already in Kentucky, where he owned 10,000 acres of land in the Louisville area, and was at work on a 12-foot square log house for his wife and their new child.

Eventually he would move the log house to become slave quarters and build a brick mansion resembling the home they had left behind in Virginia.

The twelfth president was descended from people who came to the United States on the Mayflower, and his family was well-established among the First Families of Virginia when he was born in 1784.

Taylor was a second cousin to James Madison by marriage, but he didn't follow the usual First Families tradition of public service. Possibly living on the Kentucky frontier had a lot to do with it but, when he was 24 years old, he joined the army just in time to make a name for himself in the War of 1812, and he made up his mind to make a career of the military in time to become a hero again in the 1832 Black Hawk War in Illinois. He added his name to the list of leaders who tried to turn back the Seminole in Florida in the mid-30s, and nearly succeeded. He became an all-star national hero in the Mexican War in 1847 when he led 5000 men into battle against a force of 20,000 and won the day.

His military career lasted nearly 40 years. He married in 1810 at the house in Louisville, but he and his wife lived

Library of Congress

Springfield is still a private house, and though it contains some modern amenities, like electric lights and a dishwasher, the spirit of the Taylors is still there in the president's library (right), the master bedroom (below), the entrance hall (bottom left), the guest room (bottom center) and the kitchen (bottom right).

most of their early years on army outposts from Minnesota to Florida, Ohio to California. In 1815 he retired from the army for a year and became a farmer on the Springfield estate in Kentucky. In 1820, he moved to Louisiana, where he owned three different plantations before finally settling down at Cypress Grove Plantation near Rodney, Mississippi. The 1923-acre estate with a small wooden house cost him $95,000. He resold it seven years later and moved to a four-room cottage in Baton Rouge on the site of the present Louisiana State Capitol.

He bought the house in Baton Rouge because it was off the beaten path in 1848 and, as America's most popular war hero, he preferred the anonymity it gave him. Every one of the stories that circulated about him involved in some way his incredible modesty. He almost never wore a uniform, though he was a general with thousands of men at his command. Many times he was mistaken for a farmer, and there are dozens of tales of young officers reporting for duty who spent their first hours patronizing him, only to discover to their chagrin that he was their patron.

After his retirement, there was a ground swell to draft him as a presidential candidate, but the man they called "Old Rough and Ready" didn't seem at all ready to accept

the call, though he did tell a few close friends that he thought it was time for the country to have a president who represented all the people and he thought he might be just the man for the job.

On the other hand, he didn't know much about politics and cared less. But those who did knew a winner when they saw one, and in 1848 the Whigs gave him their nomination. The only problem was that Taylor was not at the convention. The Party drafted a letter telling him what they had done and dropped it in the mail. When the letter arrived with postage due, Taylor didn't bother to pick it up at the post office. He had gotten letters from political parties before and thought the extra postage was just the first cost. Fortunately, a duplicate letter was sent, with proper postage this time, and Taylor's candidacy became official weeks after the fact. He wasted no more time in accepting and, though he knew very little about any of the issues, won in November with a comfortable margin. He seems to have lived to rue the day. Enemies in the halls of Congress were not as easy to deal with as those on the battlefield, where the rules are often easier to follow. The issue of slavery was rearing its head, and already in 1849 States were talking of seceding from the Union. He was determined to prevent it and convinced he was capable, but his enemies were passionate. A friend wrote of a conversation they had: "...He spoke as a proud, brave and deeply injured man alone can speak of unmerited wrong and unprovoked persecution. ...But General Taylor is the unconquerable man. When he was through with his recital of his injuries, the soldier awoke within him and he exclaimed that he always kept his flag flying in front of his tent and would never strike it, that he had never turned a back to friend or foe and that, by God, he would not do it now."

Taylor died in office on July 9, 1850, five days after suffering heat stroke and apparently overeating at the cornerstone-laying ceremonies for the Washington Monument. His body was taken back to the family estate in Louisville for burial.

Springfield, the house where he had been married and had lived for several periods, had been sold more than 20 years earlier after Taylor's father died. Since that time it has had several owners and has been changed several times.

A Louisville journalist bought the house and was well on the way to restoring it to its original appearance when it was struck by a tornado in 1974, setting the work back many years. The discouraged owner sold it again to Dr. and Mrs. William C. Gist, who continued the work until the house today looks almost exactly as it did when Taylor was alive. They have collected memorabilia from the General's life and furnished the house with 19th-century furnishings and antiques.

Some of the character of the house at 5608 Apache Road in Louisville is a reflection of the character of Taylor's wife, the former Margaret Mackall Smith of Maryland, whose family had arrived there not long after Taylor's stepped off the Mayflower. They lived very well in all their houses. By the time of the 1848 election, Taylor's estate was worth well over $200,000 and he was one of only 1800 men who owned more than 100 slaves. Yet no one would ever know it to look at him. Even as president, he was often mistaken for a farmer. One of the soldiers who served under him reported that: "He always wears an old cap, dusty green coat, a frightful pair of trousers and on horseback he looks like a toad."

It was all part of his charm, and even if he hadn't been a war hero, Taylor probably could have had a grand career in politics if he had wanted to. He was a natural leader with broad appeal. Though in this age of televised charisma it would help if he didn't work so hard at looking like a toad.

His house, on the other hand, was all a 19th-century prince could possibly hope for.

Rough and ready was what they called Zachary Taylor during the Mexican War. But when he was at home in this lounge and the library beyond, the rough edges were obviously left out back along with the remains of the log house that was the original building on the 400-acre Taylor farm.

The Taylor house on Apache Road in Louisville is not open to the public except for special tours organized by the present owners, Dr. and Mrs. William C. Gist.

Nearby, seven miles east of the city on Route 42, is the Zachary Taylor National Cemetery, which includes the Taylor family plot.

The information center of the Louisville Convention and Visitors Bureau is located on Founders Square in the center of town.

Other points of interest in Louisville include Cave Hill Cemetery, with the grave of George Rogers Clark as well as that of Colonel Harland Sanders. The Jefferson County Courthouse is a fine Greek Revival building with an impressive rotunda. The Victorian Brennan House on Fifth Street has most of its original furnishings, including a signed Tiffany lamp. Farmington, an 1810 house built from plans by Thomas Jefferson, is six miles from town on Route 31E. Locust Grove, the Georgian home of General George Rogers Clark, is six miles from town on River Road. An 1840 cottage on East Washington is the restored home of Thomas Edison and includes a museum of his inventions. The Colonel Harland Sanders Museum on Gardiner Lane tells the success story of Kentucky Fried Chicken.

13

MILLARD FILLMORE
(1800-1874)

Stencilled walls and comfortable rockers in the living room (below) make the Fillmore cottage seem like an ordinary 19th-century farmhouse. The president's desk in the study (bottom right) lets you know there is a difference.

Millard Fillmore, the 13th president, was the first who could honestly claim to have come from humble beginnings. During his early life, his schooling was limited to no more than the three winter months each year because his help was needed to keep the family farm going.

His father had migrated down to Cayuga County, New York, from Vermont, and though his farm covered 400 acres, it was poor, unproductive land and the young Fillmore grew up in comparative isolation in a cabin his family shared with his uncle and aunt with no neighbors less than four miles away.

The elder Fillmore didn't feel that a farmer's life was the best idea for his son, and when the boy was 14 he was sent off to Sparta, New York, to become an apprentice to a clothmaker. During the next three years, he worked in a sawmill and briefly as a teacher to accumulate enough money to buy his release from apprenticeship and went to nearby Monteville to study law with a local judge. Before he was 23 years old, he was admitted to the bar and moved to East Aurora, where he set up a law practice and became one of the small town's most important citizens.

Library of Congress

He built his first home in East Aurora across the street from his law office. Two years later he was elected to the New York State Legislature and four years after that he was elected to Congress, where he stayed for the next ten years. Before becoming vice president, he also served as New York State Comptroller. Through it all, he became one of the most influential men in New York and accumulated enough wealth to rank among the top one percent of the richest people in the state.

A pleasant welcome seems guaranteed as you approach the porch of the home (facing page) Millard Fillmore himself helped build for his wife, Abigail. Over the years he made additions to it, but never changed its charming outlook.

The cottage where Millard and Abigail Fillmore lived in East Aurora is a charming cottage, and the only presidential home built in part by the president's own hands. In addition to his law practice in East Aurora, though, he also had a law firm in nearby Buffalo, the most successful in a very important city. It was there he built a house that was reflective of his position and his wealth. When he was president, his father visited him at the White House and told him it wasn't as good a place to live as the house in Buffalo. He may have been right. The Gothic palace on Niagara Square he called Hollister House was possibly the most elegant house in town and may well have outdone the White House, even though the Fillmores installed the first kitchen range and the first bathtub in the Executive Mansion.

Hollister House was the scene of grand entertainment, with formal dinners, balls, recitals and rubbing elbows with the great and near-great of the Niagara Frontier and beyond. At least it was reported to have been grand. Fillmore and his second wife, Carolyn, had a set of rules that needed to be followed. "This is a home of industry and temperance with plain diet, no tobacco and no swearing," he wrote.

Comfortably tucked under the sloping roof on the second floor, this bedroom (above), with beautiful pine-plank floors, is furnished with original pieces. Also tucked away on the second floor is the playroom used by the two Fillmore children. It contains a collection of antique toys and dolls.

But if there was plainness amid the elegance at Hollister House, which was converted to an inn in 1875 and torn down to make room for a hotel in 1922, the elegance of the house in East Aurora is a direct result of its plainness.

The home has been restored to the way it felt in 1826 when the young country lawyer built it. The comfortable living room with its stencilled walls is furnished with 19th-century antiques around a charming, inviting fireplace. But the invitation blossoms in the kitchen, which includes a warm hearth and a beehive oven where hearth cooking demonstrations are held during the summer months.

Much of the furniture in the house comes from the house in Buffalo, especially in the library that was added later to house the books and other artifacts of Fillmore's post-presidential years. His wife, Abigail, was responsible for the addition of a library to the White House.

The second floor playroom has a collection of dolls, dollhouses and other toys popular in the mid-19th century. And outdoors, the herb garden still produces the aromatic, medicinal and culinary herbs considered indispensable to any dooryard garden in the years before the Civil War. The garden also serves to add to the charm of the house, with its masses of lilacs and myrtle. And the Presidential Rose Garden is one of the treasures of the area.

The carriage barn, which was added to the restored house after it was moved to Shearer Avenue from Main Street in 1930, is made from wood and hand-hewn beams from the barn on the grounds of the old family homestead. It contains a collection of 19th-century tools, a cutter and a surrey.

When Fillmore moved into the White House, according to one old story, he decided he needed a new carriage. He was shown the best outfit in the District of Columbia. But when he asked the salesman about the propriety of the President of the United States riding in a second-hand carriage, the salesman said, "Mr. Fillmore, you are a second-hand president." Though he had just three years to prove it, Fillmore, like John Tyler before him, was determined to fill out the unexpired term of his predecessor in his own way. But the early 1850s were turbulent years in the history of the American Republic and, like his predecessor, Fillmore got mired in the issue of slavery. He said it was an institution he detested, but admitted he was powerless to do anything about it. "It is an existing evil, for which we are not responsible, and we must endure it." It turned out the Whigs couldn't endure him, and in 1852 they turned a deaf ear to his plea to be allowed to run for a term of his own.

He retired to Buffalo after that, but in 1856 he tried again, running for the presidency on the ticket of a party that called themselves "the Know-Nothings." Their basic principle was hatred of immigrants in general and Catholics in particular. It is likely that Fillmore didn't especially like the Know-Nothings, but to a man who had tasted the power of the president of the United States, it was something to grab at. We'll never know. He polled so few votes that most histories don't even mention that he ran.

In spite of their prohibition of tobacco and swearing and their strict rule about temperance, the Fillmores lived in Buffalo for more than 15 years in a style that was the envy of the society at the other end of the state. The former president became an active philanthropist, and many of the dances and dinner parties they staged in their baronial home were intended to make others feel as charitable as they.

Among the treasures housed in the homestead at East Aurora is a portrait of Millard Fillmore, painted during the last years of his life. Queen Victoria, who knew him at the time, and was clearly not one to give such compliments lightly, said that he was the "most handsome man in the world."

A later addition, the parlor (above) was part of a 1930s extension. It contains Fillmore furniture and a late portrait of the president. The kitchen (facing page top) is the scene of hearth cooking demonstrations today. The carriage barn (facing page bottom) contains the president's sleigh, called a cutter.

The Village of East Aurora, New York, is 20 miles south of Buffalo. Within the community are three museums, including the Millard Fillmore House and Museum, which is owned by the Aurora Historical Society. The house is open from 2 p.m. to 4 p.m. on Wednesdays, Saturdays and Sundays between mid-June and mid-October. Guided tours by costumed hostesses make the experience of the house more authentic to modern visitors.

Visitors can take self-guided tours through the Aurora Historical Museum, which is open during the same hours as the Fillmore cottage. It contains artifacts from the earliest origins of the town, including an extensive collection of Indian arrowheads.

The Elbert Hubbard Library and Museum, also open Wednesday, Saturday and Sunday afternoons from mid-June to mid-October, contains examples of items produced in his famous Roycroft Shops, all of which reflect his philosophy of giving the world "the beautiful and the good, the plain and the simple."

Also in East Aurora is the original building of the world-famous Fisher-Price Toy Company, the Roycroft Inn, and houses built for Millard Fillmore's father and his uncle.

14

FRANKLIN PIERCE
(1804-1869)

The National Portrait Gallery, Smithsonian Institution

"Young Hickory of the Granite Hills" was what they called Franklin Pierce in the 1852 campaign. His portrait by George Peter Alexander Healy reflects the image.

Franklin Pierce was actually born in a log cabin, but it had nothing at all to do with his family's social status. When he was six weeks old, he was taken to live in the newly-completed Pierce family homestead in Hillsboro, New Hampshire. It is a grand, two-story, 15-room frame house with enough space inside for a ballroom.

Pierce's father, General Benjamin Pierce, had been a hero of the Revolutionary War and went on to become something of a local hero as county sheriff and as a representative on the state legislature. He eventually became governor of New Hampshire.

The future president grew up in luxurious surroundings. The grand ballroom in the Hillsboro house was the scene of an almost constant round of parties, and as a young man he knew everyone of even minor importance in this area.

When it came time for him to go to college, the natural choice was nearby Dartmouth, but his father, the General, didn't like their political leanings up in Hanover and sent his son to Bowdoin College in Brunswick, Maine, instead. It turned out to be a lucky choice. While he was there, he met Jane Means Appleton, whose father had been president of the college and whose near relatives included the Lawrences of Boston. Before long the two were married and Franklin Pierce was solidly entrenched as a member of the New England aristocracy.

After he came home from school, Pierce studied law at Portsmouth, New Hampshire and at Northampton, Massachusetts. He served two terms in the New Hampshire Legislature and then was elected to the House of Representatives at the age of 29. Three years later he was elected to the United States Senate. He resigned from

A trip to France was memorialized by the wallpaper Pierce brought home to embellish his parlor. The sofa came home to New Hampshire from the White House. The picture on the table is of the president after he himself came home.

the Senate before his term expired and went back to Concord, the state capital, where he established a law firm. The house he owned at the time is in Concord Historic Park today.

When war broke out with Mexico in 1846, Pierce joined up, retiring from the army a year later as a brigadier general. His war record seems to have been undistinguished, but he went back to Concord to a hero's welcome and was even nominated to follow in his father's footsteps as governor, a post he turned down. Meanwhile, in the words of one biographer, "His fame and fortune grew." Not necessarily in that order.

His wife was no help to him during the campaign. It was said that she fainted when he got the nomination because she couldn't stand the idea that they might be moving to Washington again.

But in spite of it all, he won easily. Before the inauguration, he and his wife and their young son were on a train going home from Boston when the car they were in jumped the tracks and went over an embankment. The parents weren't injured, but the boy was killed instantly. Being of old New England stock, the Pierce's saw the tragedy as a sign from God. The president-elect thought God was telling him he had no business being president of the

A dinner party invitation to the Pierce Homestead would have brought you to this dining room, still inviting today.

In 1852, the Democratic convention wasn't able to make up its mind who should run against the Whig candidate, General Winfield Scott. It took 49 ballots to come up with the name of Pierce, who, as it happened, agreed with Scott on just about every important issue. It made for another interesting presidential election campaign.

Like the campaign of William Henry Harrison, where personalities seemed to be all that mattered, the Whig attack was on Pierce's war record, or the lack of it. Though the Democrats painted Scott as a warmonger, the Whigs tried to make Pierce out to be a coward, and not a very bright one at that. During one battle in Mexico, Pierce's horse had stumbled and he had been knocked unconscious. The way his opponents saw it, he had fainted from fear of the enemy. According to one campaign broadside, Pierce had been given an order to make a feint to throw the Mexicans off balance. He misread the command, said the opposition, and fell off his horse, an act he later explained as "Just following orders."

United States. But his wife, Jane, was able to convince him that God was simply removing a family distraction from the responsibilities he was facing.

No one will ever know whether he was completely convinced. But at his inauguration, he became the first president who refused to swear the oath of office with his hand on a Bible.

Though a son of New Hampshire, he supported the pro-slavery views of the South. When a manifesto was issued to either buy Cuba or take it by force, the president chose to ignore it, but did support an idea that the island might be admitted to the Union as a slave state. When he approved the Kansas-Nebraska Act in 1854, he mandated that the issue of slavery on the frontier should be left to a popular vote.

When his term ended, the Democrats decided to look elsewhere for a standard-bearer and the Pierces went abroad to think things over. After spending the winter of 1857 on the island of Madiera, they toured Europe, staying the following summer by Lake Geneva, Switzerland, and the winter in Italy. In 1859, they came home to Andover, Mass., and spent the summer touring the South on their way to a winter in Nassau. They finally moved back to Concord, New Hampshire, where they lived in a three-story house. It was the house where Pierce died in 1869. In the last few years of his life he had a summer home near Portsmouth, New Hampshire, which he tried to promote as the nucleus of a summer colony.

The house where he died became a memorial to the 14th president and remained open to the public until it was destroyed by fire in 1981. He supported the Union during the Civil War, but couldn't help speaking out against President Lincoln and the policies that caused war to break out. It was a highly unpopular thing to do in New England, where the idea of abolition first took root.

Fancy dress balls took place frequently in the second-floor ballroom (above). On such evenings, the kitchen (top left) was also a busy place and the master bedroom (top right) unoccupied until the small hours of the morning. Outside (bottom right), the scene was a traffic jam of horse-drawn carriages as important people from miles around enjoyed the Pierce hospitality.

Eventually all was forgiven, and New Hampshire's only president is the pride of the Granite State today. The reconstructed Pierce Manse in Concord is one of the memorials, containing many of the original furnishings and utensils typical of mid-19th-century New England.

But the real treasure of the Pierce legacy in the Concord area is the old family homestead in Hillsboro. From the day it was built in 1804 it has been a local showplace, and today the restored white frame house with its distinctive hip roof is furnished with period furniture and decorated mural wallpaper that would be the pride of any family.

The Franklin Pierce Homestead, completely restored and furnished with many original pieces, is located three miles west of Hillsboro, New Hampshire, at the junction of routes 9 and 31. It is open, for a small admission fee, Friday through Sunday between Memorial Day and Labor Day.

The Pierce Manse, near the State House in Concord Historic Park, Concord, New Hampshire, also contains many original furnishings and is open between June and Labor Day, every Monday through Friday except July Fourth. There is an admission charge.

Near Concord is the Canterbury Shaker Village, one of two such communities founded by the Shaker religious sect in the 18th century. Canterbury includes six original buildings.

South of Concord is Bow Junction, the birthplace of Mary Baker Eddy, the founder of Christian Science.

PIERCE HOMESTEAD
The Pierce Homestead was built in 1804 by Benjamin Pierce, a general in the American Revolution, twice governor of New Hampshire (1827-28, 1829-30), and father of Franklin Pierce, the 14th President of the United States (1853-57). Franklin Pierce was born in Hillsboro November 23, 1804 and the family occupied this dwelling shortly thereafter.

15

JAMES BUCHANAN
(1791-1868)

"American Empire" is the name of the style of the dining room at James Buchanan's Wheatland, in Lancaster, PA (facing page). The president's bedroom (below) is also distinctly, and very comfortably, American in style.

The portrait of America's only bachelor president is by G.P.A. Healy.

The National Portrait Gallery, Smithsonian Institution

When the new president, Abraham Lincoln, visited the White House between his election and his inauguration, the man living there at the time said, "If you are as happy about coming to live here as I am about returning to Wheatland, you are a happy man indeed." President Buchanan meant what he said. Like the men who served before him, he had become undone over the issue of salvery, and though he had hoped to settle the issue, he left the White House convinced that he would be remembered as the last president of the United States.

His father had been born in Ireland and emigrated to the United States in 1783. He settled near Mercersburg, and began a successful trading post and warehouse that enabled him, by the time James Buchanan was born in 1791, to own a 300-acre estate with a two-story brick house. He was also able to send his son to a private school and then to Dickinson College, where the boy graduated at the age of 18. Young Buchanan studied law after that and was admitted to the bar three years later. He was soon elected to the Pennsylvania State Assembly, and soon after that to Congress.

As a country lawyer he was able to speculate in real estate, and by the time he was 30 his holdings were estimated to be worth more than $300,000.

In 1815 he bought the tavern he had been using as an office in Lancaster, Pennsylvania, and lived there until his election to Congress. He went from Washington to Moscow as President Jackson's minister to Russia and lived there for three years, during which time he continued acquiring Pennsylvania real estate.

Not long after coming home, he bought his most treasured piece of real estate, a mansion with 22 acres in Lancaster that he called Wheatland. As a bachelor, the huge house with its spacious rooms might have seemed like he was overdoing it a bit, but even if he didn't have a wife, he had a family in the form of nieces and nephews who were his dependents.

Wheatland had been built in 1828 for William Jenkins, and when Buchanan bought it it was the summer home of William Meredith, who, like Jenkins, was a Philadelphia lawyer. Buchanan didn't make many changes in the French-influenced federal style house except to add central heating, a new kitchen and a library.

Every cent he spent on the house, indeed everything he ever owned, was meticulously documented down to the last penny. When he was Ambassador to Great Britain for three years, he required his valet to keep track of every expenditure, from straight pins to flowers, for the elegant parties he held at his home on Harley Street in London. It was a boon to the James Buchanan Foundation for the Preservation of Wheatland, which restored Wheatland to its original condition. They had a single source of information on such details as the colors of the walls and woodwork as well as a detailed list of the furnishings. The result is one of the most authentic restorations of almost any 19th-century house in America.

He was as meticulous about his appearance as about his surroundings. And his manners were just as elegant. It was said that he more resembled a British peer of the 18th century than a Pennsylvania country lawyer, which he took great pride in saying he was.

But after his years in the Foreign Service, his 11 years as a United States senator, and his term as President Polk's secretary of state, he was clearly well beyond his roots. He seems to have thought so, too. He was on hand at three different Democratic Conventions from 1848 on, actively politicking for their presidential nomination. They finally gave it to him in 1856, and he began his campaign from the front porch at Wheatland, framed by its small, columned portico with its beautiful Federal-style door with an impressive fanlight above it. It was only fitting, for the brick house surrounded by landscaped grounds was, in the opinion of one of his neighbors, a symbol of "success, prosperity and respectability."

Though his predecessor, Franklin Pierce, wasn't a noted entertainer in the White House, when he lost his bid for another term, he told a friend, "there is nothing to do now, but go out and get drunk." And he often said he had

Victorian elegance adds a romantic note to the parlor (facing page), where the president's niece was married in 1866. Buchanan himself selected the furniture for this room as, indeed he did for all the rooms in the house.

The Federal style of architecture is seen at its finest in the exterior of Wheatland (top). Inside, in the study (above), Buchanan wrote his presidential memoir. His personal library is still there, along with items collected during 40 years of public service.

enjoyed a friendly drink now and then "because of a maternal influence." But Buchanan made him look like a teetotaler.

The 15th president was probably the most epicurean of all his predecessors, except possibly Thomas Jefferson, and his social functions at the White House were notable for the quantities of champagne and fine wine consumed. He was also partial to rye whiskey, which he bought in ten-gallon casks. But no one ever reported seeing him under the influence of all that strong drink. And anyone who ever tried to match him drink for drink usually wound up forgetting where he was but having a very unpleasant memory the next day in the form of a splitting headache. The president himself, on the other hand, was always bright-eyed and bushy-tailed the morning after.

As a wealthy, influential bachelor, he was often pursued by ladies with marriage on their mind. And when he was in the White House there was almost a steady stream, all of whom he charmed, but none of whom he proposed to. One of them thought she came close by asking him outright if it wasn't a trial for him not to have a lady to help run such a house as the Executive Mansion. "That, my dear, is my misfortune, not my fault." he said, and the discussion was over.

Even without a lady of the house, Wheatlands is a model of 19th-century gentility. The large rooms were furnished in the latest styles of the day, and much of the Victorian and Empire furnishings he accumulated throughout his life there are still in the house where he left them. His Empire dining room still has its original table, which seats 25 and still contains memories of parties highlighted by the best wines available from his famous cellar, and the romantic Victorian parlor still has silent memories of the day his niece was married there.

The house also contains memories of Buchanan himself. Although he spent very little time at Wheatland before leaving the White House, he spent the last seven years of his life there before his death, at age 77, in 1868.

The restored house today is surrounded by four acres of the original estate, which is beautifully landscaped and includes many trees that shaded the former president during his years of retirement.

After he retired there, he wrote to a friend, "I am now residing at this place, which is an agreeable country estate about a mile and a half from Lancaster. ...I hope you may not fail to come this way. ...I should be delighted with a visit."

Wheatland, which is the property of the James Buchanan Foundation for the Preservation of Wheatland, is on Route 23 one and a half miles west of Lancaster, Pennsylvania. Tours by costumed guides are conducted every day from April through November. A small admission is charged. In early December the house is open for Christmas Candlelight tours.

The Lancaster area is rich in its colonial past, and is the heart of the Pennsylvania Dutch country. The Victorian Fulton Opera House downtown is one of the most elegant structures for miles around. There are several Pennsylvania Dutch houses and farms open to the public in the area, including Amish Homestead, the Hans Herr House and the Amish Farm and House.

Lancaster is the birthplace of the inventor of the steamboat, Robert Fulton, whose home is open during the summer months. Other attractions include the Pennsylvania Farm Museum, which has six period homes among its exhibits, Rock Ford Plantation, built in 1790, and Franklin and Marshall College.

In Lancaster, it is possible to tour America's first commercial pretzel factory, a candy museum, an engineer's museum and a brewery with catacombs beneath it. The town boasts a restored colonial village with a 1738 gristmill and an atomic power plant. It has a railroad museum and a 19th-century railroad whose trains take you to Paradise.

16

ABRAHAM LINCOLN
(1809-1865)

A humble log cabin is as much a part of the popular Lincoln legacy as anything the man ever did. His restored boyhood home (below) was built in 1931 at Knob Creek, KY.

The reconstruction of the cabin and the farm where he grew up (facing page) is part of a National Memorial in Lincoln City, IN. By the time the portrait on this page was painted by John Henry Brown, Mr. Lincoln had gone west to Illinois, leaving the memory of log cabins behind him.

The National Portrait Gallery, Smithsonian Institution

More has been written about the life of Abraham Lincoln than about any other president. But he himself said, "It is great folly to attempt to make anything out of my early life. It can all be condensed into a single sentence and that sentence you will find in Gray's Elegy: 'The short and simple annals of the poor'."

But that doesn't stop the historians who, like most Americans, find Lincoln the most endlessly fascinating of all the chief executives. Since the 16th president died in 1865, a lot has come to light on his ancestors that he himself had no way of knowing. The first of the Lincolns in America was Samuel Lincoln, a weaver from the west of England, who arrived at Hingham, Massachusetts, a few miles southeast of Boston, in 1637. Though he was not a rich man, he had a trade and was able to live comfortably. His children and grandchildren, as often happened in the 18th century, moved on from New England in search of better farmland in Pennsylvania and New Jersey and eventually as far south as Virginia. The president's great-grandfather, John Lincoln, owned a prosperous farm there, which he willed to his son, also named Abraham Lincoln.

The young man inherited the family's wanderlust, and in 1782 he sold the farm and moved his wife, Bersheba, and their five children across the Cumberland Gap into Kentucky, where they settled in Jefferson County near Louisville. Four years later, as Abraham and his children were working in the fields, they were attacked by a band of Indians, and 10-year-old Thomas Lincoln, who would become the father of the future president, was orphaned.

Young Tom grew up on the Kentucky frontier and eventually married a local girl named Nancy Hanks. Two years after his marriage, he had accumulated enough money to make a $200 payment for a 300-acre farm near Hodgenville in Hardin County. The couple had a year-old daughter and Nancy was expecting another child when Tom built a one-room log cabin for them near the spring that gave his farm the name "Sinking Spring." That winter, on February 12, 1809, she gave birth to their first son, whom they named Abraham in honor of his grandfather.

The family stayed in the log cabin for the next two years until Tom Lincoln became involved in a land dispute and they were forced to move about ten miles away to Knob Creek, where a few years later the boy first went to school, and broadened his practical education by listening to the tales of teamsters and other travelers along the Louisville-Nashville Road which ran past their front door.

Life wasn't easy on the two Kentucky farms, but no more difficult than the lives their neighbors were

experiencing, and the Lincolns probably would have stayed there, except once again a land title dispute forced them to move on. In 1816, when Lincoln was seven years old, they moved again across the Ohio River to Little Pigeon Creek, Indiana. The president later recalled the trip as one of the hardest experiences of his life. During their first winter, they lived in a lean-to, which was later replaced by an 18 by 20-foot log cabin, for which the boy helped clear the land and cut the logs. Two years later, when Abraham was nine and his sister 11, their mother died. A year after that their father went back to Kentucky and found a new wife in the person of Sarah Bush Johnston, a widow with three children. In the meantime, the household had also grown when Dennis Hanks, a cousin, came to Little Pigeon Creek after his parents died.

Though there were more hands to help with the work, there were also more mouths to feed, and more bodies in the tiny, one-room cabin.

They stayed in Indiana for 14 years, during which time young Abe grew to his full height of six feet, four inches and his adult weight of 200 pounds. He had received a better than average education and had an eagerness to learn more. He had also worked at several jobs by then and knew the independence brought about by earning his own money.

Their next stop was Decatur, Illinois, where he helped build a new, more comfortable house. But in celebration of his "independence," he moved on to New Salem, Illinois, where he took a job in a store and eventually became the

A prominent lawyer by the time he paid $1500 for his first house in Springfield, IL, Lincoln often burned the midnight oil working in the corner of his bedroom (right) while his four sons slept in their room nearby (below).

The wall and fence around his Greek Revival Springfield home (facing page) were added by Lincoln in 1850. His wife had the house enlarged to two stories in 1856.

town's postmaster. It gave him a kind of fame in the area, and in 1834 he was elected to the Illinois State Legislature. That gave him an idea that he should study law, and within two years he was admitted to the bar.

He was lucky enough to be accepted as a partner in the most successful law firm in Springfield, and later went into partnership with an even more important lawyer. By the time he married Mary Todd in 1842, his income was far above the average in the capital of Illinois.

Things would get better. Within two years he formed a new law partnership with William Herndon which represented major railroads, banks and utilities. Meanwhile, he stayed in the legislature, serving four terms. In 1846 he became a congressman for a year, then went back to his law practice and, after failing to win a Senate seat, he finally succeeded in getting the Republican nomination for president in 1860.

By that point he was living in a large Greek Revival house, the only home he ever owned, on Seventh Street in Springfield. He bought it in 1844 for $1,500 and ten years later expanded it, eventually enlarging it to two stories.

His wife, Mary, was responsible for most of the changes, and when she went to the White House she changed its appearance, too, much to the chagrin of people who believed a little too strongly in the backwoods image her husband worked so hard to convey. In reality, she was as much an aristocrat as any of the first ladies who preceded her. Her family was among the most prominent in Kentucky, and her great grandfather had been a general in the Revolutionary War.

Lincoln loved politics more than almost anything else, and he had his eye on the presidency right from the beginning. But when he finally moved into the White House it was probably the darkest point in American history, and he found more sorrow than joy there. Toward the end of his life, when a reporter asked him how he

liked being President of the United States, he said, "Have you heard about the man who was being tarred and feathered and ridden out of town on a rail? Someone asked him how he liked it and he said that if it wasn't for the honor of the thing, he'd rather walk."

He is the most honored of all the presidents. He is the only one, with the possible exception of the incumbent, whose name is familiar to every American. There are hundreds of reasons, but he said the one most important thing he ever did, "the central act of my administration, the great event of the 19th century," was signing his name to a piece of paper that said: "On the first of January in the year of our Lord, 1863, all persons then held as slaves in any state or designated part of a state the people whereof shall then be in rebellion against the United States, shall be then, and thenceforth and forever free."

The kitchen stove,which burned wood, often made the room (below) uncomfortable.

The aura of success fills the Springfield house where the Lincoln family lived for 17 years. It was a source of pride for a self-made man. He even had a guest room (top left), a parlor big enough for entertaining (top right) and a spacious dining room (right). The dirt-floored log cabins of Lincoln's youth were obviously far behind him.

The Lincoln Birthplace National Historic Site is about three miles south of Hodgenville, Ky. on Route 31E, which, in turn, is about 40 miles south of Louisville. It is open every day except Thanksgiving, Christmas and New Year's Day. The log cabin where the 16th president was born is preserved here in a granite Memorial Building.

Seven miles away, on Route 31E, is a replica of the Lincoln boyhood home which is open for a small admission charge every day from April through October.

The Lincoln Boyhood National Memorial and Lincoln State Park are in Lincoln City, Indiana, on Route 162, two miles east of Dale, Ind. The 1747-acre park has facilities for camping, swimming, picnicking and fishing. The memorial features a working pioneer farm with demonstrations of living and farming activities from early spring until late fall. The visitor center with a museum and theater is open every day except Thanksgiving, Christmas and New Year's day. The site also includes the grave of Nancy Hanks Lincoln, the president's mother.

In Springfield, Ill., the Lincoln Home National Historic Site, a well-maintained 19th century house with Lincoln family furnishings, is open every day except Thanksgiving, Christmas and New Year's day. Nearby is Lincoln's Tomb State Historic Site, open on the same schedule as the Home, containing the graves of President Lincoln, his wife and three of their four sons.

Also in Springfield is the restored Lincoln law office, a Lincoln wax museum and the Old State Capitol building where Lincoln served the State of Illinois.

The Lincoln Heritage Trail, a 325 mile drive east from Springfield, is a marked route into Indiana and Kentucky covering special sites associated with the early life and career of President Lincoln.

ANDREW JOHNSON

17

ANDREW JOHNSON

(1808-1875)

Library of Congress

If you were to ask anyone in Raleigh, North Carolina, in 1824 if anything good would ever come of sixteen-year-old Andrew Johnson, you'd have gotten a worried smile and a sad shake of the head for your answer. In those days, no one in town would have given a dime for the lad's chances. In fact, the local tailor, James Selb, had run an ad in the local paper offering a $10 reward for information leading to the capture of a whole gang of teenagers, which ended by saying "...or I will the above reward for Andrew Johnson alone."

Andy's crime, as folks around Raleigh knew it, was to throw rocks at the Widow Well's windows. All he and his friends were doing was trying to get the attention of her daughters, who they considered "right smart," and no windows were broken. But Mrs Wells let them know she was going to "persecute" them to the extent of the law.

By that time Andy had had his belly full of persecution. He had lost his father at the age of three and as soon as he was old enough his mother apprenticed him to the tailor Selby. When the boy ran away, he was careful to take his tailoring tools with him, which angered his master even more than the loss of a hired hand. He had been a trouble-maker anyway, leading the other apprentices into such things as going swimming if he felt like it.

Andy ran off to the town of Carthage, about 60 miles away, but he thought he could feel Mrs. Well's breath on his neck, so he kept moving south to Laurens, South Carolina, supporting himself all the way by tailoring.

When he heard that his mother was destitute, he went home again, only to find the tailor Selby out of business, but in no mood to release him from his apprenticeship, which meant he wasn't free to work his trade in Raleigh. He told his mother to sell all she had and, with the proceeds as a nest egg, he packed her, her second husband and his brother, William, into a cart and set off across the Great Smokies in the direction of Tennessee. A month later they arrived, and settled down in the town of Greeneville, where the 18- year-old Andy got a job as a tailor, saved his money and went into business for himself.

From the earliest times, every town in America had a central gathering place for the exchange of news and gossip. After 1827, the place in Greeneville for such things was the Johnson Tailor Shop. At almost any time of the working day there was a lively conversation going on there, and just to make sure everyone had their facts straight, the proprietor hired a man to read aloud from newspapers and books for a fee of 50 cents a day.

It made Andy a kind of hero of the working class, something he prided himself for until his dying day. At the age of 21 he was elected to the Greeneville Board of Alderman and then served as the town's mayor for three terms before being elected to the state senate and then to the House of Representatives.

When he came home from Washington to become governor of Tennessee, he bought the house of James Brannon on Main Street in Greenville and moved his family there. His wife, the former Eliza McCardle, the orphaned daughter of a shoemaker, had kept the tailor shop going for him. The new house was his pride and joy. "It is a spacious residence," he wrote, "with generous fireplaces, high pitched ceilings and a pleasing view from every window."

After two terms as governor, he became a United States senator and then two years later was appointed by President Lincoln as Military Governor of Tennessee with a mandate to re-establish the Federal Government in the state. In 1864 he became Lincoln's running mate in his

A rebellious teen? Some people in Raleigh, NC said the lad who lived in the house (these pages) near Casso's Inn was just that. They put a reward on his head, and the Johnson boy left town. His birthplace, and his reputation, have since been restored.

His life improved when Johnson moved to Greeneville, TN. He was able to buy a house (facing page top), and trade it later for a bigger one (facing page bottom right). And he furnished them well (remaining pictures).

second campaign for the presidency. When the president was assassinated on April 15, 1865, Andrew Johnson became the 17th president of the United States.

In 1861, when Tennessee voted to secede from the Union, Johnson was forced to leave the state, but after his appointment as military governor he was able to convince the legislature that joining the Confederacy was a mistake. It was in keeping with his own life-long principles, but ardent secessionists became Johnson's enemies and he was burned in effigy all over Tennessee. In many places where he appeared to promote the Union cause he had to keep his gun in sight so the crowd wouldn't attack him before he had a chance to speak. When he did speak, his words usually had the desired effect. One reporter who heard him wrote that "...he has never been so cool, so determined, so eloquent, so impressive in bearing. ...As he appealed with burning words for the preservation of the Union, all hearts turned towards him."

As the first president after the Civil War was over, Johnson ran into a maelstrom of vengeance on the part of members of Congress from the Northern States, who felt the South should be punished for having started the whole affair. Johnson seemed inclined to go along with them, and made several strong statements on the importance of punishing traitors. But he never had the heart to go as far as the Radical Republicans wanted to go. In 1866 he discovered that the majority of the people agreed with them and not him as he took to the hustings to campaign against his enemies in the Congress. The Radicals won enough support from the voters to be able to override all of Johnson's vetoes against their reconstruction laws. Among the laws they were able to pass that way was one that limited the president's power to remove people from office. The Supreme Court, many years later, agreed with Johnson's first reaction that the law violated the Constitution. But in 1866, when Johnson fired Secretary of War Edward Stanton, Congress began impeachment proceedings against him.

The trial lasted two months and Congress was very nearly successful in making the first impeachment in American history. But they missed by one vote in convicting Johnson of "high crimes and misdemeanors."

Johnson retired to Greeneville a year later after his term expired, determined to clear his name. He took his case to the people and ran for Congress in 1869 and then again in 1872. He lost both times, but in 1874 he was elected to the United States Senate again, where he was serving when he died on July 31, 1875.

His body was taken home to Greeneville and buried on a hill overlooking the town he loved. His gravesite is part of a complex that makes up the Andrew Johnson National Historic Site today. The recently-completed memorial is a park that includes his tailor shop and his two homes. The shop, which became the property of the state in 1921, is enclosed in a brick building that also serves as a visitor center. The restored family home on Main Street is also part of the park.

The Greeneville Historic Site is administered by the National Parks Service. The Johnson birthplace has been moved a short distance from its original location and is now part of Mordecai Historic Park in Raleigh, North Carolina, and is administered by the non-profit Mordecai Square Historical Society and the Raleigh Historic Properties Commission. Like the houses in Greeneville, the simple log cabin where the 17th president was born has been restored to its original appearance and is furnished with pieces that were in the house or in the area in the early 19th century.

Together the memorials bring back the origins and the life of the man who more than any other could honestly claim to be a man of the people. He was always proud of his origins and during the campaign of 1864, when the

opposition warned the electorate that the country was about to fall into the hands of "rail-splitters and tailors," he accepted it more as a compliment than an insult. As he told one audience, "Adam, the father of the race, was a tailor by trade, for he sewed fig leaves together for aprons."

Unfortunately, the master tailor of Greeneville wasn't able to sew up the wounds of the late Civil War. But if he hadn't fought so hard for what he believed with all his heart, history might have taken a quite different turn.

A comfortable life is evident in every restored room, many with inviting hearthsides (above), at the Andrew Johnson National Historic Site. And it was appropriate when he died while serving in the United States Senate that his burial place (right) would be in his adopted Tennessee hometown.

The Andrew Johnson National Historic Site is in Greeneville, Tennessee on Route I-81 southwest of Johnson City. The park, which contains two homes, Johnson's tailor shop and his burial place is open every day of the year except Christmas Day. Except for the Johnson Homestead, for which there is a small entrance fee, the facilities are open at no charge.

Ten miles east of Greeneville is the place where Davy Crockett was born in 1786. The 62-acre park includes a replica of the Crockett log cabin and his picnic and camping facilities.

Mordecai Historic Park in Raleigh, North Carolina, includes the cabin where Andrew Johnson was born. The park, which is closed on Thanksgiving Day and from Christmas Day until the end of February and on Tuesdays from June through September, is the site of the neo-classical Mordecai House, which contains many of its original furnishings. A small donation to the upkeep of the park is required of visitors.

Not far from Raleigh is Durham, the home of Duke University, and Chapel Hill, home of the University of North Carolina. Also nearby is Asheboro, the gateway to Great Smoky Mountains National Park, and Biltmore, the 10,000-acre estate of George W. Vanderbilt, designed by Richard Morris Hunt in 1890, and considered by many to be one of the most beautiful homes in America.

18

ULYSSES S. GRANT

(1822-1885)

The silver service in the dining room (below) at Grant's home in Galena, IL, was used at the White House. The Haviland china was made for Nellie Grant's wedding in the East Room. The oak dining set is original to the Galena house.

The Grant portrait is by Ole Peter Hansen Balling.

The National Portrait Gallery, Smithsonian Institution

Ulysses S. Grant never wanted to be a soldier. It took some convincing to make him want to be president, too. His father engineered his appointment to the United States Military Academy at West Point and applied a strong dose of parental pressure to make his son get on the trail to make the trip east from Georgetown, Ohio. The young man, whose name was changed from Hiram Ulysses to Ulysses Simpson because of a mixup in the official appointment to West Point, got even by finishing in the lower third of his class. He liked the new name, though. It made his initials "U.S.", and it was nice not to have to answer to the name "Hiram".

He served nine years in the Army after graduation, and was sent to fight in the Mexican War under Generals Taylor and Scott. He later said that he felt the war was the most unfair piece of business he had ever been involved in, and that the Civil War was probably God's way of punishing the United States for what it had done to Mexico. After the war he was transferred to Fort Vancouver, in Washington, and then to Fort Humbolt, California. He was married by then, but couldn't afford to have his wife with him. In an effort to remedy that, he tried potato farming in California to supplement his army pay. However, the frustrations of army life had already driven him to drink, and his commanding officer ordered him to either give up the bottle or give up his military career. He said he would do both, packed up his kit and moved to a small farm near St. Louis which his wife had received as part of her dowry. They stayed there for four years trying to make a living on what he called "Hardscrabble."

A hilltop villa was a gift of the people of Galena to Grant in 1865. The brick Italianate mansion (right) was, he said, "furnished with everything good taste could desire." At the time Grant was Commanding General of the Army, stationed in Washington, D.C.

His next move was to Galena, Illinois, on the Upper Mississippi River, where his father owned a tannery and a leather goods store. His brothers ran the place, and his job was to run around Wisconsin, Minnesota and Iowa serving his father's customers. It was a better living than he had made before, but still not perfect, and after a winter of the life of a traveling salesman, he was among the first to volunteer in 1861 when President Lincoln issued a call for help. He organized a company of soldiers in Galena and marched them off to Springfield, where he put his West Point training to good use organizing other Illinois regiments.

He earned a reputation in Springfield as a no-nonsense officer who was able to make disciplined soldiers from raw volunteers, and prove their worth, and his own, in the field. He led the fight at Shiloh, took Vicksburg and, after an impressive victory at Chatanooga, he was made Commander of the Union Armies, with the rank of Lieutenant General. It wasn't until after he accepted General Lee's surrender at Appomattox that he was made a full general by an act of Congress. Until then, it had been a foregone conclusion that no man would could ever attain the rank that had been earned by General Washington.

During the war years his family lived in Burlington, New Jersey, and after the war they moved to Washington, where he served as Commanding General of the Army until 1868. But "home" to the Grants was Galena.

Before he rejoined the Army they lived in a rented brick cottage, but when he returned in 1865, the citizens of the town had bought a five year-old house for them. His wife, Julia, described it as "a lovely villa exquisitely furnished with everything good taste could desire." Though the Grants didn't actually live in the house it was a retreat for them over the next 15 years, and caretakers kept it in perfect condition in case they should suddenly decide to make a surprise visit.

At home in Galena, Grant held conferences in the library (above). Jesse Root Grant, one of his three sons, used the bedroom (right). The president and his wife, Julia, shared the master bedroom (far right).

Though he never surprised them, he did delight them with periodic visits, which continued for most of the rest of his life. Two years after his wife died, their children gave the house back to the citizens of Galena "with the understanding that this property is to be kept as a memorial to the late General Ulysses S. Grant, and for no other purpose. ...Kept as nearly as possible as it was when General Grant resided in it." The house by that point had become run-down and though the town restored it, they were finally forced to deed it to the State of Illinois, which became responsible for its upkeep in 1931.

In 1952, the Illinois Department of Conservation began making plans for a major restoration, which was finished in 1957. The house as it stands today reflects "a typical Victorian household of the 1870s with a particular emphasis upon the individual traits the Grants would have left upon it." Fortunately, most of the original furniture was still in the house and all the original plans

Grant's daughter, Ellen, whom he called Nellie, used this bedroom when she was there. The Rodgers sculpture, "Council of War" (bottom right) in his library depicts General Grant, President Lincoln and Secretary of State Edwin Stanton.

The easy chair that helped make life comfortable in the White House (facing page bottom) followed Grant to Galena when he retired. He didn't need to move the White House kitchen – the house had a perfectly equipped one already (facing page top).

still available. Grant himself had said to his neighbors "I hope to retain my residence here, spend some days with you every year ...and I expect to cast my vote here always."

Galena was, and is, a town that is easy to love. It started life in the 1820s as a mining boom town around the lead mines of the Upper Mississippi. Steamboats kept the boom going, and by the 1850s it was known as the "Queen City of the Midwest." But, as often happens with boom towns, history passed her by and the queen became something of a dowager. There was enough local business to keep Galena very much alive, but not enough to encourage change in the name of progress. The result is a very charming town that looks very much as it did in 1860 when the Grant family first arrived.

When the Republican Party first suggested to General Grant that he could have its nomination for president, he took a long pull on his cigar, looked them in the eye and said, "I'd much rather be mayor of Galena." It took him almost four years to change his mind, and in 1869 he moved from a row house on Washington's I Street to the White House on Pennsylvania Avenue, which he and his wife began immediately to redecorate.

Historians generally concede that the Grant presidency wasn't the most outstanding. There were scandals and charges of cronyism, but the president himself was above reproach. For all the talk that he drank too much and smoked too many cigars, he was an uncommonly gentle man who never allowed profanity in his smoke-filled rooms and never got angry except if someone was mistreating an animal. Through all the scandal and criticism, when he ran for a second term he became the first of only four presidents to win all of the electoral votes.

During his eight years in office, he became the first president to take vacations away from Washington when he bought a summer home at Long Branch, New Jersey. The government establishment was scandalized, and it was suggested that any bills signed in Long Branch couldn't be considered official laws. Fortunately for Grant, and for the presidents who followed him, it was decided that working vacations were perfectly legal.

Once he left the White House in 1877, he took a world tour during which time he was amazed at how popular he was among the people everywhere he went. It gave him an idea that possibly he ought to be a presidential candidate again. Instead, the Republicans suggested that maybe it was time for him to run for mayor of Galena.

Instead he went to New York to live in a town house on East 66th Street, a few steps from Central Park. He died four years later of lung cancer in a cottage north of Saratoga Springs, New York.

The Grant birthplace at Point Pleasant, Ohio, has been restored and is maintained by the Ohio Historical Society. The home where he grew up, in Georgetown, Ohio, is privately owned.

Grant's Farm, which he named Hardscrabble, is now part of a 281-acre park in St. Louis, Missouri, owned by the Anheuser-Busch Co. In addition to Grant's cabin, the park includes a barn with Clydesdale horses, a carriage house, and deer, buffalo and cattle roaming free. It is open every day except Monday in the summer months and Thursday through Sunday in the spring and fall. There is no admission charge.

The Ulysses S. Grant Home State Historic Site in Galena, Illinois, is open every day without charge except Thanksgiving, Christmas and New Year's Day.

Also in Galena is the Historical Museum, open, for a small fee, with the same schedule as the Grant Home, and the free Old Market House, an 1897 blacksmith shop, a general store museum, a stockade, a 19th-century print shop and a half dozen restored mansions. The area also has a ski resort, a doll museum, an auto museum and an old lead mine still open.

The Grant summer home in Long Branch, New Jersey, has been destroyed, as has the townhouse in Manhattan. The cottage north of Saratoga Springs, New York, where General Grant died, is still standing.

19

RUTHERFORD B. HAYES
(1822-1893)

Victorian splendor would make Spiegel Grove in Fremont, OH, (facing page top) worth visiting even if it weren't the home of a president. The stately drawing room (bottom) and the friendly parlor (facing page bottom), known as the red room, are impeccably furnished with priceless antiques.

The Hayes bust (right) is by Olin Levi Warner.

Like Andrew Jackson, Rutherford B. Hayes was born a few months after the death of his father. The elder Hayes, a descendant of a family that emigrated from Scotland to Connecticut in the 1680s, had made a respectable living in Vermont before leaving for Delaware, Ohio, where he built the first brick house in town and furnished it more elegantly than any other for miles around.

Ironically, one of the sources of his income was a distillery. As president, Hayes imposed a strict ban on alcohol at the White House, much to the chagrin of Washington partygoers, one of whom commented after a state dinner that "the water flowed like champagne." Hayes took all the credit for the ban along with the prohibition on smoking and cussing inside the White House gates. But most people put the blame at the door of Mrs. Hayes, the former Lucy Ware Webb, the daughter of a family prominent in Virginia and Kentucky whom most Washingtonians referred to as "Lemonade Lucy."

As a young man, Hayes hadn't suffered any of the usual hardships associated with fatherless boys in the 19th century. He was looked after by his mother's brother, Sardis Birchard, one of the richest men in Ohio. He owned the biggest store in Cleveland and had bought so much of the land in that part of Ohio that the Seneca Indians nicknamed him "the man who owns all the land."

With money came influence, and there was almost no one in Ohio who didn't owe at least a small favor to Sardis Birchard. His uncle saw to it that the boy had the best possible education, first at expensive private academies,

The National Portrait Gallery, Smithsonian Institution

The Hayes Library on the 25-acre estate is America's first presidential library. Books were removed from the house when it opened in 1916, but the library in the home (below) is still an impressive collection. The drawing room (right) was a quiet retreat from the large dining room (facing page top), as was the comfortable master bedroom (facing page bottom).

then at Kenyon College. He studied law at Harvard and then opened a law practice in Lower Sandusky, moving quickly on to Cincinnati.

From that point on, he didn't need Uncle Sardis's money any longer, though it was always available to him if he did. His law practice was a great success, and his sideline of land speculation hugely profitable. When he married Lucy Ware Webb, he was able to buy the most elegant house in Cincinnati and he was beginning to think of a career in politics.

His first elective office was city solicitor, a job he gave up just before the outbreak of the Civil War. Like his predecessor, Ulysses S. Grant, he joined the army. He rose from captain to major, then became an adjutant general. Later he became a lieutenant colonel, colonel and major general. The last title was the one he always said he treasured most and enjoyed being called "General Hayes" more than anything else. A major wound received in combat made him a folk hero back home and the local politicians made him a candidate for Congress. He accepted the honor, but pointed out that there was still a war to fight and he would neither campaign nor serve until his country didn't need him to help fight that war. They kept his name on the ballot anyway and he was elected. True to his word, he didn't go to Washington until almost a year later after the war had ended.

It is the kind of stuff American voters have always loved, and they re-elected him to Congress again in 1866 and then gave him two terms as Governor of Ohio. He turned down a bid for the U.S. senate in 1872, but was elected governor again four years later. The following year he was nominated for the presidency.

The election of 1876 was one of the strangest in American history, and it is still possible to get an argument in some partisan circles about the outcome. The Democratic candidate, Samuel Tilden of New York, drew the majority of the popular vote, but under the Electoral College system the actual winner was in doubt. There were charges of election fraud on both sides in some Southern states, which were still occupied territory in those post-Civil War days. The job of settling the issue went to an electoral commission appointed by Congress. The commission, made up of 8 Republicans and 7 Democrats, voted along party lines and Hayes was declared the winner by one vote.

It took more than a year for the Democrats to accept the loss. But it is usually conceded, even among Democrats, that a Hayes presidency was, in the end, better for the country. He was as non-partisan as he could possibly be,

appointing Democrats to important offices, appropriating funds for rebuilding the South and ending the Federal occupation there.

Hayes chose not to run for a second term as president. He had already inherited his uncle's house at Spiegel Grove in Fremont, Ohio, and had added two additions to make room for a new kitchen, a library and an office. As soon as he left the White House in 1881, he doubled the size of Spiegel Grove by duplicating it with an identical connected building and binding both together with a veranda. Eight years later he expanded and changed it again, leaving just two rooms, the Victorian parlor and the bedroom above it, from the original house his uncle had built in 1859.

During his lifetime his library was part of the house, but after his death in 1893 it was expanded to more than 70,000 volumes and housed, along with 75,000 photographs and one million manuscripts, in the Memorial Library on the grounds of the 25-acre estate. It is the first presidential library in the United States.

The estate is surrounded by an iron fence with six gates that were originally at the entrances to the White House. Many of the trees on the property were planted by Hayes himself, who named many of his trees for close friends and associates. Some of the trees he planted are cuttings from other famous trees.

The 19th president and his wife are buried on the grounds of Spiegel Grove not far from an old Indian trail that winds through the woods across a corner of the estate. The massive library building on the grounds also contains a museum with two floors of exhibits on the president and life in the second half of the 19th century. The house itself is furnished in Victorian elegance with pieces collected from the Hayes home in Cincinnati, which has been destroyed, and from their years at Speigel Grove.

Speigel Grove, which was named, using the German word for "mirror" to describe the pools of water there, reflects the life of the Hayes family home from 1873 until the former president died in 1893. The following three generations of the family made it their home, too, until it was opened to the public in 1966.

It is a place full of memories and of inspiration. It is where Hayes formed the philosophy that helped him through his public life. "The solution to social problems," he said, "is in the home, the school, the lecture hall, the pulpit and the press." It was a philosophy that helped bind a nation back together after decades of uncertainty. It is a philosophy that lives in the Victorian comfort of the big house, its peaceful setting, its quiet elegance.

Spiegel Grove, the Rutherford B. Hayes Presidential Center, is in Fremont, Ohio, just off the Ohio Turnpike between Akron and Toledo. The Residence is open, for a small fee, every day except Thanksgiving, Christmas and New Year's Day. The Library, which is open without charge, is closed on Sundays and holidays. The museum, which also charges an admission fee, is open on the same schedule as the Residence. Guided tours of the Residence are given every day.

Across Buckland Avenue from Speigel Grove is the beautiful Victorian Dillon House, an 1873 mansion that has been restored and furnished in the style of the period. There are guided tours three times a day, Tuesday through Friday. The house is also available for meetings and receptions.

On her bedroom wall (left and far left), the president's daughter, Fanny, proudly hung a portrait of herself and her famous father.

Sardis Birchard, the president's uncle, also had a room there (top left). The dining room (top right) was for the whole family.

20

JAMES A. GARFIELD

(1831-1881)

A self-made man, James A. Garfield was portrayed at the height of his career by O.P.H. Balling.

The National Portrait Gallery, Smithsonian Institution

The 20th president was the sixth and last to be born in a log cabin. He was fond of pointing out that he had been born to poverty. It's true his father died when the future president was just two years old, but the elder Garfield had been a hard-working man who was apprenticed to an Ohio farmer as a boy, and by the time James Garfield was born, he had saved enough money to buy a small farm of his own and to own his house free and clear.

The boy grew up on the farm in Cuyahoga County, Ohio, where he was born. His mother was a fiercely proud woman who scrupulously avoided debt and any of the things she considered symbols of poverty. She made sure her son worked hard to help support the family, and she managed to save enough to send him to Geauga Seminary in Chester, Ohio. He also went to Western Reserve Eclectic Institute, to Hiram College in Ohio and then to Williams College in Williamstown, Massachusetts. At Williams, for a variety of reasons, not the least of which was that he was older than most of the students because he had worked a few years to earn the tuition, he became friendly with the college's president, Mark Hopkins.

He was 24 years old when he graduated from Williams and went back to Western Reserve to teach. He eventually became the school's president, and managed to study enough law to pass the Ohio bar. He further enhanced his status by marrying Lucretia Rudolph, the daughter of a prominent man.

He was married less than a year when he was elected to the Ohio State Senate and seemed headed for a comfortable career when the Civil War broke out. He volunteered as a lieutenant-colonel and rose in a short time to the rank of major general. In 1862, though still in the

Garfield's library (facing page top) contains many presidential mementoes, including the desk he used in Congress. The reception hall (facing page bottom) has a portrait of Lucretia Garfield over the fireplace. The home itself (below) was expanded from nine rooms when the Garfields bought it.

White House china designed by Haviland is in the dining room cabinet (below). Lucretia Garfield's bedroom (bottom), used after her husband's death, contains a white cradle used by 39 family members.

army, he was elected to Congress, a seat he held for 17 years, the last three years of which he was Minority Leader of the House.

His Congressional career ended at the 1880 Republican National Convention, to which he was a delegate on behalf of another Ohio Congressman. The convention was deadlocked, and it was beginning to look as though it couldn't agree on any candidate, when out of nowhere the name of James Abram Garfield came up. No one, least of all he, expected it would come to anything. But when the votes were counted after the 36th ballot, Mr. Garfield was the man they chose to oppose Winfield S. Hancock in the November election.

Garfield was a spellbinding speaker and managed to overcome an attempt at character assassination from the opposition camp. A dozen years before, Garfield had been charged with having accepted a bribe of $329 from a railroad construction company. He denied the charge and proved his innocence to everyone's satisfaction at the time. But in the presidential election it was a handy hatchet for the Democrats. Soon grafitti began appearing everywhere, from the front porch of Garfield's house to San Francisco piers, in the form of the number 329. Everyone knew what the numbers meant, but they didn't mean enough to tip the balance in favor of W.S. Hancock, and in 1881 James A. Garfield became the 20th President of the United States.

The first job of any president is keeping office-seekers at bay, and President Garfield had more than the usual number since his nomination had represented a compromise between two factions of the Republican Party. Neither had any love for the other, and neither was satisfied with all of the new president's appointments.

In the midst of it all, the dark horse president had to deal with a dark horse candidate for the post of consul in Paris. A man named Charles Guiteau felt he was ideal for the job, but couldn't get the president's ear to state his case. On July 2, 1881, as Garfield was boarding a train for New England, Guiteau appeared at the railroad station with a gun in his hand.

He fired two shots at the president, who dropped to the floor, and ran out into the street where he was captured by police. The president was taken back to the White House where he stayed, near death, until the end of August. In September he was taken to the Elberon Hotel in Long Branch, New Jersey, which had been the summer home of his predecessor, Rutherford B. Hayes. He died there 80 days after the shots were fired, on September 19, 1881. The assassin Guiteau was tried, found guilty of murder and hanged the following June.

In addition to being a lawyer and a teacher, Garfield was also an ordained minister in the Disciples of Christ church. He was the only minister to live in the White House.

His house in Mentor, Ohio, which a newspaper reporter named "Lawnfield" during the 1880 campaign, was a rundown farmhouse on 118 acres when he bought it in 1876. Because he needed space for his wife and five children and his mother, who had come to live with them, he doubled it in size. Four years after his death, while it was still the home of his widow, Lucretia, a new wing was added and the house that had contained seven rooms when the family first moved there now had 30 rooms. The house remained the home of the Garfield family until the 1930s, when it was donated to the Western Reserve Historical Society, who opened it to the public as a museum in 1936.

The wide hallway on the second floor (above and above right) was a busy place when the 1880 presidential campaign was conducted from the second floor study at Lawnfield. When he wanted to get away from it all, Garfield often went downstairs to his bedroom (right) to juggle the Indian clubs that are still there on the floor.

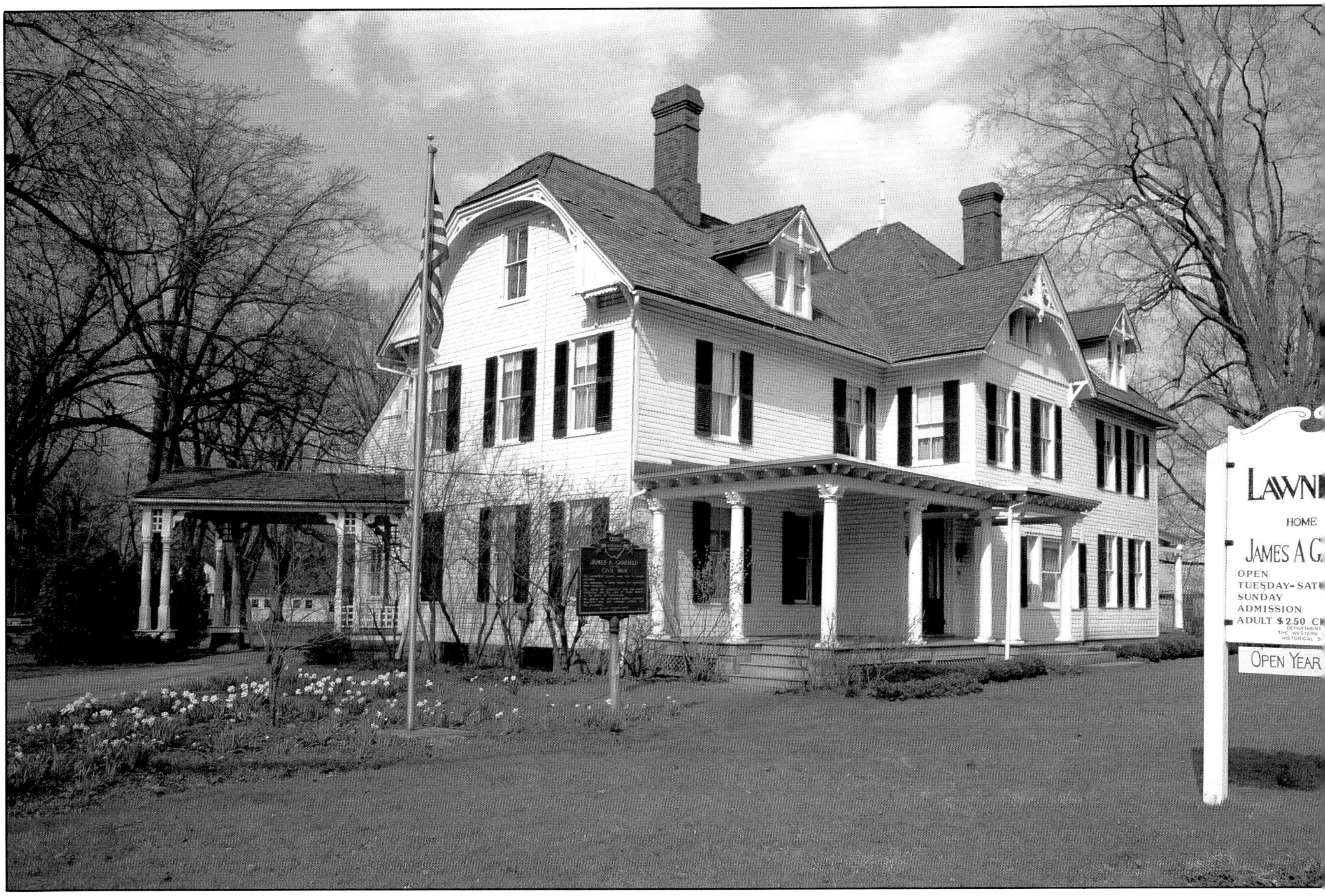

Everything in the house, from family portraits to heirloom china, belonged to the Garfield family, though some of the furnishings were added after the president's assassination. In the first floor bedroom of President and Mrs. Garfield are, among other things, the wooden Indian clubs he used to help keep in shape. The Memorial Library on the second floor was built with money that had been sent to the president's widow after the assassination by ordinary citizens concerned for the family's welfare. The total came to more than $400,000, which she used to construct what she thought would be the most appropriate memorial to the fallen president.

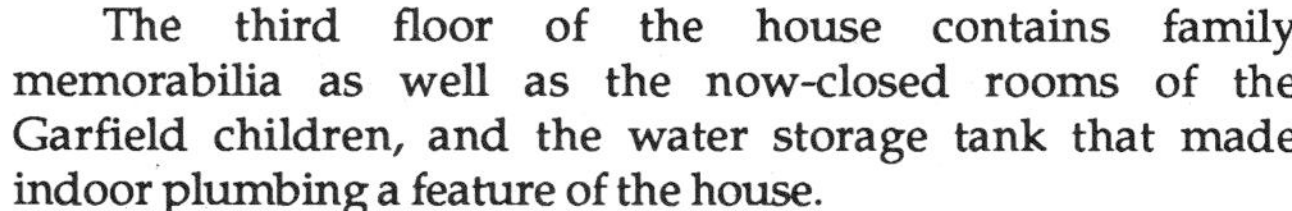

The third floor of the house contains family memorabilia as well as the now-closed rooms of the Garfield children, and the water storage tank that made indoor plumbing a feature of the house.

The second floor, in addition to the library, also has Garfield's study where the campaign of 1880 was planned and the bedroom his widow used after his death, which has on display a handmade cradle that was made for her and eventually used by 39 Garfield babies.

The Western Reserve Historical Society has special events in the house every month, sometimes a special exhibit or a lecture, sometimes a concert. During the entire month of December, the house is decorated for a Victorian Christmas.

After his election to the presidency, Garfield asked, "Will my name have a place in history?" The answer, of course, is yes. But nowhere in the United States is he better remembered than at Lawnfield, the home he loved, in Mentor, Ohio.

Lawnfield, the home of James A. Garfield, is a 30-room Victorian home at 8095 Mentor Avenue in Mentor, Ohio. It is open all year, except Mondays and major holidays, for a small admission fee.

Also in Mentor, which is a few miles northeast of Cleveland, is the Holden Arboretum, a 2800-acre sanctuary of forests and nature trails. It is open every day but Mondays, except Christmas and New Year's Day. There is a small admission charge.

In nearby Chardon is an 11-story Geodesic Dome, designed by R. Buckminster Fuller, which is the headquarters of the American Society for Metals. Its mineral garden is open every day.

In Geneva, the Western Reserve home, Shandy Hall is open every day except Monday from May through October.

In Painesville, the Fairport Harbor Lighthouse, with a lighthouse keeper's home and ship's pilothouse, is open from Memorial Day through Labor Day on weekends and holidays.

Public appearances in his campaign were made on Garfield's front porch (top left), and planned in his study (top right). The piano in the parlor (far left) belonged to daughter Mollie, whose bedroom is shown (left).

21

CHESTER A. ARTHUR
(1829-1886)

Third in a year. Chester A. Arthur, subject of this portrait by O.P.H. Balling, was the third man to assume the presidency in 1881. It happened before, in 1841, when John Tyler became president.

The National Portrait Gallery, Smithsonian Institution

Chester Alan Arthur probably would have preferred the office of vice president of the United States to being its president. But fate intervened on September 19, 1881 in the form of an assassin's bullet, and on the death of James Garfield, Chester A. Arthur became the 21st president of the United States.

He had been a compromise candidate in the first place, yet another reward for faithful service to the Republican party machine in New York. But when an old crony of his went to Washington on a job-seeking mission and was turned down by the new president, he said: "If the roles were reversed, you'd be here asking for the same thing." "I know," said the president, "but Chester A. Arthur is one person and the President of the United States is quite another."

Arthur was born on October 5, 1830 in North Fairfield, Vermont, the son of a prosperous Baptist minister. His father had been born in Ireland and graduated from the University of Belfast the year before he emigrated to Canada. Very soon afterward he moved again, to Vermont, where he had a job as a teacher and a dream of becoming a lawyer. A religious revival meeting changed his plan. He had been raised a Presbyterian and became an Episcopalian when he married, but the revival convinced him that God meant him to be a Baptist, and his success in the pulpit convinced everyone else that God was probably right.

The family moved to Western New York State when the boy was very young, and when he was 18 he graduated from Union College and moved to a Hudson River village north of Albany, where he became principal of a private school. He saved his money and a year later went to New York City to study law. Later he established a law firm in the city, which he gave up to seek his fortune in Kansas. But he missed New York and was back in a few months and on his way upward.

His first upward move was to marry Ellen Herndon, the daughter of one of the celebrated First Families of Virginia. With the marriage came an expensive town house at 34 West 21st Street in Manhattan, and the beginning of the Arthurs' enviable reputation as elegant entertainers.

His penchant for dinner parties and balls helped his law career and it also encouraged him to look for a career in politics. He began as an unpaid inspector of elections, but quickly, through a new-found friendship with the Governor of New York, he was appointed to a variety of posts culminating, after the outbreak of the Civil War, in the post of quartermaster general. He engineered a promotion after that to inspector general, a post that required that he spend the war years in New York City.

When the war was over, he and his wife bought a five-story row house at 123 Lexington Avenue in New York, where they turned their penchant for entertaining into a fine art. It was in this house, which is still standing, that Chester A. Arthur became the only president except George Washington to take the oath of office in New York City.

In the late 1860s, their parties had guest lists that included the likes of J.P. Morgan and Cyrus Field, August Belmont and Peter Cooper. In 1864 Arthur became counsel to the New York City Tax Commission, and by 1871 he was collector of the Port of New York, a job that, in the days before income taxes, was probably the greatest opportunity on earth for a young lawyer with expensive tastes. He was suspended from the job by President Hayes in 1878, some said for political reasons, others claimed because of "wrongdoing." It was a fact that Chester A. Arthur averaged $50,000 a year in the job. But it is also a fact that a year after the suspension, he was named chairman of the Republican State Committee and the president who suspended him also offered him the job of consul in Paris, ironically the same job that three years later the murderer who catapulted him to the presidency had claimed he was entitled to.

After he became president, Arthur refused to move into the White House until it was redecorated. Few people blamed him. It had turned into a rather dreary place during the Hayes administration, and the Grants had added some garish touches in contrast. Before the restoration was finished, 24 wagonloads of furnishings were removed and sold. During the three months the work was going on, Arthur shared a house on New Jersey Avenue with a senator from Nevada.

The restoration was a stunner, with Art Noveau furnishings produced by Louis Comfort Tiffany. And the parties that followed fit the setting perfectly. Unfortunately, Mrs. Arthur had died in 1880 and missed the honor, which she most certainly would have enjoyed, of being First Lady. The job of being hostess at Arthur's White House entertainments fell to his sister, who proved as much a bon vivant as her brother.

In spite of the fun, Chester Arthur chose not to run for a second term. He retired at the end of his term and died soon after, on November 18, 1886. His body is buried at Albany, New York.

The house in North Fairfield, Vermont, where the 21st president was born, vanished many years ago. In 1903 a monument was erected on the site, and in 1953 the Vermont Division of Historical Preservation constructed a replica of the parsonage that was probably his birthplace. The state is quick to point out that the building is intended to be more of a symbol than a faithful restoration. There were no records of what the building actually looked like, though old photographs gave some clues. The problem was made more difficult by the claim of one important biographer that the future president was born in a temporary structure and that the house that was duplicated wasn't built until 1830. On the other hand, most biographers agree that at

A year was lost when the future president subtracted it from his age in 1880. This replica of his birthplace had already been placed at the site of a house built in 1830 when historians proved that he was born in 1829.

some point in his career Arthur claimed he had been born in 1830 and not 1829, the officially accepted date. Who can blame the man for wanting to appear younger? Most of us do, after all.

Chester A. Arthur surprised the party hacks, who had considered him to be one of their number, by strongly supporting the creation of a Civil Service system, an act that prompted Mark Twain to say "...it would be hard to better President Arthur's Administration." He was also responsible for the Tariff Commission and for the transformation of the U.S. Navy from wooden ships to steel. And, as an old collector of customs duties, he began new programs to encourage American ships to engage in foreign trade.

He was the first president to fly an official flag, the first to visit a national park, indeed, the first to travel extensively in the West as president of the whole country.

And everywhere he went, people were charmed by his well-tailored appearance, his courtly manners and his friendly outlook. The voters had never had much chance to get to know him because the only time he ever ran for public office was on the Farfield presidential ticket. Four years later, it was obvious to everyone that he could easily have won any election he had his heart set on.

The Chester A. Arthur Birthplace is in North Fairfield, Vermont, about ten miles from Saint Albans on Route 36. Nearby is the Old Brick Church, built in 1830, where the 21st president's father was the preacher. The house is a replica of the original, but the church is authentic, with original pews, altar and organ. The site is open Wednesday through Sunday from mid-June to mid-October. There is no admission charge.

Nearby Saint Albans is in the heart of the Vermont maple syrup country and is the site of a three-day maple sugar festival in early April. The town also has a 45-acre park on the shores of Lake Champlain and another on an island in the lake.

22 & 24

GROVER CLEVELAND

(1837-1908)

The National Portrait Gallery, Smithsonian Institution

"Horse Neck" was where he was born at the Presbyterian Manse (facing page), but the little New Jersey town became Caldwell after Grover Cleveland left to seek his fortune.

The man he became is the subject of this Eastman Johnson portrait.

Grover Cleveland was the first Democrat to become president in 24 years, and there couldn't have been a more unlikely candidate for the job. Republicans called him "his accidency." The day he took the oath of office in Washington was the second time in his life he had ever been to the capital. The audience he addressed was the largest he had ever seen, and almost no one in that audience had ever seen him before. The only elective offices he had ever held were as mayor of Buffalo, New York, and governor of the state of New York.

Yet here he was, all 240 pounds of him, double chins hanging below a walrus moustache, looking for all the world like the "Hangman of Buffalo" his opponent had called him in the recent campaign. The slur stemmed from the fact that once, while Cleveland was a county sheriff, he took the job of hanging a man away from a nervous executioner.

But if he had been elected by accident, his term as the 22nd president was probably the happiest accident that ever happened to the country. After all those years of one-party rule, the Republicans were living off the fat of the land. After winning the 1884 election, the Democrats got the idea that they could begin doing the same thing. But Crover Cleveland wasn't the man to help them do it. In the first four years he was in the White House he vetoed more bills than all 21 of his predecessors combined. He also set a record for replacing officeholders, and not one of the firings was based on anything more than a careful look at each man's record. Who did the looking? No less a person than the president himself. He was a demon for work. During his first months in the White House he didn't even have a secretary. It didn't occur to him that he needed one. He wrote his own letters in longhand, and since there was only one telephone in the White House, he was perfectly capable of answering it himself.

Words like "industrious," "honest," fair" come to mind in connection with Grover Cleveland. A newspaper that supported him in the campaign ran a short editorial under the headline, "Four Good Reasons For Electing Cleveland." It said, "1. He is honest. 2. He is honest. 3. He is honest. 4. He is honest."

He seems to have come by it honestly. He was born Stephen Grover Cleveland to a Presbyterian minister and his wife in Caldwell, New Jersey, in 1837. His father, a Yale graduate, was the product of old Yankee stock. His maternal grandmother was a Quaker from Germany who married an immigrant from Ireland.

His father died when he was still young, leaving his widow with nine children. He went to work to help her support them and he was never without a job again. When he was 18 years old, he decided to go West to find greener pastures. On his way he stopped off in Buffalo to visit his uncle, Lewis F. Allen, a successful farmer. It happened that Uncle Lewis was writing a book and hired the boy to help with it. Before it was finished he encouraged his nephew to stay and offered to help him realize a dream to become a lawyer.

Once he was admitted to the bar, his uncle helped him get a job in one of Buffalo's best law firms, and by the time he was 26 he was appointed assistant district attorney. Three years later he was chairman of the local Democratic Committee, and in three more years he had taken on that fateful job as sheriff.

Cleveland was what they used to call "a man's man." He enjoyed the conviviality of men's clubs and saloons. He enjoyed hunting and fishing almost as much as he enjoyed hard work. And he had a reputation for gourmandise that was the talk of Erie County.

But if he loved the good life, he had enough of his Puritan ancestors' blood to give him a reputation of having unusually high moral standards, and when he ran for mayor in 1881 he won in a landslide.

City Hall had never seen anything like him. He was like Hercules cleaning the Augean stables. He put in 14-hour days, and was so successful in rooting out municipal corruption that he became famous all over the state. It was inevitable that he would be elected governor, and just as inevitable that he'd put in the same long hours and act with the same ruthlessness with anyone who cheated, lied or stole a cent of the taxpayer's money.

He was at work in Albany when the Democrats nominated him for president. When he was told the news, he barely skipped a beat and went right on working.

His Republican opponent, James G. Blaine, was a man the word "charisma" might have been coined for. Cleveland, on the other hand, was, at least by comparison, a dull man. If the election were held in the 1980s instead of the 1880s, there probably would be no contest. But his campaign slogan made Cleveland a candidate to reckon with. A newspaperman said it first, but everyone agreed it summed up the Cleveland philosophy: "Public Office is a Public Trust."

Cleveland hadn't been in the White House long when, at age 48, he decided it was time to get married. It made him the first president to be married in the White House, and his bride, Frances Folsom, who had just graduated from college, more than made up for what her husband lacked in personal charm. She charmed him, too. He once told a reporter that his life was "one grand sweet song." It was a marked contrast to the feelings most of his predecessors had about life in the White House. Almost to a man they agreed with Lincoln that, rather than glory, the office brought nothing but "ashes and blood."

Cleveland easily took his party's nomination for a second term and fought well in the campaign. He was

201

No small man, the 240-pound Cleveland filled a big chair in the White House. It is on display (right) at his birthplace (above). Other rooms in the house contain furnishings that were there when the future president was born

immensely popular with the voters in the big Eastern states, and though the West was suspicious of some of the ideas, he won the election by nearly 96,000 votes. But the votes were in the wrong places. He lost the election to Benjamin Harrison by 70 electoral votes. Among the states that went for Harrison was New York, Cleveland's own political base, where the machine had worked against him on principle; or rather its lack of principles.

Because of his showing in '88, the Democrats renominated him in 1892. His victory made him the 24th as well as the 22nd president.

His second term wasn't the same "grand sweet song." It was marked from the beginning by a depression, which led to unemployment, labor union troubles and distress in the West, where they never quite liked Cleveland anyway. He handled the problems in the same way he always had, one at a time. But the country was changing. He managed to keep it from changing for the worse, which a lesser man might not have done, but when he retired to his classic Georgian house in Princeton, New Jersey, he was a broken man. When he died there 11 years later, his last words were: "I tried hard to do right."

The house where Cleveland died in 1908 is now a private residence. The house where he was born, not far from Princeton, in Caldwell, New Jersey, is the former Presbyterian Manse, built in 1832 when Caldwell was known as Horse Neck.

The Grover Cleveland Birthplace is at 207 Bloomfield Avenue in Caldwell, New Jersey. The future president lived in the two-story clapboard house from 1837 to 1840. The house, which still contains the original furnishings, is maintained by the New Jersey Bureau of Parks and is open, without charge, Wednesdays through Sundays except Thanksgiving, Christmas and New Year's Day.

Caldwell is a suburb of New York City, southwest of Paterson, New Jersey.

A few miles further south, in West Orange, is the Edison National Historic Site, which includes Thomas Edison's laboratory where he worked for 44 years. The laboratory includes the first phonograph, some early incandescent lamps and a reconstruction of the world's first motion picture studio.

Edison's home, Glenmont, furnished as it was when he lived there between 1886 and 1931, is open every Wednesday and Sunday except holidays. The laboratory is open Wednesday through Sunday, except Thanksgiving, Christmas and New Year's Day. A small admission fee is charged for both buildings.

23

BENJAMIN HARRISON

(1833-1901)

The shoe fits! Though he protested campaigning on the fact that his grandfather had been president, Benjamin Harrison, (whose Eastman Johnson portrait is shown right and his home below), couldn't escape the comparison. But his oratory would have been enough to get him elected.

A sure winner in any game of presidential trivia would be to name the man who was the son of a president of the United States as well as the father of a president. His name was John Scott Harrison, son of the ninth president and father of the 23d, Benjamin Harrison.

The National Portrait Gallery, Smithsonian Institution

John Scott Harrison missed his place in history because of his father rather than in spite of him. He began his career as a partner in one of the most prestigious law firms in the state of Ohio and was well on his way to political fame and financial security when he was forced to give it all up to help run his father's estate. William Henry Harrison had inherited a substantial estate and had built an impressive one of his own. But financial setbacks made keeping it all together a full-time job, and that job fell on the shoulders of his son. The son did, however, manage to find time to serve as justice of the peace for two decades, to serve in the Congress of the United States, and to father twelve children.

Benjamin Harrison was born at the home his grandfather had built in North Bend, Ohio. Within a few months of his birth, the family moved to a big brick farmhouse in North Bend, which was torn down in 1959, exactly 101 years after his birthplace nearby burned to the ground. Young Harrison was, like his brothers and sisters, educated on the 600-acre farm, and when he was 14 he was sent to a private school to get ready for college. His father had hoped to be able to send him back east to one of the prestigious New England colleges, but financial

An artist's life would have suited the president's wife Carrie, who, in addition to raising two children and serving as First Lady, was also an accomplished painter. Her studio (facing page) is virtually unchanged since the time she found so much joy there.

Political life in the Harrison family was usually conducted here in the library (above), where he planned the campaign that led to the White House.

considerations made it necessary for him to go to Miami University in Ohio instead. He studied law in Cincinnati after that, living with a married sister until he was admitted to the bar at the age of 21.

By the time his law career began, he was married to the former Carrie Scott. They moved in 1855, after the birth of their first child, to Indianapolis, Indiana, where the young lawyer had begun a lucrative practice. They lived in three different houses in Indianapolis and, just before he enlisted in the Army in 1862, he began making plans for a new house that would better reflect his position as the grandson of a president, not to mention one of the most successful lawyers in town and reporter of the State Supreme Court. His army career interrupted his plans, but didn't hurt his political fortunes a bit. He enlisted as a second lieutenant and during the two years he served, he rose to the rank of brigadier general through his actions in campaigns at Atlanta, Nashville, Peachtree Creek and Kennesaw Mountain.

Not long after he came home, he bought two building lots on North Delaware Street in Indianapolis and went back to planning his new house. But he had other plans, too. In 1872, already an influential figure in the state Republican party, he made a bid to become governor of Indiana. The bid failed, but he succeeded in getting the nomination four years later, at which time the voters rejected him. In 1881 the legislature sent him to Washington to serve in the Senate. The voters didn't send him back when he ran for a second term in 1886. But he didn't seem to mind. His heart was in Indianapolis. In fact, the night he was elected to the presidency, he went to bed right after the Indiana election was called in his favor, in spite of the fact that the national election was still very much in doubt. "My own state is for me," he said. "It is all that matters." Fortunately for Benjamin Harrison, all the right states were for him. His opponent, Grover Cleveland, had been the voters' favorite by more that 95,000 votes. But in electoral votes, where it really counts, Benjamin Harrison woke up the following morning with a majority of 65.

He woke up that morning in the house at 1230 North Delaware Street in Indianapolis, a 16-room mansion he built in 1875. Except for the following four years as president, and the six years he had served in the Senate, it was the only home he knew until he died there in 1901. During their White House years, his wife, Carrie, put her experience of building the Delaware Street house over a

period of more than 20 months to good use by having plans drawn to expand the executive mansion. Congress wouldn't go along with the scheme, though, and she had to content herself with improving what she had. She started by exterminating the rats in the basement, an accomplishment that many have tried, but few have ever accomplished in the history of the Republic. She also managed to have the kitchens modernized, the greenhouse rebuilt and new floors installed. She also had electric lights installed in the White House, an innovation she would never see back home in Indiana. Carrie died at the White House in 1892 and her husband returned home to Indianapolis a year later alone. A few years after that, he married Mary Lord Dimmick, the niece of his late wife. She completely redecorated the Indianapolis house, added an impressive columned porch and, following in her aunt's footsteps, had the gaslights replaced by electricity.

When the former president died, his wife moved to New York and rented the Indianapolis house as a boarding house. In 1937 she sold it to the Arthur Jordan Foundation

Original furniture, in the back parlor (top left), dining room (bottom left), master bedroom (left), guest room (top) and nursery (above) was all stored in the ballroom after a major 1897 renovation.

HOME
OF
BENJAMIN HARRISON
23RD PRESIDENT OF THE
UNITED STATES
INDIANA'S OWN CITIZEN

The front porch (facing page) was added by Harrison's second wife, Mary, when she also brought electric lights to the house.

as a memorial to the 23d president. Work on its restoration began almost immediately and original furniture, some of which had been placed in the ballroom for storage, was returned to take the house back to its 19th-century splendor. The entire home was open to the public in 1974 after a second renovation that included the destruction of some neighboring buildings to allow the house to stand free in its original setting. The 1974 renovation also eliminated the original dirt-floor cellar in favor of community meeting rooms. The third floor ballroom was converted to a museum. The other floors were restored to their original appearance. The formal dining room, where much of President Harrison's political life was centered, contains the original mohogany table and chairs. The master bedroom is once again dominated by a massive, hand-covered maple bed inlaid with rosewood. The front parlor has its original gaslight fixture and the back parlor has all the comforts of the original home.

The house captures the personality of the man whom history has often treated sneeringly. Some of his contemporaries said that Benjamin Harrison was possibly the coldest human being they had ever met. Yet everyone conceded that he was the most dynamic speaker they had ever heard. During the campaign of 1888, the Republican leadership devised a perfect formula of whistlestops that were carefully overlapped so that their candidate was forced to leave for the next stop as soon as his speech was finished, so that no potential voters would have a chance to look him in the eye and experience his handshake, which some said was as limp as a dead fish.

But what he lacked in charisma he seems to have more than made up in honesty. He was unapproachable in every way, much to the consternation of office-seekers who found it took more than a wink, a handshake and reminder of owed favors to get things done their way in the Harrison administration.

All through his political career he never seems to have doubted for a minute that he owed that career to the memory of his grandfather. Yet he began his first major political speech by telling his listeners that "... I want it understood that I am the grandson of nobody. I believe that every man should stand on his own merits." And he wasn't speaking only for himself, as he proved time and again during his White House years.

The front parlor (above) reflects the formal elegance of the 1875 era, when Harrison built his brick mansion for $21,123.10. The gaslight survived later renovation.

The President Benjamin Harrison Home at 1230 North Delaware Street in Indianapolis, Indiana, is open every day February through December except Easter, Thanksgiving and Christmas Day. There is a small admission fee. The site also includes an old-fashioned herb garden and a gift shop.

Also in Indianapolis is the impressive limestone World War Memorial Plaza with a unique room dedicated to the American flag. It is also the national headquarters of the American Legion. Lockerbie Square is a six-block neighborhood of cobblestone streets and brick sidewalks in front of restored 19th-century homes, one of which was the home of James Whitcomb Riley, "The Hoosier Poet."

The Morris-Butler House at 1204 N. Park Avenue is a museum of Victorian furniture and decorative arts in a restored house built in 1865.

25

WILLIAM MCKINLEY
(1843-1901)

The National Portrait Gallery, Smithsonian Institution

A $500 bill will show you what William McKinley looked like. But, for now, this portrait by Charles Ayer Whipple will serve as a reasonable substitute.

In all the history of America, few men have ever proven as well that "nice guys finish last" as the 25th president, William McKinley. To be sure, he had a brilliant career. He was elected to Congress for Ohio in 1876 and served in the House of Representatives until 1891. While he was there, he was chairman of the House Ways and Means Committee, making him one of the most powerful men in the capital. His opinion was respected by everyone on both sides of the aisle. The rich and powerful across the country curried his favor. But he put it all aside to run for governor of Ohio, a job he held from 1892 until 1896. He gave that up to run for the presidency. He beat the immensely popular William Jennings Bryan by a comfortable margin, twice.

Not many men would consider any of that evidence of finishing last. But on September 6, 1901, William McKinley became the third President of the United States to be assassinated. Even he didn't believe it. As they were carrying him off to the hospital with two bullets in him, he looked toward the anarchist, Leon Czolgosz, who had shot him, and said, "must be some poor misguided fellow."

He had married well, too. But there was a problem there. His wife, Ida, the daughter of a wealthy banker, had inherited enough money to make them comfortable. But a year or two after their marriage she became ill and for the rest of her life was subject to headaches and fits of epilepsy.

But to know him was to love William McKinley. Though few people ever loved him more than Ida, fewer still could ever come up with a harsh word for the man. And the love was genuine. Office-seekers he turned away usually went away smiling for having had the opportunity to talk with the man. Political opponents never seriously got angry at his opposition. It's highly likely that even the misguided Leon Czolgosz would have liked him if he hadn't had a pistol in his hand when the president reached out his to shake it.

Of the 40 presidents, McKinley is the only one without some place, somewhere, except for the White House, of course, that he once lovingly called home. He was born on Main Street in Niles, Ohio, in a two-story building with a store in front. The building was moved twice in his lifetime, and was eventually destroyed in a fire started by vandals. When the future president was nine years old, his family moved to Poland, Ohio. The house they moved to was eventually torn down to make room for a fire house. Another house they called home in the same town was removed to build a parking lot. Such is often the story of America. But in McKinley's case, the story doesn't end there.

After having served in the Ohio Infantry during the Civil War, during which time he received a battlefield commission to the rank of major, he moved to Canton, Ohio, to begin reading law. The house he lived in there has vanished. Next he went to Albany, New York, to law school. There is no trace of the place he lived in while he was there, and there is no sign of the rooming house he lived in when he hung out his shingle in Youngstown, Ohio.

When he married the former Ida Paxton, they first lived in a hotel in Canton, which no longer exists. Then his father-in-law presented him with a house in town that was their home for six years. He sold it when he was elected to Congress in 1876. It was torn down to make way for a hospital, but carefully this time; someone had an idea to rebuild it some day. The parts were put into storage, but not carefully enough, and when they were removed for reconstruction they were too badly weathered to do anything with them. While he was in Congress, they stayed during the summer in Ida's family home in Canton. That building still exists, but is in private hands, and not many people remember that a President of the United States once lived there.

During his years as governor of Ohio, they lived in a hotel in Columbus that burned down while they were living there. They leased a house near the capitol, but it has since been destroyed, too. During his years as governor, he bought back the house he had sold in Canton. His plan was to retire there some day, but of course, he never had the chance to retire. He also bought a farm near Canton which is still in existence, but sadly run down.

But it's not as though William McKinley is without memorials. You may not get to see one very often, but his picture is on the $500 bill. You may never get to Alaska, but if you do, the highest mountain there, or in all the United States, for that matter, is the 20,320-ft. Mount McKinley, which, as is typical of the 25th president's luck, is in a National Park that was once named for him but has since become known as Denali National Park. There is a county in New Mexico named for him, too.

A spacious porch, with an octagonal gazebo, made the McKinley house one of the finest in Canton, OH. It was removed to build a hospital.

The great memorial of the McKinley presidency is, ironically, the one thing that the man would have opposed almost to the death had he not been subjected to the pressures of the office. He was a man who loved his fellow man, almost to a fault. The way he treated his wife prompted one colleague in Congress to say, "He makes it hard on all us husbands." Though he had been a hero in the Civil War, he hated the idea of sending young men into battle. When agitation began, during his first year in the White House, for the U.S. to go to war with Spain, he said that he had "seen one war, and don't ever want to see another." But when the U.S. battleship Maine was blown up in Havana harbor on February 15, 1898, even he couldn't stay out of the conflict between Cuban rebels and the Spanish government. He was responsible for ordering a U.S. blockade of Cuba that spring, which resulted in the Spanish-American War. Within weeks, the U.S. Navy confronted the Spanish fleet and destroyed it in the Philippines, and by the end of the year the Spanish had agreed to give the United States the Philippines, Guam and Puerto Rico as well as giving independence to Cuba. Most Americans at the time, the president included, weren't even too sure where such places as Puerto Rico and Guam might be. But the troubles in Manila started a groundswell for the annexation of Hawaii, which also took place in the McKinley administration.

The war and the expansionism that followed it seems to have suited the American psyche. When he ran for a second term in 1900, William McKinley received the highest plurality of any candidate for president up to that point. But, of course, that second term lasted less than a year. Somebody, obviously, didn't like William McKinley.

Photo courtesy of the Stark County Historical Society, Parent Organization of the McKinley Museum of History, Science and Industry, Canton, Ohio.

He lived for nine more days after the assassin's bullets struck him down in Buffalo, New York. And before he died, with his wife at his side, she said to him "I want to go, too." To which he responded, "We are all going." She lived another six years. They are reunited in Canton, Ohio.

THEODORE ROOSEVELT

(1855-1919)

The enthusiasms of Teddy Roosevelt are everywhere in his Queen Anne-style mansion, Sagamore Hill (facing page) in Oyster Bay, Long Island. Among his hunting trophies in the North Room (below) is the presidential flag he designed himself. His portrait (right) was painted by Sally James Farnham.

The National Portrait Gallery, Smithsonian Institution

Any American who grew up in the era of comic books remembers the advertisement for the Charles Atlas body-building method that introduced a 97-pound weakling who had sand kicked in his face at the beach – until he tried "dynamic tension" to get a better body and to help get the girl of his dreams. Young Teddy Roosevelt would have answered that ad. But as it turned out, he didn't need it. When he was ten years old, his father put his arm on the frail boy's shoulder and said, "You have the mind, but you have not the body, and without the help of the body, the mind cannot go as far as it should. ... You must make your body."

The lad didn't waste a day. At first he went to a local gym and began lifting weights, hoisting himself on parallel bars and pounding at a punching bag. It was a painfully slow process that continued for the rest of his life, and no Roosevelt home was ever again without equipment to help keep the master of the house in shape.

When he was 14 he was given the gift of a gun and a pair of glasses. He had already developed a love for birds and small beasts ... stuffed. But until that moment, he had never known that his eyes were as weak as his body had been. The glasses helped him stalk better and better specimens; the gun helped him capture them for his collection. And no Roosevelt home from that moment was ever without stuffed birds and animals, trophies of T. R.'s hunting instinct, many of which were mounted by the amateur taxidermist who would eventually become President of the United States.

His first home was the place where he was born, a brownstone house near Madison Square in New York City. It was there on the third floor that his first personal gymnasium was installed and where he established the first "Roosevelt Museum of Natural History." When he was a teenager, the family moved uptown to another brownstone on West 57th Street just off Fifth Avenue to be closer to Central Park, where the family felt the air would be better for the still frail young man.

After his graduation from Harvard and a year at Columbia University's law school, he married Alice Lee and took her home to the house near Central Park. Four years later, on Valentine's Day, eleven hours after the death of his mother, she died, and the young Roosevelt, who had already served for two years in the New York State legislature, gave up New York for the life of a rancher in the Dakota Territory. He had already become a partner in an outfit called the Maltese Cross Ranch, and in 1884, he got out his pearl-handled six shooter, his tailor-made buckskin jacket, his silver-plated belt and returned to the open range, where he lived in a rather luxurious log cabin surrounded by books, fine clothes and other trappings that gave a new meaning to the word "dude." He also gave a new meaning to the word "bully" by using his fists against anyone who would be one. He much preferred using the word as an adjective.

After two years of being at home on the range, he went back to New york to run for mayor in 1886. He lost the election, but a month later became a bridegroom again by marrying the former Edith Carow, who eventually bore him four sons and a daughter. His firstborn, Alice, his only child from his first marriage, was three years old when her brother, Theodore, was born.

By the time of his second marriage, T.R. had bought 150 acres of land on Cove Neck at Oyster Bay on Long Island. In 1882 he began work on a house he originally intended to name "Leeholm" in honor of his first wife. The house was finished in 1885 and became the base for his campaign for Mayor of New York City. But the original name didn't seem appropriate any longer. His plans for a second marriage made him change it to "Sagamore Hill," in honor of the Indian chief who had given the land to the white men who settled the area.

From the time the Roosevelts moved into the house in 1887 it was their home until he died there in 1919, and the home of his widow until her death in 1948. T.R.'s career took them to Washington, first as Civil Service Commissioner and then as Assistant Secretary of the Navy. In 1898 he moved to the Governor's Mansion in Albany and in 1901 moved back to Washington to become Vice President of the United States. On September 14, six months after arriving, the Roosevelts moved into the White House after the assassination of President William McKinley. Sagamore Hill became the Summer White

A summer cottage was what they considered this house (left), but they were here as often as at home in New York, enjoying family meals in the dining room (above).

The Rough Rider tossed his hat in the air and it landed on a set of antlers, a trophy in the North Room. It's one of the memories still there.

House from 1901 until 1909, and it was also, like the White House itself, the center of a maelstrom of family activity. The Roosevelt children were encouraged to play hard no matter where they were, and T.R. once said: "I don't think any family has ever enjoyed the White House more than we have." He described the pillow fights, which he often instigated, as "vigorous." He encouraged them to rollerskate in the East Room, to take the family pony up in the elevator to have a look at the family living quarters, and to let their pet bear wander the halls to the consternation of official visitors.

Because Sagamore Hill was their own, life there was even more uninhibited. But there was always a rule book to be obeyed. T.R. described their life in Oyster Bay when he wrote: "I should say there was just the proper mixture of freedom and control in the management of the children. They were never allowed to be disobedient or to shirk lessons or work; and they were encouraged to have all the fun possible. They often went barefoot, especially during the many hours passed in various enthralling pursuits along and in the waters of the bay. They swam, they tramped, they boated, they coasted and skated in winter,

they were intimate friends with the cows, chickens, pigs and other livestock."

It is hardly the usual image of a Victorian family, yet Teddy Roosevelt himself had been brought up that way. One measure of the success of it all is his son Theodore Roosevelt, Jr. who earned the Congressional Medal of Honor for bravery during the Allied invasion of France on June 6, 1944.

The house in Oyster Bay, on the other hand, is as fine an example of Victorian living as any in the United States. It is a solid, 23-room frame and brick structure that has changed very little since the day Edith Roosevelt died there at the age of 87 in 1948, and not much more than it looked when the 60-year-old Theodore Roosevelt died there in 1919.

In describing the house himself, T.R. wrote, "I wished a big piazza where we could sit in rocking chairs and look at the sunset; a library with a shallow bay window looking south, the parlor or drawing room occupying all the western end of the lower floor ... big fireplaces for logs (there are four on each floor, with dumbwaiters to haul the logs) ... I had to live inside and not outside the house, and

Roosevelt's hero, his father, "the best man I ever knew," is the subject of the big portrait in his Sagamore Hill library (below).

while I should have liked to express myself in both, as I had to choose, I chose the former."

The grounds of Sagamore Hill seem perfectly to reflect the personality of the 26th president, who was an ardent conservationist, and the nearby Old Orchard Museum, built as the home of Theodore Roosevelt, Jr. is a tribute to his enthusiasm passed on. But the spirit of T.R. lives inside the big house, which is filled with flags and trophies, books and paintings and furniture that bristle with the passions of the man. His collection of guns is there, too, and all round the feeling of family life that was probably T.R.'s greatest passion.

Wandering through the comfortable rooms, it's easily possible to expect to turn around and see the grinning man with the big white moustache and hear him say, as he once did while president: "come with me and I'll teach you how to walk on stilts."

Japan's Emperor gave him the quilt for his bedroom (facing page top). The parlor furniture (facing page bottom) is original.

Sagamore Hill is at the end of Cove Neck Road in Oyster Bay, Long Island, a short taxi ride from the Long Island Railroad or a short drive from Exit 41 on the Long Island Expressway, a small distance from New York City. It is open, with a small admission charge, every day from April through September and on Mondays by appointment during the rest of the year. It is closed on Thanksgiving, Christmas and New Year's Day. The Old Orchard Museum on the grounds includes an exhibition of Roosevelt memorabilia and a film on the president's life. A tour taped by his daughter, Alice, is available for rent.

Nearby, the National Audubon Society had established a wildlife Sanctuary and conservation museum which is open daily at no charge.

Also nearby is Planting Fields Arboretum, a 150-acre former estate that is one of the largest collections of azaleas and rhododendrons in the United States.

In Manhattan, at 28 East 20th Street, the national park Service maintains a reconstruction of the brownstone house where Theodore Roosevelt was born and spent the early years of his life. It is furnished with pieces that were in the original house and decorated as it was when the future president was born in 1858. The house is open for a small admission fee on a year-round basis.

27

WILLIAM HOWARD TAFT

(1857-1930)

The man was big. William Schevill's portrait shows how big. Our largest president weighed over 300 pounds.

The National Portrait Gallery, Smithsonian Institution

A year before he became president, William Howard Taft's mentor, Theodore Roosevelt, asked him what he would like to be above all. The answer was not President of the United States, but Chief Justice of the Supreme Court. He would eventually be both. But he never enjoyed being chief executive. In 1921, when Warren Harding granted him his real wish, he became the only man ever to be both president and chief justice. Before his death, he told a reporter that "In my present life I don't remember that I ever was president."

He was well-qualified to be both. But, as many of his predecessors had discovered, it helped to have an influential father. Taft was the son of a man who was well-known as "the first citizen of Cincinnati." The son of a well-established family himself, Alonzo Taft was a man who knew a good investment when he saw one and took advantage of good opportunities that came his way. He was a prominent judge, Secretary of War and the Attorney General of the United States. He was the United States Ambassador to Austria and then to Russia and raised his family in elegant surroundings in an 1840 brick mansion he bought and considerably improved in 1851. The house was situated on a large lot with manicured lawns on Auburn Avenue, one of the most fashionable addresses in Cincinnati, Ohio.

As a young man, the future president was sent to Yale University where he graduated with honors, returning home for further study at Cincinnati Law School. Money was no object to the young lawyer, who turned down better paying jobs to work as a court clerk. It led to his appointment, at the age of 23, to the job of assistant county prosecutor, and from that day forward he began working toward his goal of becoming Chief Justice. In later years he even turned down two Supreme Court appointments because he wanted to be more than just an ordinary Justice.

By the time he was 31 he was soliciter general of the United States, then served for eight years as a judge on the federal court of appeals, during which time he also served as dean of the Cincinnati Law School.

In 1900, he was appointed commissioner of the Philippine Islands and soon became the territorial governor. After that he was a special envoy to the Vatican and then Roosevelt's secretary of war. In the latter job, he became a particular favorite of the president, who gave Taft special assignments that took him to such places as Japan, Cuba and the Canal Zone. The ultimate assignment was to run for the presidency when T.R. decided not to run himself in 1908. He defeated the perennial Democratic candidate, William Jennings Bryan, and became the 27th President of the United States.

Though he had been in public service all his life, William Howard Taft was not a politician by instinct. He had grown up a gentleman and had throughout his life adopted the idea that a public service was exactly that, and that a man should conduct himself in office according to his own intelligence and instincts. Taft was strong on both counts, but weak in public relations. One of his contemporaries once said that "he is a large amiable island, surrounded entirely by people who know exactly what they want." Among those people was his mentor, former president Roosevelt, who became more and more disenchanted with the man. He said that Taft was "a good lieutenant but a bad captain."

By 1912, when the Republicans met in convention to choose their standard-bearer, T.R. discovered to his chagrin that Taft was a better captain than he thought. The party nominated William Howard Taft and the former Rough Rider formed his own party, becoming the third candidate against Taft and Woodrow Wilson as the Bull Moose candidate.

Both Taft, who probably didn't care, and Roosevelt, who most assuredly did, went down in defeat in the 1912 election. Roosevelt went back to New York, but not for long. He was soon off to Brazil on another hunting expedition, returning in time to campaign for American involvement in the 1914 war in Europe. Ex-president Taft went up to New Haven to become a law. professor at Yale University. He went back to Washington again to become co-chairman of Wilson's War Labor Board. His appointment to Chief Justice in 1921 was all he ever wanted. For the next nine years he worked tirelessly to make the Court function more smoothly, and during that time made the work more efficient by supervising the construction of the present Supreme Court Building in Washington.

In the book of records about American presidents, William Howard Taft ranks as the heaviest. He weighed between 300 and 340 pounds. He was four inches shorter than Abraham Lincoln, who was the tallest at 6'4", and more than three times the weight of James Madison, who was the smallest of all the chief executives. When Taft went to the White House, a special bathtub had to be installed. It held four normal-sized people. He was described by one historian as "a kindly, well-meaning, soft-voiced, rather simple-hearted, lumbering fat gentleman." He was a man of bulges and wrinkled clothes, with a red face accented by a big white moustache and twinkling blue eyes that were surrounded by gentle wrinkles. One of the stories that went around Washington when he was there was that he decided to go swimming near the summer White House in Massachusetts one day, which meant that his neighbors were beached because "the president was using the ocean." One of his own favorites was of a time when he asked for a train to make an unscheduled stop to pick up "a large party." When the railroad honored the request and only he was on the platform, he blithely told the conductor that he was the large party and the train could continue on.

"Big Bill" Taft, as he was called, was a football player during his years at Yale, but his first love was baseball, a passion he carried with him to Washington

His home is small. Taft built this tiny Italianate house in Cincinnati, OH, for $6000 in 1886, but went to Washington to larger quarters when he became Solicitor General in 1890.

when he established the tradition of opening the season each spring by throwing out the first ball. He was also the first president to use a car rather than a horse and carriage, and was responsible for the replacement of the White House stable. He expanded the executive mansion while he was there, doubling the size of the west wing and creating the present Oval Office. His wife, Nellie, who had been with him on a mission to Tokyo, was the prime mover in getting the Japanese to make a gift of 3000 cherry trees to the District of Columbia.

Though the family retained ownership of the house in Cincinnati until 1899, William Howard and his wife and their three children lived after 1886 in a three-story house on East McMillan Street before moving to Washington in 1890. It was sold a few years later and is now a private residence. The Taft birthplace was sold to the Taft Memorial Association in 1961 and became a National Historic Site in 1969.

Though the exterior has been completely restored, the interior is still closed to the public. The National Park Service, which administers the site, expects to have the first floor restored and furnished as it was between 1851 and 1877, by 1988. A museum nearby contains art and artifacts housed in an 1820 Federal-style mansion.

The William Howard Taft Historic Site in Cincinnati is open seven days a week, 10 a.m.–4 p.m. Admission is free. The nearby Taft Museum at 316 Pike Street is open every day, also without an entrance fee, except Thanksgiving and Christmas Day.

At 2950 Gilbert Avenue in Cincinnati is the restored home of Harriet Beecher Stowe, author of Uncle Tom's Cabin. It contains its 19th-century furnishings and is open, without charge, Tuesdays through Thursdays. On weekends and holidays it may be open by appointment.

Nearby, in the city's historic district, the John Hauck House contains 19th-century furnishings and memorabilia. It is open, with a small admission charge, every Tuesday, Thursday and Sunday, or by appointment.

A Cincinnati landmark is the domed Union terminal, open free every day for the admiration of its mosaics, marble walls and terazzo floors.

28

WOODROW WILSON

(1856-1924)

The National Portrait Gallery, Smithsonian Institution

A preacher's son, Woodrow Wilson, whose portrait here is by Edmund Charles Tarbell, was born at the Presbyterian Manse (below) in Staunton, VA, where the family Bible is still in the parlor (facing page top), and the kitchen (facing page bottom) looks like his mother has just stepped away.

His grandfather established the pace. When James Wilson arrived in Philadelphia from Northern Ireland in 1807, it seemed inevitable that he carried with him the seed of a future president. His first act was to take over the Philadelphia Aurora, one of the most influential newspapers in the country. His second was to join the movement to the West. He migrated to Ohio where he built a small fortune in real estate, became a bank executive and got himself elected to the state legislature. He never had a law degree, but was known as one of the most intelligent judges in the entire state.

James Wilson had seven sons, all of whom were as successful as their father. The youngest was given a different challenge than the others. It was decided that he should follow an academic life. Joseph Wilson proved as successful at that calling as his two brothers who became generals in the army. He was class valedictorian at Jefferson College and established an enviable record in post-graduate work at Princeton University. He became a college professor after that, and in 1855 answered the call to become pastor of the First Presbyterian Church in Staunton, Virginia. The following year, his wife presented him with his first son, their third child, three days after Christmas. They named the child Thomas Woodrow Wilson.

During his tenure as the pastor at Staunton, Joseph Wilson expanded the parish by some 30 members and earned a reputation for miles around as the best preacher

The back porch was designed to be the front of the house when it was built in 1841. But the Staunton town plan decreed that Coalter Street would be on the other side, creating an opportunity for a wonderful garden.

Virginia had ever seen. But his talent became Virginia's loss in early 1858 when he was asked to take over a larger and more prosperous church in Augusta, Georgia. The future president spent his early years in Augusta, where his father was a chaplain in the Confederate Army. The churchyard next to their house was a temporary stockade for prisoners of war, the church itself a hospital for wounded Confederate troops.

In 1870 the family moved again, this time to Columbia, South Carolina, when Reverend Wilson became a professor at Columbia Theological Seminary. Three years later, Tommy Wilson, who by then was beginning to prefer being called Woodrow, went to Davidson, North Carolina to begin college in preparation for a career as a Presbyterian minister. He left within a year because of poor health and went to live with his parents, who by then had moved on to Wilmington, North Carolina. In 1875 he was ready for school again and enrolled at Princeton, where he expanded his interests and changed his goal. He now wanted to become a lawyer. Before he graduated in 1879, everyone at Princeton agreed it was a wise choice. He was one of the university's best debaters, not to mention the remarkable skill he had developed as a writer.

He went from there to the law school at the University of Virginia and, though he didn't graduate, he passed the bar in Georgia and briefly practiced law in Atlanta. It was there he met Ellen Louise Axson, also the child of a Presbyterian minister, whom he married two years later. In the meantime, he had decided against law as a career and went to Johns Hopkins University in Baltimore, where as a student he published his first book, Congressional Government. Soon after, armed with a Ph.D. degree, he became professor of history at Bryn Mawr College.

Family dinners in the dining room (above), and in other Wilson homes, always included stimulating discussions.

In 1890, he went back to Princeton University again as professor of jurisprudence and political economy. Twelve years later he was made president of the University and had published a five-volume History of The American People. By that point, six different universities had offered him their presidency, including the University of Virginia, which made the offer three different times.

His eight-year tenure at Princeton was marked especially by liberalization of time-honored, but restrictive, traditions and earned national recognition which didn't go unnoticed by the New Jersey Democratic Party, which asked him to be their candidate for United

States Senate. When he turned them down, they countered with a nomination that got him elected Governor of New Jersey in 1911. At the Democratic Convention in Baltimore in 1912 he won the party's nomination for the Presidency on the 46th ballot. The divided Republicans gave him 435 Electoral Votes compared to eight for the incumbent, William Howard Taft, who later said that more people had voted for him to become an ex-president than for any man in the history of the United States.

Wilson's own sense of history was colored a great deal by his Presbyterian background and his strong belief in predestination. Even before he was elected, he reminded the leadership of his party that he wasn't at all interested in repaying any political favors. They were stunned when he told them that "God ordained that I should be President of the United States," and that they would be fools to go against His wishes.

Once he was elected he was single-minded about what he considered God's mandate that the United States, through him, should work to achieve peace in the world once and for all. The world seemed to have other ideas. Within a year of his election war broke out in Europe, and though he was inclined to stay out of it and to take on the role of peacemaker, public opinion went against him with the sinking of the British ship Lusitania in 1915. The loss of 128 American lives made it impossible for him to stem the tide.

Wilson was born in his mother's bed (above) on December 28, 1856. Among the reminders of his later life now displayed in the house is his old rolltop desk with papers still in the pigeonholes (right).

Meanwhile, his wife died, leaving him grief-stricken. And his grief was expanded when he was finally forced to ask Congress for a declaration of war. His speech resulted in a standing ovation to which he responded, "My message today was a message of death for your young men. How strange it is to applaud that."

But life goes on, of course, and within 18 months of his wife's death, he married again. His new bride, the former Edith Bolling Galt, became one of the most controversial of all the first ladies when the president suffered a stroke in 1919 and she took on the responsibility of not letting anyone see or talk with him without talking with her first. "He can still do more with a maimed body than anyone else," she said, and blocked every attempt to have him declared incompetent to continue as president. "His mind is clear as crystal," she argued. And she was probably right.

When the war was finally over, Wilson asked Congress to ratify his program for peace, which included the formation of a world body that would be known as the League of Nations. Later, after he agreed to concessions from the allies, he wasn't able to convince the senate that the plan would work. They rejected the treaty, and the president, though his mind was clear as crystal, didn't have the strength to fight any longer and spent the last 18 months of his presidency a broken man. He retired in 1921 and continued to live in Washington until his death in 1924.

Wilson lived in the Staunton house until his family moved to Georgia when he was a year old. He never romped in the family room (right), ate in the dining room (below) nor played in the gardens (below right), but the house is furnished with things like the typewriter and desk (bottom) that were part of his later life.

The Manse in Staunton, Virginia, where the 28th president was born, was home to three different families after the Wilsons moved away. It was modernized a few times, beginning with the enclosing of the lower balcony and installation of indoor plumbing in 1887. Later the roof was replaced and a widow's walk added, the porch changed, windows altered and the brick exterior painted white. Central heating was eventually added, and bathrooms and an inside stairway built.

When Wilson died in 1924, the trustees of Mary Baldwin College bought the building as a memorial to the president, and in 1938 the Woodrow Wilson Birthplace Foundation began restoration of the house, a project that culminated in 1964 when the building was designated a National Historic Landmark. By 1981, they were able to restore it to its original 1850s look. Today it is visited by more than 20,000 Americans every year who understand very well why President Franklin D. Roosevelt called it a "shrine to freedom" when he dedicated the restored building in 1941.

Wilson himself visited the home several times after his family moved from Staunton. He told the story himself of the day he went there after his election in 1912 and addressed a record crowd of his former neighbors. He said that a small boy pushed his way through the crowd and shouted at him, "where is it?" "I think I'm it," said the future president. "Oh," said the disappointed boy, "I thought it was a dogfight."

The Woodrow Wilson Birthplace is at 24 N. Coalter Street, near Route 11, in Staunton, Virginia. The house has been restored to its original appearance and contains mementoes of President Wilson and his family, including the president's 1919 Pierce Arrow limousine. The house, which may be seen for a small entrance fee, is open every day except Sundays in December, January and February, Thanksgiving, Christmas and New Year's Day.

The Woodrow Wilson Boyhood Home at 1705 Hampton Street in Columbia, South Carolina, also contains memorabilia of the Wilson family. It is open, for an admission charge, every day except Monday. It is closed Thanksgiving, December 24 and 25 and New Year's Day.

The Princeton Faculty Club in Princeton, New Jersey, was Wilson's home from 1902 through 1910 when he was president of the University.

The Woodrow Wilson House at 2340 S St. NW in Washington, D.C. contains an extensive collection of books and other Wilson possessions. The house where the president died and where his widow lived out her days is operated by the National Trust for Historic Preservation and is open daily except Monday for a small admission fee. It is closed on Thanksgiving and Christmas Day and for the month of January. In February, it is open only on weekends.

E PLURIBUS UNUM

29

WARREN G. HARDING

(1865-1923)

Looking the part of a president, along with his impressive speaking style, helped get Warren G. Harding elected in 1920. The look was captured on canvas (right) by Margaret L. Williams.

Harding looks out at visitors from another portrait in his Marion, OH, home (facing page). The quilt in the guest room (below), used by many impressive visitors, was a gift from the people of Utah. The women who made it stitched their names radiating from the American flag.

The National Portrait Gallery, Smithsonian Institution

When he was beginning his rise in politics in the State of Ohio, one of the party leaders said to Warren G. Harding, "You know, you'd make a dandy-looking president." The young newspaper editor from Marion smiled his best "Aw, shucks!" smile and went back to concentrating on the poker game.

At the time, Warren Gamaliel Harding didn't want much more out of life than he already had. He was one of the people who "gets things done" in Marion, Ohio. His newspaper, the Marion Star, was the most influential in the heartland of Ohio, and even if he had won it in a game of cards, he built it from a nonentity to double the circulation of its two nearest competitors combined. He was a 33-degree Mason, an Elk, a Rotarian and the shining light of the Marion Chamber of Commerce. He was a man who liked people, and those who mattered, as well as those who didn't, liked him even more.

He was one of them, after all. He was born the son of a doctor in nearby Blooming Grove. As a young man he was well-known all over the county as a man who knew how to have a good time. Fathers of other young men were pleased to see him with their sons. Mothers of young women were pleased to see him on their front porches, but couldn't help worrying just a little.

He had been to college, had worked as a grade school teacher, was a great cornet player and was manager of the town's baseball team, for which he played first base. He had read some law books and earned a few dollars as a country lawyer and kept himself in better-than-average style by selling life insurance.

One of the very few people in Marion who didn't like young Harding also happened to be the richest man in town. But Harding married his daughter anyway. He was 25 years old at the time. Florence was 30. Many say it was

the turning point in his life, in spite of the fact that Amos Kling, his father-in-law, swore that his life would end very soon if he had anything to say about it. Among other things, young Warren put an end, or at least a curb, to his former wicked ways. And his bride, whom he began calling "the Duchess," rolled up her sleeves and went to work to mold all of his obvious talent into something resembling success.

By many standards, Warren G. Harding already was a success. He had made some good investments and, even though he was only 25 years old, he had the means to build a stylish two-story frame house, complete with stained glass windows and solid oak trim, for his bride and her young son from a previous marriage.

The 1965 restoration of the Harding house included bringing back original dining room furniture (left), returning the bedroom funishings (top), and his campaign hat, and replacing the gaslights in the parlor (above).

But Florence wanted more and she was willing to work to get it. She talked him into changing the Star from a weekly to a daily paper and then signed on as circulation manager. She helped him sell advertising and encouraged him to use the time she was saving him to put his social skills to better use.

He became a public speaker. His voice was probably his best asset. He had a pitch that made it easy to hear without becoming grating. He had the appearance to go with it, too. He was just over six feet tall with impeccable posture. He knew how to wear clothes and looked perfect for every occasion. His teeth were even and pearly white, his hair neat and richly black. His skin had a dark, healthy glow and he had a smile that inspired confidence in men, and made women weak at the knees. Before very long the audiences for his speeches were much wider than the audience for his newspaper, in spite of Florence's impressive efforts at building the latter. It was strange, too, because Warren Gamaliel Harding had nothing to say.

He thought he had a way with words, but the fact was he didn't. He did invent a few words during his career, the most fascinating of which described his own style. He called it "bloviating," which means being able to talk for any length of time on any subject and not saying anything. He liked to use alliteration, and in one speech he pushed the idea to its limits by saying: "Progression is not proclamation nor palaver. It is not pretense nor play on prejudice. It is not personal pronouns not ,perennial pronouncement. It is not the perturbutation of a people passion-wrought nor a promise proposed." What, then, is progression? Don't ask.

H.L. Mencken, who did have a way with words, said the Harding speechmaking style was "rumble and bumble, flap and doodle, balder and dash." A leading Democrat said that it was "the big bow wow style of oratory." "His speeches leave the impression," he said "of an army of pompous phrases moving over the landscape in search of an idea."

Yet, as the man said, he had all the qualities of a dandy-looking president. And if his speeches weren't very illuminating, very few could resist giving rapt attention to the tall, well-dressed man and his incredible sincerity.

It was inevitable that he should get into politics. When he was only 22 he served as a delegate to the Republican state convention, at 26 he was president of the local Young Republican Club and a few years later was sent to the Ohio State Senate, at which time he added an elegant front porch to his house in Marion. After all, William McKinley started on the road to the White House by making speeches from his front porch over in Canton. In 1903 Harding was elected lieutenant governor of Ohio, and in 1914 went to Washington to serve in the United States Senate.

It was there that he attracted the attention of the powers-that-be in the national Republican Party and he was hand-picked to serve as chairman of their 1916 National Convention with the specific assignment to keep Theodore Roosevelt from being nominated. He won the battle for them in June, but they lost the war in November. Four years later, the Republicans met again very much divided, but eager to get back into power. It was there that the famous "smoke-filled room" entered the annals of American politics. Four months before the convention one of the party's leading lights said, "...At about eleven minutes after two o'clock on Friday morning at the convention, when fifteen or twenty men, somewhat weary, are sitting around a table, one of them will say: 'Who will we nominate?' At that decisive time friends of Senator Harding will suggest him. In fact, I think I might suggest him myself."

Harding got the nomination on the tenth ballot on Saturday morning.

It was then he coined his most famous word. "America needs not heroics," he told them, "but healing. Not nostrums, but normalcy." He was proposing to take a war-weary America back to the days when life centered around the front porches of towns like Marion, Ohio; back to the peace and contentment of the 19th century. To the Republican leadership, "normalcy" meant one of their own in the White House, which had been the case for all but 16 of the previous 60 years.

Harding had always been a loyal party man, but he himself admitted that he was a man of limited talents and that it takes more than looks to be President of the United States. He did the best he could, but so did every special interest from Big Oil to small farmers. Eventually it all started to unravel as scandal after scandal began showing from under the rug. His black hair turned white, lines began to show in his handsome face. But his face to the world was calm and reassuring. The round of parties and beautiful people gave a new luster of normalcy.

Harding appeared on the front porch of his Marion house to make his famous campaign speeches. He had the house built when he married Florence Kling in 1891. They lived there until he went to the White House 30 years later. The rounded front porch extension was added, probably to set the stage for the future, while he was an Ohio state senator.

In 1923, he set off on a speaking tour that took him all the way to Alaska. But at every stop he seemed older than at the stop before it. At one point he told a reporter, "I'm not worried about my enemies in this job. I can handle them. It's my friends who are giving me trouble." But Warren G. Harding was always loyal to his friends and said no more. On the way back from Alaska it was said he ate some tainted food, and he arrived in San Francisco a very sick man. He died quickly at the age of 57.

It was never made quite clear what killed him. Possibly a broken heart. In the months that followed, scandals involving his official family shocked the nation. His own name was dragged into it and dragged down with the rest. But it is highly likely that Warren G. Harding's only crime was loving his fellow man.

The President Harding Home and Museum is at 380 Vernon Avenue in Marion, Ohio, off Route 23 north of Columbus. The restored house is open at no charge Wednesdays through Sundays between memorial Day and Labor Day.

The Harding Memorial, the burial place of the President and his wife, is nearby.

Marion also has the True Home, a 13-room 1848 Gothic Revival house furnished with period furniture. It is open Monday through Thursday at no charge.

Also in town is the Stengel True Museum, a collection of Indian artifacts and other antiques. It is open on weekends except holidays at no charge.

30

CALVIN COOLIDGE
(1872-1933)

Silence is golden, was the opinion of Calvin Coolidge, who frustrated official Washington by never saying anything he didn't think was worth saying.

Library of Congress

Plymouth Notch, VT, where Coolidge was born in the house (below), understood silence and respected it. After all, it was part of the Vermont character.

Once during a White House dinner party, a Washington matron confided to President Calvin Coolidge that she had a bet with some friends that she could get him to say more than two words. "You lose," said the President.

He once told a frustrated reporter that he thought it was best not to say much. "If you don't say anything, no one can call on you to repeat it," he explained.

But Silent Cal proved one of the great axioms of human relations. No one knows how good you are unless you yourself tell them.

On August 3, 1923, when he was told that President Harding had died and that he was now chief executive, he said "I think I need a drink." The drink he chose was a popular soft drink of the day known as Moxie. Though the name is also a slang word for courage, Mr. Coolidge was not making an editorial comment. He avoided that like the plague.

But he was a man of unusual courage and perseverance. When he moved into the White House he was confronted by party hacks and hangers-on in the midst of one of the greatest scandals ever to involve the presidency. He didn't call any press conferences, nor clear air time to reassure the people that he was their hero. He simply cleaned up the mess and let the courts take care of the rascals. Without a word.

It was frustrating to his friends and to his enemies, and it wasn't long before word got around that this was a president who would never amount to anything. It wasn't

Talk of the town in 1872 usually took place around the stove in kitchens like this one (right) at the Coolidge Birthplace house (facing page) in Plymouth Notch.

The big kitchen (above) in the Coolidge Homestead is set for breakfast. Plates, usually set in place the night before, are upside down to keep them clean.

true. Where his predecessor had promised a return to "normalcy," Coolidge in his quiet way reminded the country that old-fashioned honesty was good business. If he had been a man of words, stability would have been one to use often.

He was a hard man to understand in the America of the 1920s. But those who knew their history knew him very well as the kind of stock that made the country work in the first place. He was a Vermonter through and through. He was hard-working, thrifty, unmoveable, practical. His silence was the silence of the granite hills that produced him. He had a bit of the maverick in him, but that was normal, too. The first Coolidge to arrive in the United States was a Massachusetts Puritan who came from England in 1630. Some of his offspring migrated to Vermont in search of freedom. It was this branch that produced the future president, who was born in 1872 in the living quarters in back of the general store his father operated at Plymouth Notch, Vermont. He graduated from Amherst College and read law in Northampton with the firm of Hammond and Field. He was admitted to the bar in Massachusetts and stayed in Northampton to establish his practice. It was there he met and married Grace Goodhue, a fellow Vermonter who was teaching school in his adopted town.

As is typical of the man, he waited until he was 33 years old to get married, but he jumped into politics at a much earlier age. He became a member of the Republican City Committee for Ward 2 in his first year as a lawyer and soon after was elected City Councilman from Ward 2. It wasn't long before he was mayor of Northampton, which led to four terms in the state legislature. He served three terms as lieutenant governor and in 1919 became Governor of the Commonwealth of Massachusetts.

The job gave him national attention in 1919 when the police in Boston went on strike. It took him nearly a week to make a bold move, but he finally called out the National Guard and served notice on the Union that he'd have no more of such behavior. A year later the Republican Party made him its candidate for Vice President.

When he was elected and went to Washington, it was the first time he had ever been there. He didn't change much, though the pace forced him to change his bedtime hour from 9:30 to 10:00. And he found the pace of official banquets a bit tiring, though he kept up the pace because, as he explained, "a man has to eat."

Though he never drank anything stronger than Moxie, Coolidge did enjoy a good cigar and spent many a summer evening on the front porch of the White House, savoring a fine Havana cigar in his favorite rocking chair. The summer White House in 1927 was the State Game Lodge in the Black Hills of South Dakota, where the president did all he could to look like one of the boys. He dressed like a cowboy, proving once again that it takes more than clothes

The oath of office was administered in a former dining room (bottom) in the Homestead with the Bible that is on his desk. When it was over, Coolidge went upstairs to bed (below).

to make an image. He had learned to fish in his childhood and claimed he enjoyed the sport, but to the chagrin of photographers insisted on wearing white kid gloves while doing it. He never developed a stomach for baiting hooks, either, and that job became one of the duties of the Secret Service.

The National Park Service got into the act, too, by stocking the stream to make sure there would be an occasional fish at the end of the line where the worm had been.

It was after one of his fishing expeditions in South Dakota that he surprised everyone, including his wife, by

issuing one of the strangest statements ever uttered by a president. He didn't say it, but had it written on slips of paper which he handed to reporters. It said, simply, "I do not choose to run for President in 1928." It was the fourth anniversary of his having taken the oath of office, but still ten months before the Republicans would meet to choose their standard-bearer. He had won the elelction of 1924 in a landslide and could easily have won again. But what was odd about the statement was that it never said he wouldn't be a candidate. Other hopefuls needed to tread

After retiring, Coolidge often vacationed in a rocker on the porch of the Homestead, smoking cigars and watching the world go by.

softly lest the incumbent should decide to let someone else make the choice for him. State delegations stayed in the president's control, and Coolidge kept them that way until the following June with his dozen-word statement.

The Coolidges made the White House their home for six years, and during that time had the roof raised and a third floor added. Though he was well-known as a man who liked to sleep a lot, Coolidge began the custom of White House staff meetings over breakfast, but not until he discovered that the government would pay for the coffee and Danish.

But he was happy to go home again when it was all over and the Republicans had agreed with the choice of Herbert Hoover as his successor. The house they went back to, on Massasoit Street in Northampton, was little changed from the time he and Grace had moved there right after they were married. Without a budget for entertaining he did very little, and went back to his old habit of staying in bed every morning until after nine. Those who did visit never seemed to notice that the silverware and linen

When not talking, Coolidge's neighbors liked nothing more than singing, which they often did around the old piano in the family parlor.

carried the monogram of a local hotel that had long-since gone out of business. The ex-president was a man who knew a bargain when he saw one. This was the same man who, when asked to become a depositor in a local bank to enhance their prestige, suggested that they consider making him an "honorary" depositor.

The house in Plymouth Notch, Vermont, where he grew up, stayed in the family all his life. The room above the general store was the summer White House in 1924 and the house he lived in as a boy is where he was in 1923 when his father administered the oath of office to the new president. The house in Northampton, which he always rented but never owned, is now a private residence.

After he retired, Coolidge often went to Plymouth Notch for vacations. Once, a friend who was visiting with him there mentioned that he must be very proud to see so many cars passing that way just to have a look at the presidential birthplace. "It's not as good as yesterday," said Cal. "There were 60 of 'em then." The site attracts more than 50,000 visitors every year these days. It would make Calvin Coolidge proud. But he'd never tell you so.

If the town of Plymouth, Vermont, has changed any since Calvin Coolidge was born there on the Fourth of July in 1872 it would be hard to see where the change took place. The general store his father owned is still in business, and the Coolidge Homestead has been restored to its original appearance. The birthplace of the president's mother is there, too, as is the Carpenter Gothic Union Church and a barn filled with early farming equipment. All of the buildings in the Historic District, along with a visitor center and museum, are open every day for a small admission charge, from mid-May through mid-October.

The District is north of Plymouth on Route 100A.

The cemetery where six generations of the Coolidge family are buried is nearby.

The 16,000-acre Calvin Coolidge State Forest is near the Historic District. It has camping and picnic facilities and hiking and snowmobile trails.

31

HERBERT HOOVER

(1872-1964)

The great engineer was what the people called Herbert Hoover when they elected him president in 1928. But the man in this portrait by Douglas Chandor was much more than that. His brilliant career began in a small Iowa farmhouse, whose living room (below) doubled as a kitchen.

The National Portrait Gallery, Smithsonian Institution

During the Harding administration, Herbert Hoover was secretary of commerce. Though Harding felt he was a great speechwriter, he allowed the secretary to write a portion of one of his speeches. But when he delivered the address, he had a problem with the alien passage. During a pause he glanced over his shoulder and said, "Damn it, Hoover, why don't you speak English the way I do?"

It was lucky for the president the man his successor called a "wonder boy" hadn't included some British colloquialisms in it. It would have been easy. He had lived in London for eight years. He could have given it an Australian twist, too. He lived "Down Under" for two years. Or he could have injected some Chinese into it. He lived in Peking for a while, too.

By the time he joined the Harding Cabinet, he had been around the world five times, in fact. And to take the job in the government at $15,000 a year, he had turned down a $500,000 a year offer from the biggest mining firm in the world.

But Herbert Hoover hadn't always been rich. He was born in West Branch, Iowa, the son of a Quaker blacksmith. His father died when the boy was six, his mother two years later. He spent the next two years on a nearby farm owned by his uncle, and when he was ten he was shipped off to Newburg, Oregon, to the home of his mother's brother, Dr. Henry Minthorn, who became a father to the boy.

The doctor was also in the real estate business, which gave the boy a job, and he ran a private school, which gave him a basic education. When he was 17, he enrolled at the new Stanford University in Palo Alto, California, where he was one of the first residents of the men's dormitory. He held all kinds of odd jobs as a student, but the most important one was in the office of one of his professors, who happened to be one of the most important geologists in the country. It led to a summer job with the Arkansas Geological Survey and then with the United States Geological Survey.

He took a job as a miner after he graduated, but he didn't stay underground very long. He was soon promoted to mine surveyor and within a year or two went to Australia to work for a huge combine. He had a talent for hard work, but he also had good business sense and invested part of his salary in a gold mine that turned out to be a bonanza, with the result that he was not only financially secure, but a partner in the firm that had employed him. He was just 25 years old.

After two years in Australia he sent a cablegram to Lou Henry, the daughter of a prominent California banker he had met in his student days. "Will you marry me?" it said. When the reply was "Yes!," he cabled back that she would have to go with him to China, where he had taken a new job. The answer was still "Yes!," and they were married, and off to China, in 1899.

They were in Peking during the Boxer Rebellion, survived it and moved on to London where he became a partner in a management consulting firm. By then he was a millionaire many times over and had time for public service. The outbreak of World War I gave him an opportunity. Even before the United States got into the war, he was in charge of Belgian War Relief and commuted regularly between London and Brussels, and often Berlin. When the war ended, he was named a delegate to the Paris Peace Conference, and in 1921 became a member of the Harding administration and occasional contributor to presidential speeches.

He kept his post in the Commerce Department during the Coolidge years and, when the president decided to retire, became his hand-picked successor.

When he and Lou moved into the White House in 1929, the Twenties were roaring at full-tilt. Prosperity was the watchword and if anybody in the United States was unhappy, the future was almost certain to get better.

Then, on October 30, the whole thing came apart. The stock market collapsed and the country was dropped into the greatest depression it has ever seen. Hoover couldn't have prevented it, and he didn't seem able to get out of it. Even Calvin Coolidge, who never had much to say, had to say "The country is not in good condition." A story about Hoover that was repeated time and again was that he was walking down the street with a banker friend and asked to borrow a nickel to call a friend. "Here's a dime," said the banker. "Call both of them."

But Hoover wasn't friendless at all, of course. During

their years in Washington, which began right after World War I when President Wilson appointed him Director General of Postwar Relief, the Hoovers were among Washington's most important entertainers. Lou Hoover had long experience, with more than 17 different homes during their 44-year marriage, with entertaining guests and winning friendships for both of them. She had survived the siege at Peking, where no less than five artillery shells landed in their yard; the war in London, where they often slept in the basement during the bombing raids; and a three-alarm fire in the White House on Christmas Eve in 1929.

His friends in the Republican Party had enough confidence in him to give him their nomination in 1939, but unfortunately he couldn't muster enough friends to get reelected.

The only bedroom (facing page top) in the 14- by 20-foot Hoover farmhouse had a rope bed for the parents and a trundle bed for the son. The cooking stove (facing page bottom) was moved out to the back porch (above) in the summer months.

After his defeat the Hoovers moved back to California, to a house they had built on the campus of Stanford University. But a short time later his activities prompted them to move to New York City, where they rented a suite in the Waldorf Towers, which would be the former president's home for the next 30 years. In 1946 he joined the Truman administration as a special consultant in averting a post-war famine. The following year, and again in 1953, he headed commissions to study ways to reorganize the Executive Branch of the government.

After he retired in 1955, Herbert Hoover became an elder statesman in his 31st-floor tower suite. He had two offices there, from which he wrote books, kept track of his business interests and active in the affairs of the Boys Clubs of America. He died there in December, 1964 at the age of 90.

His memorial is at West Branch, Iowa, where his life began and he and his wife are buried. "I prefer to think of Iowa as I saw it through the eyes of a ten-year-old boy," he said, and the Herbert Hoover National Historic Site has been restored to reflect exactly what he saw.

The Site, which was designated in 1965, contains the tiny 1871 cottage which is furnished with much of the original furniture. The future president's father had a blacksmith shop nearby, and it has been restored, too. Also on the Site is the 1857 Friend's Meeting House and an 1853 schoolhouse. The Presidential Library contains thousands of papers collected during Hoover's years of public service as well as books and objects associated with his career. A short distance across the prairie is the simple gravesite where the former president and his wife have been reunited.

The Site is a memorial to the 31st president, but it is something more than that. It is a memorial to hundreds of midwestern farm towns that existed in the late 19th century. It is a trip back in time to an era when life was simpler. It is a peaceful place in a fast-paced world. It is where our roots are.

West branch, Iowa, is a short distance east of Iowa City on Route 80. The historic buildings on Herbert Hoover National Historic Site are open every day, at no charge, except Thanksgiving, Christmas and New Year's Day. The Presidential Library and Museum is open on about the same schedule and has a small admission fee.

The former home of Dr. Henry Minthorn at 113 S. River Street in Newburg, Oregon, where Herbert Hoover lived between 1885 and 1888 is open to the public.

The Hoover home on the campus of Stanford University in Palo Alto, California, is the campus President's house.

Hoover's summer White House on the Rapidan River in Virginia is now part of Shenandoah National Park, and is open to the public once a year on Herbert Hoover's birthday, August 10.

32

FRANKLIN D. ROOSEVELT

(1882-1945)

The National Portrait Gallery, Smithsonian Institution

Once, when he was a young man, Franklin D. Roosevelt described himself as a "Hudson River gentleman, yachtsman, philatelist and naval historian." Modesty was never, ever, anything anyone accused F.D.R. of, but he was much more than that, even then.

It was just that he never had to bother to earn a living and never did anything that didn't interest him. The term "Hudson River gentleman" summed it all up.

His family had been squires of the Hudson Valley for generations. Isaac Roosevelt, the future president's great-great grandfather, started it all with a successful sugar refining business. His son, as future Roosevelt generations would do, married well and went into the banking business. It was he who established the family estate in Dutchess County, a comfortable distance up the Hudson River from New York City. His son, James, studied medicine, but never mended a broken leg. He used his talents to improve the livestock and the landscaping of the country estate. His son, F.D.R.'s father, did the same thing, but devoted a lot of attention to investing, an activity he had an exceptional talent for.

The future president was born on the family estate on January 30, 1882, the son of Sarah Delano Roosevelt, one of the wealthiest young women of her day, with a family background and social connections that may well have been one of the most impressive in American history.

Her son had every advantage imaginable: trips abroad every year, a private tutor so he wouldn't have to associate with youngsters his mother considered beneath him, and a summer home on Campobello Island in Canada where he could enjoy the good life among his peers. He was their only child, after all.

His education was at the exclusive Groton School and then at Harvard University. He went to the Columbia University Law School after that, but dropped out when he was offered a job with a Wall Street law firm that was willing to take a chance on him without a law degree. At about the same time he married his cousin, a niece of Theodore Roosevelt, who gave the bride away at their wedding.

To the manor born, F.D.R. lived the life of a gentleman at his Hyde Park, NY, estate (facing page), where he had a White House "hot line" on the wall next to his bed (right).

Painter Douglas Chandor found the gentleman's hands very expressive.

He didn't have any problem getting time off from his new job to take an extended wedding trip to Europe. He never asked for time to move into the town house on Manhattan's East 65th Street that he and his bride would share with his mother. The fact was, the firm he worked for didn't care if he came to work at all. His social connections were what they were paying for, and in that regard he earned his salary hundreds of times over.

A lot of men with Franklin Roosevelt's background would have become insufferable playboys. But Franklin Roosevelt wasn't like a lot of men. He enjoyed a good time, to be sure, but his greatest joy, as he would prove years later in the White House, was people. It was inevitable he would get into politics and, once having decided to do it, it was just as inevitable that the political establishment would welcome him with open arms.

He was elected to the New York state legislature in 1910 and reelected when his term expired. He went from there to Washington as assistant secretary of the Navy in the Wilson administration and during his seven years there established himself as a man to watch in Washington. His reward for faithful service was the vice presidential nomination, running with James M. Cox in 1920. They lost, and Washington thought it had seen the last of Franklin D. Roosevelt, who went back to New York where he had another Wall Street job waiting. He also accepted partnerships in several different law firms, none of which required much of his time, but all of which helped him add to his personal fortune.

He spent his spare time in charitable work, and kept his hand in the political pie. He was a particular favorite of New York Governor Al Smith and worked with the man they called "the happy warrior" in his bid for the presidency in the 1928 election. He became governor of New York himself that year, and two years later was reelected in a landslide. Two years after that he took the Democratic nomination for the presidency. The state, and the nation, had been surprised by the millionaire's dedication to hard work and his compassion for the people he served.

Elegant comfort is apparent in every room at Hyde Park. The living room (top left) has it, as do the dining room (far left), bedrooms (above and left), and dressing room (above left).

Not long after going home from Washington after the 1920 election, Roosevelt became the victim of polio. He never was able to walk normally again. He never called attention to the fact that he was confined to a wheelchair and couldn't walk without the benefit of two canes. But he never let the handicap get in his way, either. The only time he ever officially mentioned it was in response to a reporter's question about the difficulties of the presidency. "If you had spent two years in bed trying to move your toes," he said, "you'd understand how easy the rest has been."

It wasn't easy. F.D.R. went to the White House in the midst of the Great Depression and immediately began breaking every rule in the book to get it behind him. He called his program the New Deal. The country had never seen anything like it before and in getting his ideas made the law of the land, he made as many enemies as friends. No one was ever indifferent about Franklin D. Roosevelt. In the process, he gave the country its first experience with such things as unemployment insurance, retirement programs, wage and hour laws, housing for the poor, jobs for the needy; all as the responsibility of the Federal Government. "It is the Government's first duty to keep people from starving," he said. Enough people loved him

Roosevelt's desk in the library (above) is a reminder of the long hours he worked at Hyde Park while president. The china-filled Dresden Room (facing page) is one of the reasons he loved being there and entertaining heads of state at home, including, in 1939, the King of England.

for it to make him the first president in history to run for a third term, and he made history again in 1944 by running for, and winning, a fourth term.

His performance as an administrator and a morale-builder was even more impressive after the United States entered World War II in 1941, and his personal style with other world leaders established the pattern for the peace that followed it. But he didn't live to see the peace he designed. In April, 1945, less than a month before the German surrender and five months before the end of the war with Japan, Franklin D. Roosevelt died at the Little White House in Warm Springs, Georgia.

He was buried in the family rose garden at Hyde Park. Seventeen years later, in 1962, his wife, Eleanor, was buried beside him.

World leaders still make the trip up the Hudson to pay homage to the 32nd President of the United States, just as they often did in his lifetime. The estate, which his ancestors had called Springwood, was considerably changed from the original house where he was born after FDR moved there with his new bride. A three-story tower that had dominated the original clapboard structure was changed to make a full third floor. The exterior was refaced with brick and stucco and the style altered from Italianate to Neo-Classical. He added two wings and a portico and terrace. Later he built a cottage on the grounds so he could "get away from the show." In his will he gave the house to the American people, and in 1945 the building, which had been in the family since the early 1800s, was no longer their property.

During his presidential years Roosevelt maintained an office at Hyde Park, and was host to such people as the King and Queen of England there. It hasn't changed a bit since those days, and nowhere in the world is the spirit of F.D.R. more alive than in his comfortable house overlooking the beautiful Hudson River.

The 188-acre Franklin D. Roosevelt National Historic Site is on Route 9 in Hyde Park, New York, a few miles north of Poughkeepsie. A small entrance fee gains admission to four different buildings: the Roosevelt Birthplace, the Franklin Roosevelt Library and Museum and Val-Kill, the country home of Eleanor Roosevelt. The fourth building is the nearby Vanderbilt Mansion, a Beaux-Arts palace designed by McKim, Mead and White for Frederick W. Vanderbilt in 1898.

The Site is open every day April through October, and Thursday through Monday in November and March. It is closed between December and February and on Thanksgiving Day.

The Mills Mansion, a 65-room McKim, Mead and White creation in the Neoclassical style, is a short drive north of the Roosevelt Home on Route 9. It is furnished in Louis XV and Louis XVI style with rare tapestries and art objects. It is open, at no charge, every Wednesday through Sunday between Memorial Day and the end of October.

The house at 47-49 East 65th Street in New York City, which Franklin and Eleanor Roosevelt shared with his mother, and where he recovered from polio, is now the Sarah Delano Roosevelt Memorial of Hunter College.

The "Little White House," in Warm Springs, Georgia, which FDR built in 1932 and where he died in 1945, is now a museum, open every day except holidays for a small entrance fee. The Roosevelt properties on Campobello Island, New Brunswick, Canada, off the northern coast of Maine, are also open to the public in a joint Canadian/American park.

33

HARRY S. TRUMAN

(1884-1972)

The National Portrait Gallery, Smithsonian Institution

The stars fell, Truman said when he became president. But Greta Kempton saw an unchanged man when he sat for his portrait.

Of all the presidents, none knew as much about his predecessors as Harry Truman. He had a wonderful sense of history, but little understanding of his own place in it. When he retired in 1953, he told an interviewer that "I wasn't one of the great presidents, but I had a hell of a good time trying to be one." Oh, if he could hear them now! Even Republicans are saying nice things about him these days.

He never really wanted the job in the first place. When Franklin Roosevelt suggested his name as the vice presidential candidate on the 1944 ticket, he told FDR to go to hell. It took a great deal of arm-twisting and reminders of the obligations of party loyalty to get him to change his mind. Eighty-two days after the Roosevelt fourth term began, Harry S. Truman was the 33d President of the United States.

Truman was a man who believed in the simple values of the 19th-century Midwest. Hard work and honesty were as important as life itself. He was born on his father's farm in Lamar, Missouri and, when he was six, the family moved to a big white frame house in Independence. After high school, Harry went to work as a timekeeper for the railroad, moving on soon after to work for a contractor, then to the Kansas City Star, where he found a job in the mailroom. After that he worked as a bookkeeper, and when his family came into a modest inheritance he moved to his grandfather's farm and ran it for about a dozen years.

When war broke out in 1917 Harry joined the Army, where he rose through the ranks to captain and saw action in France. He was 35 years old when the war was over, and decided it was about time to marry Bess Wallace, making good on a promise he had made to himself as a young boy. After their marriage, they moved into Bess's old home at 219 Delaware Street in Independence, an 1867 house that needed little improvement beyond central heating and electricity.

It was about the same time that Harry invested $15,000 in a haberdashery store in nearby Kansas City. The business failed in two years and Harry, as they say, lost his shirt. Characteristically, he blamed it on the Republicans. By then he was already active politically, and the party machine helped soften the blow of the business failure by making him a candidate for judge of the county court. He lost his bid for reelection three years later, and took a job with the Kansas City Automobile Club, which tided him over until 1926 when he became presiding judge of the county court, a job he held for the next eight years. In 1934 he became a United States Senator, the job he seems to have enjoyed more than any other in his entire life. During his ten years there he earned some notoriety as chairman of a special committee to investigate war contracts. He uncovered billions of dollars worth of fraud and put a stop to much of it. In one instance, he found enough surplus olive-drab paint to cover every mailbox in the United States for the next 30 years, not to mention the Army's equipment during the Second World War.

In his first press conference after taking the presidential oath, he said, "Boys, if you ever pray, pray for me now!" They obliged for a short time, but before his second year in office had ended the press, and the public, too, seemed to be preying for the President. The post-war world wasn't the same as the good old days everyone remembered. They gave Harry Truman the credit he deserved for ending the war, but the controversy that still rages over his decision to drop an atomic bomb on Japan didn't do much to enhance his popularity. He signed the United Nations Charter, helped establish the Marshall Plan to help European recovery, established NATO, made possible the creation of the State of Israel and held the infamous Senator Joseph McCarthy at bay. His popularity slipped when he ordered troops into Korea in 1950 and slipped even more when he fired the popular General MacArthur in 1951. But his popularity had been lower in the past.

Toward the end of his second year in office, when people couldn't think of enough nasty things to say about Harry S. Truman, he made a speech in which he said, "There is going to be a Democrat in the White House in 1949, and you're looking at him." The partisan audience cheered, but there wasn't a soul in the room who believed a word of it, and quite a few who were determined to prevent it.

Indoor plumbing and electricity didn't exist in this Lamar, MO, house when Harry Truman was born there in 1884.

Even before the conventions in 1948, the Republican hopeful, Thomas E. Dewey, was taking measurements for new curtains on the White House windows. The Democrats glumly renominated their incumbent and quietly began reading the want ads for jobs they were sure they'd have to find when it was all over.

The day after the convention, Truman called Congress back into session to take care of unfinished business. They didn't accomplish a thing and he had a perfect campaign issue. He boarded a train and announced he was going to criss-cross the country to "Give 'em hell." He accused the Republicans, who controlled Congress, of doing nothing, and predicted that they'd keep on doing nothing without someone like him to keep on giving them hell.

On election night in 1948, Harry Truman retired early. Though early returns had him ahead, the pundits were convinced that the tide was in Dewey's favor. Newspapers came out with early edition headlines that the president had been retired. Tom Dewey himself didn't believe he had lost and didn't concede until nearly noon the next day. It may well have been the happiest moment of Harry Truman's life.

It was a short-lived happiness. The world crashed in on the man from Independence soon after, and by the time he was forced to recall General MacArthur for insubordination in Korea in 1951, there were cries of impeachment in the air.

Yet Harry Truman survived it. And he never stopped smiling. He kept a sign on his desk that said, "the buck stops here," and another right next to it that said "if you can't stand the heat, get out of the kitchen." He accepted responsibility and fought long and hard for what he believed was right. A fiercely-loyal Democrat, he never compromised the good of the country for the good of his party. He gave courage a new luster and his straightforwardness was the like of which almost no president, before or since, has been able to master.

When the Harry S. Truman Birthplace was formally dedicated in 1959, the former president himself was on hand for the dedication ceremonies. "They don't do this for a president until he's been dead for 50 years," he said. "I feel like I've been buried and dug up while I'm still alive and I'm glad they've done it to me today."

He was honored several years later by a visit from President Nixon, who brought a gift of the White House piano for the Truman Library of Independence. The President, an accomplished piano player, sat down at the keyboard and dashed off a rendition of the Missouri Waltz, which the former president hated, as it turned out. It didn't matter much, though. Harry was 84 at the time and quite hard of hearing. When Nixon finished his recital, Harry turned to Bess and asked "What was that he played?"

Harry Truman died at Independence in 1972 at the age of 88. His beloved Bess died ten years later. Both are buried on the grounds of the Truman Library where the former president had his office through the years of his retirement.

The Truman family moved from the Lamar house when their son was a year old, leaving behind this bedroom, where little Harry probably slept. His father planted a pine tree, which is still standing in the yard, when the boy was born, and the backyard well, dug by hand, is still producing water.

The Harry S. Truman State Historic Site lies at the intersection of Routes 160 and 71 at Lamar, Missouri. The Site, which includes the Truman Birthplace, comprises a small, six-room frame house, an outdoor smokehouse and hand-dug well. The house was purchased from descendants of Marshal Wyatt Earp by the United Auto Workers of America and donated to the State of Missouri. It is open daily, at no charge, except Thanksgiving, Easter, Christmas Day and New Year's Day.

The Harry S. Truman Library and Museum is on Route 24 in Independence Missouri. It contains a reproduction of Truman's White House office and shelters the graves of President and Mrs. Truman. It is open, for a small charge, weekdays except Thanksgiving, Christmas and New Year's Day.

The Truman Home at 219 N. Delaware Avenue in Independence is a late-19th-century Victorian house that was home to the Trumans from 1919. It is open every day except Mondays for a small charge.

The Harry S. Truman Courtroom and Office Museum on Independence Square in Independence has the restored office and courtroom where Truman began his political career. A free sound and light show traces the early Truman career.

34

DWIGHT D. EISENHOWER

(1890-1969)

Five-star general Eisenhower, in this portrait by Thomas Stevens, went on to an impressive second career as president after his retirement.

The National Portrait Gallery, Smithsonian Institution

When Dwight D. Eisenhower was finally convinced to run for the presidency in 1952, the whole country seemed to be shouting "I like Ike!" He liked hearing it, but it took him a while to get used to the "Ike" part. It was a nickname that was attached to him as a boy, but he had long-since outgrown it. His friends called him "Dwight," his associates "General." But neither had the right folksy ring to it, and there was no denying that to know him was to like him.

So "Ike" it was for the rest of his life. It was all part of the image, based on fact, that in spite of his impressive accomplishments in the military, he was still a regular guy. A guy like your father, many people said. And they were right, too. He had a warm, inviting manner that either reminded you of your father or made you wish your father had been like him. His smile defied description, though many tried. It was boyish, but it was more than just that. It was infectious, but that word didn't quite describe it, either. If the like of it ever comes along again, it will probably be described as an "Eisenhower" smile.

He was born in 1890 in a house by the railroad, where his father worked, in Denison, Texas. That same year, the family moved to Abilene, Kansas, where his father, David, had found a job in a local creamery. When the future president was nine years old, the family moved to a large Victorian house which is where he and his five brothers were raised.

During his school years young Dwight worked with his father at the creamery, and when he graduated he went to work there as night foreman. Two years later, an appointment to the United States Military Academy at West Point started him a career in the military that would span the next 33 years.

The first assignment he gave himself when he graduated in 1915 was to marry the former Mamie Doud, which he did the following summer. The Army's first assignment for him was a post at Fort Sam Houston in Texas. Over the next several years, he and Mamie moved from one Army base to another, from Georgia to Kansas to Maryland and Pennsylvania. They lived in the Rocky Mountains near Denver, in the Canal Zone, in Washington and eventually in Paris.

The day they were married, he was promoted to lieutenant. By 1940, he was a full colonel and chief of staff of the 3d Division. Prior to that, he spent four years in the Philippine Islands as aide to General Douglas MacArthur. He later confessed that one of his jobs was to write the General's speeches, an impressive assignment since MacArthur's speeches were legendary. The delivery was also a large part of it, of course. Eisenhower described his Philippine assignment as "a course in dramatics."

By the time the United States entered World War II at the end of 1941, Eisenhower had reached the rank of brigadier general and was immediately promoted again to major general and put in charge of planning for the conduct of the war. Very shortly after, with the four stars of a full general on his shoulders, he was sent to Europe and made commander of American forces there. At the end of 1943, he was given a fifth star and named Supreme Commander of the Allied Expeditionary Forces.

He was well-liked and highly respected by his fellow officers and the men and women who served under him. And the folks back home regarded him as a super hero, especially during the days after the allied invasion of France in June, 1944, when the tide of the war changed and the question was not would we win the war, but how soon.

When it was over over there, General Eisenhower came home to a hero's welcome. He was made the Army's Chief of Staff and moved into Quarters One on Officer's Row in Arlington Heights, Virginia. It was then that talk began that he and Mamie really should be living across the Potomac at 1600 Pennsylvania Avenue. When the idea was first suggested, the General responded by saying "Baloney!" "I'm a soldier," he said, "and that's all I ever want to be." As his former boss, General MacArthur, told Congress a few years later, "Old soldiers never die, they just fade away." But General Eisenhower wasn't ready to do a fading act just yet. When he announced his retirement from the Army in 1947, he also announced that he was going to move to New York, where he would be president of Columbia University. He held the job for three years, retiring from Columbia in 1950, at which time he bought a farm in Gettysburg, Pennsylvania, and seemed, though only 60 years old, quite ready to retire.

But he wasn't really ready. The following year he went back to Paris to become Commander of NATO. In 1952, he cleared up two mysteries. The first, whether he would run for the presidency, was answered with a resounding "yes." And with that, he answered the second. Ike was a Republican. Up until that point, no one knew for sure, and the Democrats secretly hoped he would land in their camp.

He ran against the former Governor of Illinois, Adlai E. Stevenson, in '52 and won easily. Four years later, Stevenson and Eisenhower met again on the campaign trail and Eisenhower's majority was even greater.

As president, he never lost his smile and though he was reputed to have an unusually violent temper, it never showed at all in the public man. He had a serious heart attack in 1955, which seemed to confirm that his life wasn't all sunshine.

Politically, Ike was a conservative, but he called it "dynamic conservatism." It gave him a problem because he was too liberal for the conservatives, and too conservative for the liberals. Once, in frustration, he threatened to form a whole new political party. He wasn't the first president to make a threat like that and realized that history was certainly not on his side.

His first act as president was to end the unpopular Korean War and he spent all of the rest of his years in the White House keeping a tight rein on any moves that could lead to the outbreak of another war. "I know what war is," he said. "And like others who have experienced it, I don't want it to ever happen again." It was the era of Senator Joseph McCarthy, who went to great pains to uncover Communists in America, especially where they might bring him publicity. Eisenhower, who believed in a dialogue with the leaders behind the Iron Curtain, was clearly opposed to the witch hunts, but kept his peace. "I won't get down into the gutter with that man," he said.

Through it all, Ike's popularity never wavered. All America loved him, and when he took a world tour near the end of his presidency, it was clear that the man from Abilene had the respect and affection of the entire free world.

When he retired in 1961, Ike and Mamie moved to their farm at Gettysburg, Pennsylvania, the 27th house they lived in during their marriage. Beginning in 1955, he expanded the original farmhouse considerably. He added a putting green on the lawn to keep active in his favorite game of golf, and he added a studio where he could spend time painting.

It was their home, except for California winter vacations, until the former president died in 1969 and was taken home for burial in a building called the "Place of Meditation," across from his boyhood home at 201 S.E. Fourth Street.

The Eisenhower Center in Abilene was established with the construction of a museum in 1952 and the restoration of the Eisenhower home in 1947, before he was elected to the presidency. The Presidential Library, which houses books, papers and other memorabilia from the Eisenhower years, was dedicated in 1962. The Site has been expanded over the years, and now includes five separate buildings, including a Visitors Center, which was opened in 1975.

Eisenhower Center in Abilene, KS, includes the restored family home (facing page), furnished with original pieces, and a heroic plaza behind it (right), flanked by a library and a museum.

The Eisenhower Center in Abilene, Kansas, 80 miles west of Topeka on Route 1-70, is open every day except Thanksgiving, Christmas and New Year's Day. The small admission fee covers all the buildings, and includes an orientation film at the Visitors Center.

The Eisenhower National Historic Site at Gettysburg, Pennsylvania, gives visitors a self-guided tour of the farm Ike and Mamie loved, possibly more than any of their other houses. There is no fee for the house itself, but a charge is made for the shuttle bus. The house is open every day between April and October and Wednesday through Sunday at other times of the year. It is closed Thanksgiving, Christmas and New Year's Day.

The Eisenhower farm is adjacent to the Gettysburg battlefield on Pennsylvania Route 134.

35

JOHN F. KENNEDY
(1917-1963)

His famous rocker was an appropriate place for J.F.K to sit for this William F. Draper portrait.

The National Portrait Gallery, Smithsonian Institution

In a speech to the Massachusetts Legislature just before his inauguration as president, John F. Kennedy said, "It was here in Massachusetts my grandparents were born, and it is here I hope my grandchildren will be born."

He himself was born on May 29, 1917 at 83 Beals Street in Brookline, Massachusetts. The house was designated a National Historic Landmark in 1965, and today has been restored to the appearance his mother, Rose Kennedy, remembers it having when her second son was born there.

The neighborhood has changed considerably in the years since. There were vacant lots to give it an openness, and a small-town atmosphere to make it a pleasant place to raise youngsters. But the Beals Street house wasn't big enough for a growing family, and not long after the birth of their fourth child, Kathleen, they moved to bigger quarters a short distance away. John was only four when they moved. He was ten when they moved again, this time to Riverdale, just outside Manhattan in New York City. By the time they moved, there were three more Kennedy children. Two more would be born at the New York house.

J.F.K. was born in this Brookline, MA house (facing page). He toured local streets in the carriage now in the nursery (below).

But their roots never left Massachusetts. Both the Kennedys and the Fitzgeralds, the two families that became one when Joseph Kennedy, Sr. married the daughter of Boston's mayor, were forces to be reckoned with among the Boston Irish, a society as distinguishable from other Irish-Americans as from the non-Irish population of Boston. Both of John Kennedy's grandfathers had served in the Massachusetts Legislature. P.J. Kennedy served in both houses. Jack's other grandfather, the man they called "Honey-Fitz," went on to serve in the U.S. Congress and became the first Irish-American mayor of Boston.

Joseph Kennedy, Sr. was one of the first of the Boston Irish to graduate from Harvard University. His father, P.J. Kennedy, had become a successful businessman as well as a powerful influence in local politics. His son inherited his talent for the former. While he was a student he bought a sightseeing bus and built a lucrative summer business showing off the sights of his beloved Boston. After his graduation, he got a job in a bank his father owned and within two years he bought his own bank. By the age of 24 he was well on his way to becoming a millionaire, a feat he would accomplish many times in his life. The acquisition of the bank also emboldened him to ask Honey-Fitz for permission to marry his daughter, Rose. Permission was granted and the young bridegroom opened new ground for the Boston Irish by buying the house in Brookline, a suburb that had up until then been considered the private turf of the Protestant wing of Boston society.

On the day their son John was born, Joe Kennedy was made a member of the board of the Massachusetts Electric Company, another Protestant preserve. Not long after that, he landed a lucrative job as assistant manager of Bethlehem Steel's shipyard at Quincy, a place humming with activity in those early years of the First World War. When the war ended, he went to work for a stock brokerage firm and on the side went into a partnership that controlled a chain of movie theaters, which eventually led to a franchise to distribute films in New England.

But the stigma of being Irish in Boston still worked against him. He announced that Massachusetts was no place to bring up children and packed his family off to New York where he knew he could make more money. He did. He invested in the film industry, he invested in the stock market and the money kept rolling in. By the end of the 1920s, when the market crashed, he had already cashed in his investments and survived the Great Depression with most of his fortune intact.

By then he was ready to get into politics, but the political establishment turned its back on him. He went about his business, adding to his fortune and taking verbal pot-shots at the Roosevelt administration. Finally

Roosevelt appointed him head of the Securities and Exchange Commission and all was forgiven. He found government too slow and announced that his life as a public servant was over. But Roosevelt wasn't listening, and in 1937 appointed him Ambassador to Britain, a job he held until 1940.

By the time his son ran for the presidency 20 years later, he had built a fortune estimated conservatively at $400 million. Long before that he had decided that his son, Joseph, Jr., should become President of the United States. But in 1944 Joe was killed in a plane crash on a bombing mission to the coast of Belgium. The mantle fell on Jack's shoulders that day as he lay in a hospital bed still recovering from injuries received in the sinking of a PT boat he commanded in the Pacific.

After the war was over, young Jack Kennedy went into politics by running for the House of Representatives. He was reelected twice and became a United States Senator in 1952. It was as a freshman senator that he met and married Jacqueline Bouvier, the daughter of a socially prominent family, who became one of his great political assets. He himself was a man with political assets in abundance. His huge fortune was only part of it. He was a gifted political speaker, but he impressed his audiences less by what he said than by the way he said it. As a campaigner he brought most of us as close as we'll ever get to understanding the zeal of the Biblical evangelists. His speeches were short and to the point, a real novelty to people who had become accustomed to long-winded politicians. He was relaxed, confident, earnest. Though he is often remembered for his wit, his speeches never had them rolling in the aisles. He made it a point to use plenty of quotes from statesmen and famous writers. And he was among the first to mention his opponent by name, breaking an unwritten rule that was a cornerstone of American politics.

His audiences loved him. They were mostly young and, like himself, had come of age during and after World War II. Indeed, many of his most enthusiastic supporters had no memory of the war at all. But even though many of his detractors wrote off his supporters as a bunch of "kids," they elected him anyway. And on January 20, 1961, the style of the country changed dramatically. It was a spirit

The silver bowl across the table (right) was baby Jack's. Cookies came to the dining room (facing page bottom) hot from the oven (above). J.F.K. was born in his parents' room (facing page top).

Family singing took place around the piano when the Kennedys lived here. All that is different now is J.F.K's cigar box on top.

of adventure, a feeling that nothing was impossible, a sense that it was good to be alive and wonderful to be an American. He turned Washington into a city that was fun to visit for the first time in American history. The arts, from classical music to ballet, the theater to fine painting, became part of the Washington scene for the first time. He admitted to a love for blood-and-thunder movies and spy novels. He made physical culture a fashionable pursuit. He made a love for life important.

There are all kinds of facets to the Kennedy legacy. He made all America richer for having known him. Before he came on the scene, people used to wear little "smile buttons" to help boost their morale. When Kennedy was president, they went off style in favor of smiles on people's faces. He gave us a feeling that this is the greatest country in the history of the world and that there could be real joy in making it even better.

It all came to an abrupt end on November 22, 1963 with an assassin's bullet. Though the memory is still painful to those who remember that day, the memory his widow shared with the readers of Life Magazine is the one most Americans share when they visit the old neighborhood in Brookline.

"All I keep thinking of is this line from a musical comedy," she said. "At night before we went to sleep, Jack liked to play some records, and the song he loved most came at the very end of this record. The lines he loved to hear were, 'Don't let it be forgot, that once there was a spot, for one brief shining moment that was known as Camelot.'"

The John Fitzgerald Kennedy National Historic Site is at 83 Beals Street in Brookline, Massachusetts, near the Alliston-Brighton exit on the Massachusetts Turnpike west of Boston. The house where the 35th president was born has been restored to its appearance in 1917. Though some of the furnishings are original, many are simply typical of the period and were assembled with the help of the late president's mother, who has also recorded an audio tour of the house. It is open daily except Thanksgiving, Christmas, and New Year's Day, for a small entrance fee. In the same Brookline neighborhood is the house on Naples Road where John F. Kennedy lived between the ages of 4 and 10. It is privately-owned and not open to the public. Nearby is St. Aidan's Catholic Church, where young John was baptized and served as an altar boy, and the Dexter School where John and his older brother began their education.

The Edward Devotion School in Brookline, where young John first went to public school, includes a historic building dating back to the early 1700s, which is open to the public on Wednesday afternoons.

The famous "Kennedy Compound," a group of three homes overlooking the harbor at Hyannis Port on Cape Cod, Massachusetts, is still in the Kennedy family and is not open to the public.

36

LYNDON B. JOHNSON

(1908-1973)

A "real" Texan, the man in this portrait, and the first Texan to serve in the White House brought a new style to Washington.

During his presidency, Lyndon Johnson's greatest pleasure was taking visitors on tours of the Texas hill country where he was born and began his political career. On one of the tours, he grandly pointed to a rundown old log cabin and said "That's the house where I was born." His mother happened to be in the car with him and spoke right up. "Why, Lyndon," she scolded, "you were born in a much nicer house than that." "I know that, momma," he said. "But that house was torn down, and everybody needs to have a birthplace."

In 1964, he got his birthplace. The original house had, indeed, been torn down, but a new one was built on the site using some of the original materials. The president had the old house reconstructed on his LBJ Ranch to use as a guest house, but a year later it became a place the president proudly showed off as a symbol of his humble beginnings.

The National Portrait Gallery, Smithsonian Institution

L.B.J. was born in a cabin like the one (top) on his ranch. His grandfather's was more rustic (above).

There is no question that LBJ came from humble beginnings, but not as humble as many of his biographies suggest. He was born in 1908 in what was known in Texas as a "dog-trot" cabin, a very common structure in that part of the world in those days, consisting of a pair of log cabins connected by a roofed-over open space reserved for the family dogs. The restored birthplace isn't quite of the same style. At the time he was born, his father, Sam Johnson, was doing very well in the cotton business. But a recession in 1921 wiped him out. When his son was five, he moved from the cabin on the Pedernales River to a comfortable home on 9th Street in Johnson City.

The future president lived in Johnson City until after his high school graduation, at which time he migrated to California in search of greener pastures. It's hard to transplant a Texan, though, and he was back home again not long after his 17th birthday. His mother, who was one of the few college-educated women in the state at the time, convinced him that he ought to get more education. He chose Southwest State Teachers College in San Marcos, Texas, because it was "inexpensive and close to home." Because his family was poor, he needed to work his way through school and took a job as janitor. Because he was Lyndon B. Johnson, it was only a matter of time before he was special assistant to the president of the college. One of his duties was screening applicants for jobs on campus, and it was there that he discovered the uses of power, a talent that made him one of the most outstanding presidents the country has ever seen.

After college he became a teacher and discovered another of his talents by teaching public speaking at Sam Houston High School in Houston. It was there that he decided to get into politics. His father had served several terms in the state legislature. His great grandfather, George Washington Baines, had, in addition to founding Baylor University, served in the Arkansas legislature. But young Lyndon didn't begin his career by running for office. Instead, he engineered the campaign of another man to get him elected to the Texas State Senate. In gratitude, the Senator got the young teacher a job in the office of a congressman in Washington.

The L.B.J. Park in South Texas is filled with memories, including a chuck wagon. At the Ranch his saddle and family pictures, among them one of him at age four, are in his birthplace. The guest book lies on a poker table.

At the age of 22, Lyndon B. Johnson discovered a new calling. As administrative assistant to a congressman, he found out how the world of Washington politics works. He also found out that he had a special talent for it. He worked harder than anyone in town and made sure that people who mattered knew what he was doing and how well he was doing it.

It was in Washington that he met fellow Texan Claudia Taylor and proposed to her on the same night. He and Lady Bird were married soon after and he had a perfect partner to help him on the upward trip he was obviously about to take. She was the daughter of a wealthy landowner, who provided him with the capital to begin building a personal fortune that was estimated to be about $14 million when he became president.

Not long after their marriage, LBJ's friend, Speaker of the House Sam Rayburn, had him appointed director of the National Youth Administration in Texas. It gave him the visibility he needed and a year later, in 1937, he became Congressman Johnson. During his years in Congress he was a loyal supporter of the Roosevelt New Deal and a tireless worker for the Democratic Congressional Campaign Committee. He was rewarded by the administration with its enthusiastic support in the senatorial election campaign of 1940. He left the Senate in 1942 to enlist in the Navy. When the president recalled congressmen in military service, LBJ went back to Washington and, after being reelected to the Senate in 1948, he almost immediately became majority whip. Two years later he was made minority leader and in 1954 became the powerful majority leader. Possibly no man who ever served in the Congress understood more about how the institution worked, and no one knew better how to make it work for him.

Though he worked hard against John F. Kennedy for the first place on the 1960 Democratic ticket, he settled for second place and three years later became the fourth vice president to succeed to the highest office.

He arrived at the White House with the highest possible ideals. "I don't want to be remembered as the president who built empires or sought grandeur," he said. "I want to be the president who educated young children, who helped feed the hungry, who helped the poor to find their own way." He called his program "The Great

In a pensive mood

L.B.J's boyhood home is a Victorian house in Johnson City, TX (above). He bought the ranch (right) formerly owned by his aunt at Stonewall in 1951, and furnished it comfortably (remaining pictures). Despite the house being part of a National Historic Site, Mrs. Johnson retained a lifetime right to live there.

Society." It was the program that gave the elderly Medicare and expanded Social Security benefits. It gave minorities new pride and greater opportunity. It made industry accountable for what it was doing to the environment. It made the arts a beneficiary of federal aid. It should have made LBJ one of our most revered presidents.

But LBJ came to the White House with an albatross around his neck. It was the Vietnam War. No matter what he did, the spectre of the unpopular war was always there, and no matter what he did, he wasn't able to end it honorably. He also suffered from a personal style that many people found charming, but many others found offensive. He was a real "down-home" Texan: big, brash, vulgar, informal to a fault. Hard work was his own passion, and he expected everyone near him to share it. If they didn't, he could be cruelly insulting. He once defended it by saying, "If I don't bawl you out once in a while, you ain't part of the family." There were those who didn't want to be part of the family and, unfortunately for LBJ, some of them were in the press corps. He wasn't a man who took to criticism with good grace, though he knew very well how to use it constructively.

He was a man with a profound sense of his place in history. One of his great sources of pride was the Lyndon Baines Johnson Library and Museum on the campus of the University of Texas at Austin. It is still one of the most frequently-used of all the Presidential Libraries because of his own dogged enthusiasm for saving every scrap of paper

The ranch house (right), the center of a working spread, was enlarged by L.B.J. to its present 13 rooms. He also added a swimming pool next to his bedroom door. The original house had walls nearly two feet thick for protection against Indians.

The former president was buried in a simple grave (top far right) in the family cemetery in the midst of the countryside he loved so well, and which has become known everywhere in Texas as "L.B.J. Country."

Inside the house, in sunny rooms like the den (below) and the West Room (below, center and right), it's hard to imagine that Indians once howled outside the windows.

and making sure that every member of his staff shared that enthusiasm. When the Library first opened, he proudly said, "It's all here, with the bark off."

He was careful to make sure that his story was told well in the houses in Johnson City and on the 201-acre LBJ Ranch, 15 miles away.

The Ranch, which served as the Texas White House during the Johnson administration, is still the home of Lady Bird Johnson. For that reason, visitors are limited to a bus tour which is available every day of the year except Christmas Day. The bus, it should be noted, runs at a comfortable rate of speed. When LBJ lived there, he took a special delight in packing his car full of reporters and racing around the countryside at 90 miles an hour, sipping beer from a long-necked bottle.

The Lyndon B. Johnson National Historic Park is divided into two areas along the Pedernales River some 50 miles west of Austin, Texas. The unit of the park at Johnson City includes the Johnson Boyhood Home, a Victorian house where the future president lived between 1913 and 1934. The Johnson Settlement is the restoration of a cabin that was once home to LBJ's grandfather, a Texas cattle drover. Both buildings are open, without charge, every day except Christmas and New Year's Day. The LBJ Ranch, which includes the LBJ Birthplace restoration, the family cemetery and the Texas White House, is visited only on a free bus tour operated by the National Park Service every day except Christmas Day. The tour, according to the Park Service, varies "depending on the height of the Pedernales River, road conditions, ranching operations and Mrs. Johnson's need for privacy."

Adjacent to the Ranch is the Lyndon B. Johnson State Historical Park, whose Visitor Center contains Johnson family memorabilia and relics of other early settlers in the area.

The Lyndon Baines Johnson Presidential Library and Museum on the campus of the University of Texas at Austin contains some 31 million documents as well as an exhibit on every presidential political campaign in American history.

37

RICHARD M. NIXON

(1913~1994)

There are all sorts of ways to get into politics in the United States, but very few have done it the way Richard Nixon did it. He answered a classified ad in a local newspaper.

As a boy he worked in his father's grocery store and gas station on a roadside between Whittier and La Habra, California. The family was poor, and he said later that he wore hand-me-down clothes and lived on candy bars. After high school, he enrolled at nearby Whittier College and continued to work for his father while supplementing his income with all sorts of odd jobs. After college, he won a full scholarship at Duke University Law School at Durham, North Carolina.

Native Californian Richard Nixon had his likeness added to the host of New England faces that were the stock-in-trade of Norman Rockwell.

Facing page: the gardens at the Richard Nixon Birthplace in Yorba Linda, California. (Photo courtesy the Richard Nixon Museum)

The National Portrait Gallery, Smithsonian Institution

After law school, he tried to find a job in the East, but finally went home to Whittier, where he joined a small law firm. He soon became the town attorney, but wasn't much more than a big fish in a very small pond. But it was a living, and though he tried to earn more money with various business enterprises, he was resigned to the low pay of a small-town lawyer when he married Pat Ryan, a teacher at Whittier High School, in 1940.

When the United States entered World War II, Nixon went to Washington to work in one of the war-spawned federal agencies, but within a year he enlisted in the navy. He eventually became a lieutenant commander and saw action in the Pacific. But the real action for Dick Nixon was across the poker table. By the time the war was over, he had a tidy little nest egg. That's when he saw the newspaper ad. "Wanted: Congressional candidate," it said. He got the job and used his nest egg to finance his campaign.

The issue was to become a familiar one. His opponent, he claimed, was Communist-dominated. People believed it. And they believed it about everyone who came later to take Nixon's seat away from him. In 1950 he decided to run for the Senate and won easily by accusing the incumbent of carrying a red taint. Two years later he was the candidate for Vice President of the United States. It had been just six years since he answered the want-ad.

The campaign had barely begun when it was revealed that the candidate was taking money from special interests in California to supplement his Congressional salary. His first response was that it was a smear by the Communist-dominated press, and with that he hoped the issue would go away. It might have, except the ticket was headed by Dwight Eisenhower, who insisted that he either prove the charges false or get out of the race. His response was to go on television to explain himself. The speech was quite ordinary, and quite predictable until he got to the last minute or two. After categorically denying that anyone had ever given him any money except to finance campaigns, and defending himself as a poor, but honest, civil servant, Nixon looked into the camera and said:

"One other thing I probably should tell you, because if I don't they will probably be saying this about me, too. We did get something, a gift, after the nomination. A man down in Texas heard Pat on the radio mention the fact that our two youngsters would like to have a dog and, believe it or not, the day before we left on this campaign trip we got a message from Union Station Baltimore that they had a package for us. We went down to get it. You know what it was? It was a little cocker spaniel dog, in a crate that had been sent all the way from Texas. It was black and white and spotted and our little girl, Tricia, the six-year-old, named it Checkers. And you know, the kids, like all kids, loved the dog, and I just want to say this, right now, that regardless of what they say about it, we are going to keep it."

If he had had his mom deliver a piece of apple pie on camera, the speech couldn't have been more effective. He stayed on the ticket and became Vice President in 1952.

In 1960 he took on John F. Kennedy in the presidential election and lost by less that 120,000 votes. By then he had toned down his anti-Communist hard line and people were beginning to talk about a "new Nixon." Left without a political base in Washington, he sold his house there at a

very respectable profit and used the proceeds to build a mansion in Beverly Hills, California. Then he proceeded to build a political base there.

In 1962 he ran for governor of California, but lost the election in a disappointing race. People had been saying for quite some time that Nixon's political career had ended, and in November, 1962, he seemed to agree with them. After he had conceded defeat, he ended his press conference by saying:

"For 16 years you've had a lot of fun, you've had an opportunity to attack me and I think I've given as much as I've taken. It was carried right up to the last day. But as I leave you I want you to know ... just think how much you'll be missing. You won't have Dick Nixon to kick around any more because, gentlemen, this is my last press conference."

It wasn't, of course, but the former vice president really seemed to mean what he said. Not long afterward he not only left the political world, but left his native state and moved all the way across the country to New York City.

His 16 years in politics had given his some very valuable contacts and he decided to use them. He became a partner in one of New York's most important law firms,

Photo courtesy Yorba Linda Star

Richard Nixon was born in this house, which is surrounded by a lemon grove owned by his father, at Yorba Linda, and he lived here until he was nine years old. Shown left is the living room.

Photo courtesy Nixon Library

The president's birthplace is now part of a nine-acre park including the Presidential Library.

Photo courtesy Nixon Library

which gave him more influence, more contacts and the means for a very comfortable life in an elegant Fifth Avenue apartment. He was able to make some sound investments, and for the next five years was seen in all of New York's best restaurants and clubs in the company of people most New Yorkers who consider themselves successful usually only read about.

But, as in the words of the song about New York, "If you can make it there, you can make it anywhere," Richard Nixon decided it was time to take another shot at the presidency. In 1968 he ran against Hubert Humphrey and won by a small, but comfortable margin. Four years later, in a contest against George McGovern in 1972, he won by the biggest margin since 1936, when Franklin D. Roosevelt won his second term.

Interestingly for a man who created his political base as a militant anti-Communist, as president Nixon did more to relieve tensions between the superpowers than any of his predecessors, and he did it simply by talking to them. He opened the door to Communist China by going to Peking. He went to Moscow to negotiate an agreement between the Russians and Americans on arms limitations, and for the first time in more than two decades it began to look as though the end of the world in our lifetime wasn't inevitable.

Unfortunately, as Shakespeare pointed out, the good things men do are "oft interred with their bones." The legacy of the Nixon administration, for the first decade, at least, has been that of the only president ever to resign from office.

In 1972, when five men were arrested for breaking into the headquarters of the Democratic Party, the attempted cover-up that followed implicated the president's staff and, before it was over, 20 of his closest associates were given prison sentences. Though the president claimed innocence, it was clear that the office had become much more than a single man, and just as clear that he had gone beyond the bonds of simple loyalty in covering up what they had done in his behalf.

On August 8, 1974, Richard Nixon left his White House office, boarded the presidential jet for the last time, and went home to the 12-room Spanish-style house in San Clemente, California, that had served him as the Western White House and now would become his place of retirement.

The house, which was built in 1925, is on five acres of land on a bluff overlooking the Pacific Ocean. Nixon sold it in 1980 and moved back to New York City, where he bought a town house on the fashionable East Side. He sold the house a year later at a profit, it was said, of close to $2 million. Then he moved to the suburbs. In 1981 he bought a seven-bedroom house on four acres of land in New Jersey's Bergen County.

The Richard Nixon Library and Birthplace at 1801 Yorba Linda Boulevard, southeast of Whittier, California, includes 22 museum galleries displaying gifts from world leaders, a video forum providing information at the touch of a screen, a 75-seat amphiteater, the First Lady's Garden, and the president's gravesite. It is open, for a small admission charge, daily 10 a.m.–5 p.m; Sundays from 11 a.m.

38

GERALD R. FORD
(b. 1913)

Library of Congress

In December, 1973, Vice President Spiro T. Agnew became the first man in history forced to resign from vice presidency in disgrace. The president, Richard Nixon, made his choice of a successor very carefully. It had to be a man completely above reproach, a man both respected and well-liked in official Washington. The man he chose was Gerald R. Ford, who had served for 24 years as the representative of Kent County, Michigan, in Congress, and who at the time was minority lead of the House.

He was a man completely without enemies, a rare thing after nearly a quarter-century in Washington politics.

He was born in 1913 in Omaha, Nebraska, the son of Leslie L. King and his wife, Dorothy. When her marriage ended in divorce two years later, Dorothy took her son, whose name was Leslie King, Jr., back to her family home in Grand Rapids, Michigan. Soon after that she married a successful paint dealer named Gerald R. Ford, who adopted the child and gave him his name. Jerry Ford was 17 years old before he knew that the man who raised him was not his real father.

Photo courtesy Gerald R. Ford Library

A social club, organized by young Gerry Ford in the garage of this Grand Rapids, MI, house, where he lived from age ten until he turned seventeen, was one of the most popular places in town for teenagers during the 1920s.

In high school, the future president had been a star football player, and when he graduated was given a football scholarship to the University of Michigan. In 1935 he became assistant football coach at Yale University, where he became a student in the Law School. During his years there he invested in a successful model agency and worked in front of the cameras himself.

By the time the war broke out, he was back in Grand Rapids, where he had set up a small law practice. He gave it up to join the navy, where he earned the rank of lieutenant commander.

After the war he joined a successful law firm and, at the urging of his stepfather, became involved in local politics. In 1948 he became the Republican candidate for Congress and won easily.

During the campaign he met and soon married Betty Bloomer Warren, a fashion coordinator in a Grand Rapids department store and a former student of the modern dance pioneer Martha Graham. The fact that Betty was a divorcee threatened his chances of victory, but they were able to keep their courtship and marriage secret from the voters, who in that part of the country at that time didn't take well to such things. In subsequent campaigns, Betty proved much more an asset than a liability.

He was 62 years old when he became president, on the resignation of Richard Nixon in 1974, but could easily have been mistaken for a man much younger. He had been an athlete all his life and even in his early sixties was a masterful skier, golfer, swimmer. And yes, he was remarkably well-coordinated. The jokes that implied he was not were started when he was a congressman during the Johnson administration and an opponent of many of Johnson's programs. The president, who could put a man down like no one else in the world, began ridiculing the congressman from Michigan, starting with a comment to reporters that Jerry Ford had played football too often without a helmet. The Johnson jibes continued in that vein for months and the press, who consider such things good copy, reported every one of them.

They were largely forgotten after Ford became president himself, but "good copy" dies hard, and when Ford went to Salzburg, Austria, in 1975 he tripped as he was getting off the plane and fell on his face. An uncoordinated man might have been hurt, but the president recovered instantly without a scratch. Later that same day he slipped twice on a wet marble staircase and the three falls became suddenly more important than the State Visit itself.

What the press failed to do, the television and nightclub comedians managed to complete. The air was filled with Jerry Ford jokes, and the man became in the popular mind some kind of stumblebum. But Jerry Ford was never accused of not being a good sport and he accepted the treatment good-naturedly, even to the point of telling such jokes against himself.

He was less pleased about humor aimed at his intelligence. He often did get his words mixed and often didn't say exactly what he wanted to say. But he did, it should be pointed out, graduate in the top third of his class both at the University of Michigan and at Yale Law School.

And though he was defeated in a close race by Jimmy Carter in 1976, he retired from the presidency as he had entered it, one of the best-liked and best-respected men on the Washington scene.

The Fords retired to a home in Rancho Mirage, California. The other homes they lived in during their married life are all privately-owned. They also own a condominium in Vail, Colorado, where they began taking ski vacations in 1968.

While he was serving in Congress, they lived in a house in Alexandria, Virginia, which was sold in 1977. Their home base at the time was a two-family house on Sherman Street in East Grand Rapids, where they moved in 1950 after having lived in Betty's former apartment not far away. During his boyhood in Grand Rapids, the Ford family lived in five different houses in various parts of town. Some are still standing. One was replaced by a recreation center, another by East Grand Rapids High School.

The house where he was born, in Omaha, Nebraska, was destroyed by a fire and has been replaced by the Gerald R. Ford Memorial Park.

39

JIMMY CARTER
(b. 1924)

The National Portrait Gallery, Smithsonian Institution

A bucking donkey on his desk in this Carter portrait by James Templeton is not just a symbol of the president's party, but of the way he bucked the system to become the party's standard-bearer.

Although most Americans visiting their birthplace would find it necessary to time their arrival to hospital visiting hours, of the 40 presidents who have served their country, only one, Jimmy Carter, was born in a hospital.

Though there is probably nothing significant about that fact, no one thought that the boy born at Wise Hospital in Plains, Georgia, on October 1, 1924 would grow up to be president of the United States. In fact, 50 years later when he told his mother that he planned to run for president, she couldn't help asking, "President of what?"

No matter whom he told, he got the same response. But Jimmy Carter was a determined man and, even after he secured the nomination – when people were asking each other, "Jimmy who?" – his confidence that he would succeed never wavered.

It was obvious from the beginning that he would amount to something, though. His family moved from Plains to a farm two miles west of town when the boy was four years old. The farmhouse at the time didn't have indoor plumbing, or electric power. Though the years the Carter family lived there were Depression years, they were never poor. The farm produced cotton and corn, peanuts and watermelons, Irish potatoes and sweet potatoes. The house was comfortable, and the Carters owned a car as well as the only radio for miles around.

When Jimmy was five, he walked into Plains every day to sell peanuts door-to-door. The Carter smile helped him earn as much as five or six dollars a week, a lot more than some adults were earning at the end of 1929. Four years later, the boy, who had doggedly saved his money, began to buy occasional bales of cotton, which he sold at a profit. He invested the proceeds in local real estate, and by the time he was ten owned several houses in Plains, which he rented for as much as $15 a month.

His real goal during those early years wasn't to sell peanuts, nor to become a real estate entrepreneur. His eye was on military service. As soon as he graduated from Plains High School he enrolled at Georgia Institute of Technology in Atlanta, where he immediately joined the Naval ROTC program. Before his first year at Georgia Tech had ended, he had secured an appointment to the United States Naval Academy at Annapolis, Maryland.

When he graduated from the Academy, he followed the tradition of many midshipmen and got married. His bride, the former Rosalyn Smith, had grown up in Plains, just as he had.

During his seven years of Naval service he rose quickly through the ranks, but his biggest boost came in 1948 when he applied for a spot in the nuclear submarine program. It wasn't an easy job to land, even for a determined young man like Jimmy Carter. The first step was a long, and very tough, interview with Admiral Hyman Rickover, who headed the program and ran it with an iron hand. After two hours of hard questions, the Admiral looked Jimmy in the eye and asked, "Where did you stand in your class at Annapolis?" The answer was impressive: Carter was in the top 60 of a class of more than 800. But Rickover didn't seem at all impressed. "Did you do your best?," he asked. The candidate confessed he might not have. "Why not?" asked the Admiral.

The challenge never left Carter's mind and later, when he wrote a book explaining his personal philosophy, its title was "Why Not The Best?" It also became the campaign slogan that helped him win the presidency in 1976.

Carter's Navy career ended when his father died in 1953 and he resigned his commission to go back to Plains to take over the family peanut business. His father had built quite a successful business over the years and left his son a substantial inheritance along with a thriving enterprise to build on. Jimmy had saved a good deal of money in his Navy days, and though the family business didn't thrive in the first year or two, he had a cushion that helped him keep going. A decade later, the business was bringing in more than a million dollars a year.

It freed Jimmy to go back to his old love of real estate speculation and gave him time to become active in community affairs. There wasn't an important civic association for miles around that didn't have Jimmy Carter as an active member. He was head of many, and by the mid-1950s was quite the most influential man in Southwest Georgia.

In the early 1960s he was elected to the State Senate and in 1970 became Governor of Georgia. A lot of men would have stopped right there. But prevented by law from succeeding himself, Governor Carter began looking elsewhere for success. He moved from state politics to the national scene with an appointment to the post of chairman of the Democratic National Campaign Committee, and within two years was running his own

campaign for president.

There were a lot of qualities that made him a good choice. First of all, he was an outsider, which appealed to a country weary of political "old-boy" networks. He represented the "New South," which was becoming a force to be reckoned with in national politics. He was a man who took his religion seriously, but showed a side that was acceptable to those who didn't. His smile was infectious and sincere, which could appeal to voters. But most of all, the Carter quality that shone brightest was his uncommon passion for hard work. He clearly was a man who desperately wanted to give his best, and demanded it from everyone who served with him. In those post-Watergate years, Jimmy Carter was like Lochinvar himself, riding up from the South to win the nation's heart.

The election wasn't a landslide, but his 1.6 million plurality in the popular vote was respectable enough and it stopped people from asking the question "Jimmy who?" Unfortunately, his presidency was marred by runaway inflation that hurt the people he identified with most. In his campaign he had often told the voters that the majority of Americans were outsiders like himself. But in the 1970s, the shrinking value of the dollar was pushing them even further out of the mainstream. He had a problem with the "insiders," too. He couldn't seem to make Congress go along with his ideas. And, as a man who couldn't stand losing, he altered his policies to accommodate too many people, which many interpreted as weakness. In reality, weakness was not a characteristic President Carter would ever tolerate in himself.

In the 1980 election, when he was buried under the Reagan landslide, he had the strength to concede even before the polls were closed in some Western states. His presidency, which began with a moving tribute to Gerald Ford, his predecessor, whom he acknowledged publicly to have "healed our land," ended with a statement that says as much about the man as anything he said while he was in the White House. "I once promised you I would never lie to you," he said to the nation. "I can't stand here and say it doesn't hurt. I wanted to serve as president because I love this country and its people. I am disappointed tonight, but I have not lost either love."

In 1981, less than 20 years after he entered politics for the first time, Jimmy Carter went back home to Plains, Georgia, to a house outside of town not far from his boyhood home on Preston Road in Archery.

The Carter Boyhood Home on Preston Road, two miles west of Plains, Georgia, is still maintained as a working farm and is privately-owned. It is not open to the public.

The James Earl Carter Library, on the campus of Georgia Southwestern College in Americus, Georgia, contains Carter family memorabilia. It is open free every day except holidays and during school breaks.

Young Jimmy Carter lived in this farmhouse until he was twenty years old. It was a working farm, producing cotton, corn, potatoes, watermelons and peanuts. He later became a leading local farmer.

FIRST NATIONAL BANK
Birthplace of
President RONALD REAGAN

40

RONALD REAGAN

(b. 1911)

As the sign proudly proclaims, the building that now houses the First National Bank (facing page) in Tampico, Illinois, is the birthplace of America's fortieth president. The Reagan family were to move several times before settling in nearby Dixon in 1920. There, the house on Hennepin Avenue holds the most memories for "Dutch," as the future president was known. The dining room (below) is set as it was for the four family members.

There are no sure roads to the presidency. George Washington began his career as a surveyor, and so did John Adams and Abraham Lincoln. Lincoln was also once a storekeeper, and so was Harry Truman. Andrew Johnson began his political career in his tailor shop and Ronald Reagan began his as an actor. In fact, when Reagan first announced he was running for president, he drew on his acting career to explain his decision.

"I remember the movie *Santa Fe Trail,*" he said. "I played George Custer as a young lieutenant. The captain said, 'you've got to take over.' My line was 'I can't.' And the captain said, 'but it's your duty.' And that's how I feel about this."

Critics who derided his acting career as poor experience for the presidency didn't take into account that he had also served two terms as Governor of California and had been elected President of the Screen Actors' Guild eight times. He had appeared in more than fifty movies and as many television plays during his Hollywood years, but his work with the actors' union was a full-time job as well. In fact, he often said that his off-screen work sidetracked his acting career.

In 1954 he was one of the first Hollywood stars to become a television personality when he was made host of a series for the General Electric Company. His experience as a spokesman for the Guild and for the film industry was G.E.'s primary reason for hiring him. In addition to a TV host, the company was also looking for someone to tour its plants and make personal appearances as part of its employee and community relations programs. During the next eight years, Reagan visited

135 different G.E. plants in forty states in his role of corporate ambassador. The company also frequently arranged for him to be the principal speaker at dinner meetings of chambers of commerce and civic groups. In the process, he averaged fourteen twenty-minute speeches a day and learned from the experience how to keep every one of them fresh. And in addition to making speches, he toured assembly lines, signed autographs, shook hands, made small talk and got a new understanding of a segment of America he believed the country's leaders were underestimating.

Looking back on the experience, he said later, "I enjoyed every whizzing minute of it. No barnstorming politician ever met the people on such a common footing. Sometimes I had an awesome, shivering feeling that America was making a personal appearance for me, and it made me the biggest fan in the world." The feeling was clearly mutual.

What those people discovered about Ronald Reagan was that this glamorous Hollywood star was really one of them. He was born on February 11, 1911, in Tampico, Illinois, a lusty ten-pound baby his father, Jack, immediately began calling a "fat little Dutchman," shortened to the nickname "Dutch," which followed him the rest of his life. During his early years, the family moved several times, finally arriving in Dixon, Illinois, when young Dutch was nine. Dixon was a small town with a half-dozen factories surrounded by farms. It wasn't much different from hundreds of other prairie towns that lured farmers for Saturday night shopping, where the circus visited once a year and where Chautauqua pitched its tents for two weeks every summer to provide lectures and seminars and other forms of cultural uplift.

His brother Neil shared one of the three bedrooms in the house with the future president. The photo on the wall is of the YMCA Band, for which young Ronald acted as drum major.

The Reagan boys used the side yard of the house (right) as a makeshift football field. They raised rabbits in the backyard barn, which was also used for the family car. The house was built in 1891 for an estimated $1500.

Downtown Dixon in 1920 consisted of a hotel, a couple of luncheonettes, a drugstore with a soda fountain, a movie theater and a row of retail stores, including the Fashion Boot Shop owned by Jack Reagan. It was probably the least successful business in town. In those days, thrifty Midwesterners felt that owning more than two pairs of shoes was almost sinful. Jack's own son, Dutch, didn't own any shoes that hadn't been handed down by his brother, Neil. Their mother, Nelle, coped with hard times and turned to the Fundamentalist beliefs of the Christian Church of Dixon for inspiration. Her sons were at her side, especially Ronald, who took advantage of the speech lessons she gave him and followed in her footsteps as one of the most dynamic speakers in the congregation.

When he was fifteen, Dutch convinced the concessionaires at a local park that they needed a lifeguard and he was the man for the job. He was signed on at $15, plus all he could eat, for seven 12-hour days a week. He had already earned a reputation for charm as a Sunday school teacher, but this was a different stage. He worked at the park for seven summers, during which time not one person drowned. He himself admitted that he had "saved" a great many swimmers who weren't in any danger, but if they weren't overcome with gratitude, they were pleased with the attention of this handsome young man who seemed to like everybody and enjoyed having the affection returned.

Swimming was clearly his sport, but he dreamed of being a football player. Even though he couldn't see very far without glasses, his enthusiasm outweighed his nearsightedness, and the football coach at Eureka College, about a hundred miles from home, helped him get an athletic scholarship for half his tuition. The money he saved from summer jobs would cover the rest of his expenses, at least during his freshman year. Later he got a job washing dishes at the Tau Kappa Epsilon fraternity house.

Campus protests were a generation away in 1928, but the student body at Eureka was agitating for the ouster of the school's president. When they elected freshman Ronald Reagan to make a speech announcing that they were planning a strike, it was his first brush with a political cause, an experience he later remembered as "heady wine."

His college career was an active one. He earned letters on the swimming and track teams, he performed in seven plays, served as president of the student senate and of his senior class and the school's booster club. And he worked, sometimes two jobs at the same time, to cover his expenses. He graduated in 1932 in the midst of the Great Depression, in debt and with no prospects.

He hitchhiked to Chicago, where he didn't know a soul, intent on becoming a radio sportscaster. Every door was closed to him, but one friendly interviewer he did manage to see advised him to go to every small town radio station he could reach and take any kind of job they might have. It was good advice. Reagan had spent the previous four years washing dishes and didn't mind a bit asking for a janitor's job. In a few days he was riding his thumb back to Dixon. Using the family car, he began making a tour of local radio stations and after

ILLINOIS
BOYHOOD HOME OF
PRESIDENT
Ronald Wilson Reagan
HIS FORMATIVE YEARS
OPEN
WEEKDAYS: 10-4
SUNDAY 1-4
CLOSED TUESDAY

It is unrecorded whether the razor strop in the bathroom (right) in the weatherboarded Hennepin Avenue home (facing page) was ever used for anything other than putting an edge on Mr. Reagan's razor. But they were often used to keep boys on the proper edge of behavior.

visiting dozens of them, he eventually struck paydirt at WOC in Davenport, Iowa, where the station owner, like the Eureka football coach, was impressed by Reagan's enthusiasm. He challenged the young man to recreate a football game in words "that will make me see it." The audition got Reagan the assignment to announce a real game the following week. By the time the season was over, he had his first full-time job.

The Davenport radio station was later consolidated with the larger WHO in Des Moines and Dutch Reagan became its chief sports announcer, making him a celebrity all over the Midwest. But he had his eye on a bigger prize. In 1937, he convinced WHO to send him to Los Angeles to cover the Chicago Cubs spring training. While he was there, he went to Warner Brothers for a screen test, secured a seven-year contract, and went back to Des Moines to say good-bye. Exactly a week after returning to Hollywood, he began his first movie, *Love is on the Air*, in the role of a small-town radio announcer.

He worked regularly after that, appearing in an average of five films a year for the next five years. He became a certified star in 1942 in the film, *King's Row*. Among the people who granted such certification was Louella Parsons, movie columnist for the Hearst newspapers. She, like Reagan, had grown up in Dixon, Illinois, and took him under her wing from the beginning. She also engaged in marital matchmaking when she signed Reagan to join her on a national vaudeville tour. Among the others who went along was actress Jane Wyman. She and Reagan were married in 1940.

Wyman was an active member of the Screen Actors' Guild and encouraged her husband to fill a vacancy on its board. He rose to the occasion and took the first steps on the road that eventually led to the White House. As he became more and more involved in union activities, and she in her acting, their careers drifted apart, and the Reagans were divorced in 1948. Less than a year later, a young actress named Nancy Davis appeared in Hollywood. She was looking for a career in the movies, but didn't mind saying she was also looking for a husband. After meeting Ronald Reagan, his name led all the others on her list of eligibles. He himself managed to stay uncommitted for some time, but no one in Hollywood was surprised when they were married in 1952.

His tours for General Electric started two years later, and he soon developed a reputation in political circles for an electrifying speech he often gave denouncing the evils of Communism. But his corporate ties made a low profile the best policy and he repeatedly denied that he had any political ambitions. He worked hard for his friend George Murphy in his successful campaign for the Senate in 1964, and at the same time made a nationally televised speech endorsing Senator Barry Goldwater for the presidency. But he said that he had no desire to become a political star. "One serves where he feels he can make the greatest contribution," he said. "For me, I think that service is to continue accepting speaking engagements, in an effort to make people aware of the danger in a vast permanent government structure so big and complex it virtually entraps presidents and legislators." Two years later, he announced that he was running for Governor of California.

He spent his first term in Sacramento building the staff and organization that would eventually follow him to Washington. And he began establishing a relaxed, easy-going style that wouldn't change in his White House years. He also gave the country some interesting clues about his political philosophies. During his first campaign, he told the voters that he was "sick of the sit-ins, the teach-ins and the walk-outs" that were taking place at the time on California college campuses. He promised that when he was elected, he would organize a "throw-out," and he kept the promise. He shunned professional politicians, seeking instead the advice of businessmen "who have to show a profit," and accountants to "keep an eye on the bureaucrats." No one had any doubts that he had his own eye on the presidency. But his ambitions were sidetracked when

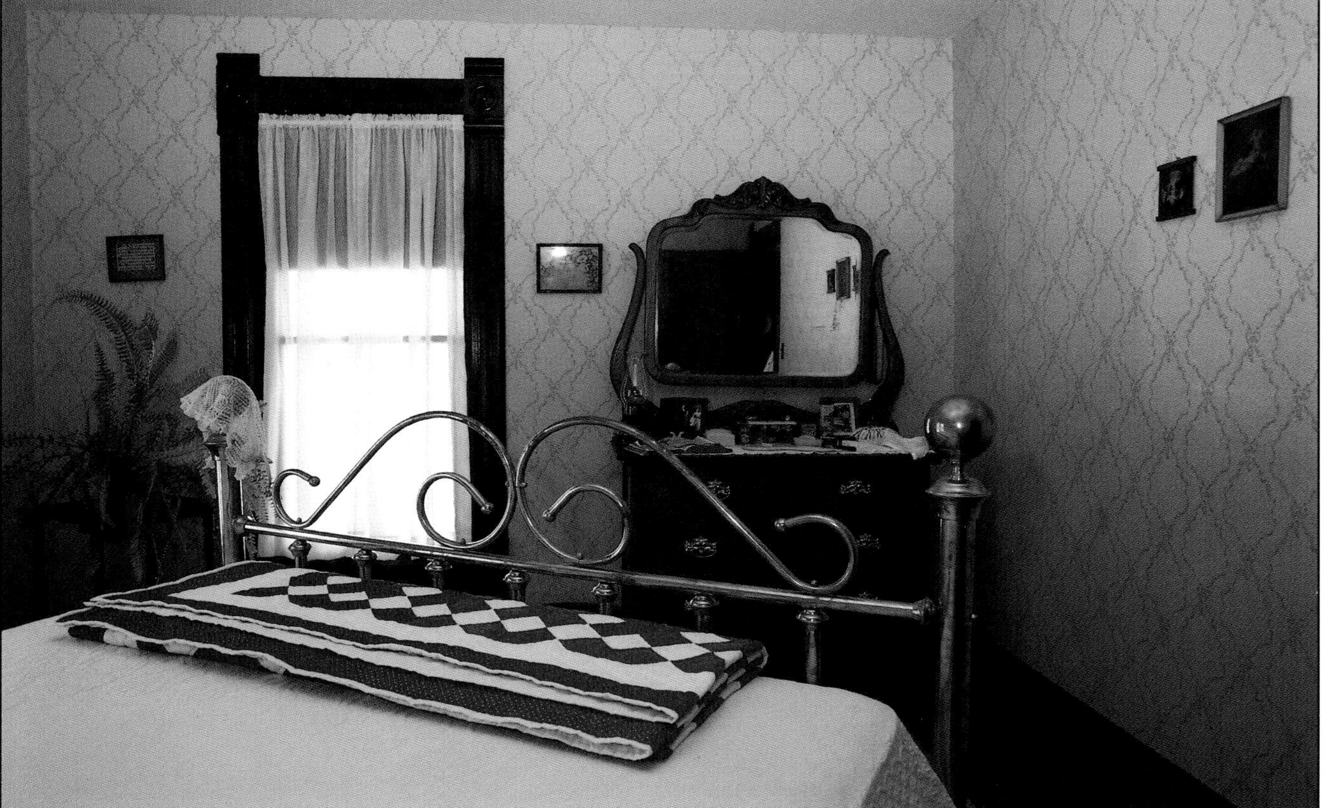

The modest kitchen (below right) and the neat, simple bedroom (right), reflect something of the warmth and homeliness of the Reagan's Dixon home.

fellow Californian, Richard Nixon, won the 1968 presidential election. At the time, there seemed no doubt that he would remain in the White House until 1976, by which time Governor Reagan would be a private citizen again. But by 1976, the incumbent was Gerald Ford, and though Reagan challenged him in the primaries, he was given the nomination. It put off Reagan's presidential plans for another four years. Most other men probably would have abandoned the plan. By 1980, Ronald Reagan would be sixty-nine years old. But unlike most other men, he was in the prime of his life.

When he was elected, he was the oldest man ever to take the oath of office. But he didn't take age seriously. He told an interviewer that Thomas Jefferson had said it was foolish to worry about old age. "And when he told me that," added Reagan, "I stopped worrying."

His presidency is remembered as one that took some of the worry out of American life. When he was elected, the country was experiencing its worst economic crisis since the 1930s. He brought new theories to the problem, and though during his first two years in the White House the country went through its worst recession in four decades, the recovery from it was dramatic and lasted through the entire remainder of his eight years in office. In the last two years of his administration, he was credited with breathing a breath of spring into the cold war that had existed between the United States and the Soviet Union for more than forty years.

They are among the reasons why Reagan left office more popular, if anything, than when he entered it. He never lost the charm that made folks back in Dixon pleased to have him rescue them from drowning, even though they weren't in water over their heads. And the image of him most Americans carry is less the man delightedly touring Moscow with the Soviet Premier than a man on horseback looking out over his ranch.

The Reagans moved from Washington to a home in California that was bought for them by a group of admirers. But the 688-acre ranch in the Santa Ynez Mountains at Santa Barbara is still his favorite retreat. He bought the ninety-year-old adobe house and its surrounding acres in 1974 after he retired as Governor of California. It is named Rancho del Cielo, "Ranch of the Sky," for its location 2,300 feet above sea level. During their White House years, the Reagans used it as a vacation home, as they still do. And when the President was in residence there, it wasn't uncommon to hear reports of his activities cutting wood and clearing brush. It is a never-ending activity at Rancho del Cielo. The only source of heat in the house is its fireplaces. And it does get chilly up there in the clouds.

Ronald Reagan's Boyhood Home at 816 South Hennepin, in Dixon, Illinois, has been furnished with family memorabilia and restored to its original appearance. It is open, free of charge, every day except Tuesdays and major holidays.

The Reagan Birthplace in nearby Tampico is open Fridays and weekends, November through February. There is a small admission charge to the second-floor apartment where the 40th president was born.

The Ronald Reagan Presidential Library at 40 Presidential Drive, Simi Valley, California, includes a replica of the Oval Office, and a section of the Berlin Wall. It is open, for a small fee, daily 10 a.m.–5 p.m.; Sundays from noon.

41

George Bush

(b. 1924)

Right: President-elect George Bush and his wife Barbara arrive at the Lincoln Memorial, Washington, at the beginning of the inaugural festivities, January 18, 1989 (Associated Press). The house (below) in Kennebunkport, Maine, built by the President's grandfather on Walker's Point, is his official home away from the White House.

Ask George Bush where home is and he'll answer, without the blink of an eye, "Texas!" But, in a country where image is often considered as important as substance, people remember men like Lyndon B. Johnson and say, "Funny, you don't look like a Texan."

Even if President Bush never sucessfully cultivated the image of a good ole boy, he is as much a Texan as any of them. He has called it home for more than forty years. And if that doesn't qualify him as a son of the Lone Star State, remember that Sam Houston was Governor of Tennessee before he got the Texas spirit, and that Moses Austin, who led the first American families into Texas, was born in Connecticut. So was George Bush. His father, Prescott Bush, served as a United States Senator from Connecticut for ten years, in fact, though he himself grew up in Columbus, Ohio.

The five Bush children, including the second-eldest, the future president, grew up in Greenwich, Connecticut, but their favorite place was the family's summer home at Walker's Point in Kennebunkport, Maine, which had been owned by Mrs. Bush's father, George Herbert Walker, a St. Louis businessman. The home there still ranks high among President Bush's favorite places. It is filled with memories of his boyhood days when he explored the rocks, hunted for starfish and collected treasures from tidal pools; and of that wonderful summer day when he was allowed, at the age of nine, to handle his grandfather's lobster boat all by himself, even if it was under the watchful eye of his eleven-year-old brother.

Six months after the Japanese attack on Pearl Harbor in

The Victorian house (facing page) in Greenwich, Connecticut, where the future president spent his boyhood is no longer in the Bush family.

1941, young George graduated from the prestigious Phillips Academy in Andover, Massachusetts, and it was expected he would follow in his father's footsteps by going on to Yale University. But when he decided to join the Navy instead, his family backed his decision. Not long after his eighteenth birthday, George Bush was learning to fly. When he got his wings, he was the youngest pilot, not to mention the youngest-looking officer, in "This Man's Navy." To make matters worse, his girlfriend, Barbara Pierce, was even younger. To upgrade his image, he even asked her to lie about her age.

George met Barbara at a dance while he was in flight school. She lived in Rye, New York, not far from his family's home, and went to school in South Carolina, not far from his Navy base. He was in advanced flight training when they decided to become engaged in 1943. But at the same time he was assigned to a torpedo squadron scheduled for active duty in the Pacific, and the wedding date was postponed for the duration of the war.

Weddings were the furthest thing from George Bush's mind on the morning of September 2, 1944. The target for the day was a Japanese communications center on Chichi Jima, part of the island chain that includes Iwo Jima, where the Marines landed six months later. As his TBM Avenger began its dive over the Chichi Jima radio tower, it was hit by anti-aircraft fire. The cockpit filled with smoke and flames licked over the wings, but Bush kept on diving. He released all four of his 500-pound bombs and headed for the open sea. Then, after his crew bailed out, Bush jumped himself. He was slightly injured, but intact, when he hit the water. He floundered there in a rubber raft for nearly two hours, without a paddle and drifting toward the Japanese-held island. Finally, an American submarine broke the surface, and the ordeal was over. The bad news was the discovery that his two crewmates had been killed. Bush himself was awarded a Distinguished Flying Cross for his efforts to save them, and for succeeding in his mission in spite of the smoke and flames.

He was back in action in a few weeks, and after flying fifty-eight combat missions, he was ordered home. He returned to Connecticut on Christmas Eve, 1944, and he and Barbara were married two weeks later. Before the war ended, his squadron was being prepared for an anticipated invasion of Japan, but the Japanese surrender came first, and George and Barbara Bush were more than ready to get on with their lives.

He enrolled at Yale University and, like so many students in the 1940s, lived off-campus with his wife and son George, who had been born in 1946. Every couple in the house's thirteen apartments had at least one child, and one had twins. It was a far cry from the typical Yale life his father had experienced. But family duties notwithstanding, George Bush still found time to become captain of the school's baseball team and a star firstbaseman at the College World Series in both 1947 and 1948. He also earned a degree in economics in just two-and-a-half years, and a Phi Beta Kappa key in the bargain.

His next logical step was to join Brown Brothers Harriman, the New York investment banking firm where his father was a partner. But when the job was offered, George Bush turned it down. He wanted to be his own man. A family friend suggested that the best place for an ambitious young man to make his mark was the Texas oil fields. When he backed up the advice with a job offer, George and Barbara packed their baby into an old Studebaker and headed for West Texas and his new job as a clerk with a company selling oil rig equipment.

They settled down in a one-bedroom "shotgun house," whose rooms were connected to each other with no hallway, on East Seventh Street in Odessa. They learned the lingo there, developed a taste for chicken fried steak and beer from long-necked bottles, and followed local football as passionately as any native-born Texans.

In a little less than a year, Bush was promoted to salesman and transferred to California, but when he was eventually moved back to Texas, he knew that he had come "home." There was an oil boom there in 1950, and the Bush family waded right into the center of the action, buying a small house on East Maple Street in Midland. It was a neighborhood filling fast with people who were all, like George, ambitious to make money. The subject even took a back seat to football at backyard

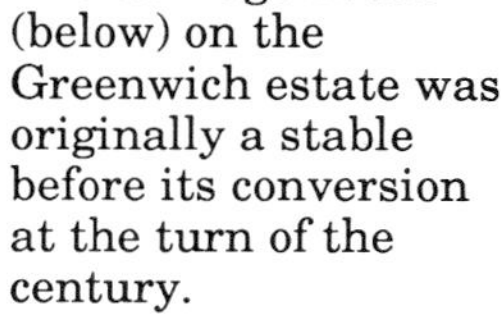

The carriage house (below) on the Greenwich estate was originally a stable before its conversion at the turn of the century.

Young George Bush often used this stairway (below) as a putting green. The mirror on the landing (right) was put in place when the Greenwich house was built.

The Bush children sometimes slept out on the back porch (facing page top) at Greenwich, and they rarely missed a family party in the dining room (facing page bottom).

cookouts in the neighborhood and, after one of them, George Bush teamed up with John Overbey to form an independent oil company. Overbey, the Bush's neighbor across the street, was as enthusiastic as he was bright, and it seemed like a perfect opportunity to twenty-six-year-old George Bush. It was. They developed oil fields as far away from Texas as Montana, and Bush's financial contacts in the Northeast helped make them highly successful wildcatters. The company operated in the black for the entire three years of its existence, a rarity among independents in the rough-and-tumble oil business.

In 1953, Bush and Overbey joined forces with two other neighbors, Hugh and Bill Leidtke, to form an even bigger independent company, which they named Zapata Petroleum for a Mexican rebel leader played by Marlon Brando in a movie they had all just seen. The company was split five years later, and George and Barbara Bush moved to Houston to take charge of a new entity named Zapata Off-Shore, and to pioneer a new type of three-legged off-shore oil rig that has since become the industry's standard.

In 1956, after Zapata's first rig began pumping, George Bush seemed destined to join the pantheon of self-made Texas oil millionaires. But of the things Texans get passionate about, politics is one of the highest on the list, and in 1962, Texan George Bush got passionate about politics. In the 1950s, the traditionally Democratic state was beginning to show Republican leanings, and Bush was approached by GOP leaders in Houston to help them build a new organization. He agreed to become the party's county chairman, and two years later its candidate for the United States Senate. He lost the election, but not the fever. On the theory that he lost because his business interests took away some of his energies, he sold his stake in Zapata in 1966 and ran unencumbered for Congress.

After serving in the House of Representatives for four years, Bush followed the advice of President Nixon, and an avuncular hint from former President Lyndon Johnson that it might be a good idea, and ran for the Senate again in 1970. He lost again, but before the year ended he was appointed United States Representative to the United Nations, where he served until 1973, a period that included the admission of the People's Republic of China to the organization. When he went back to Washington, President Nixon offered him the chairmanship of the Republican National Committee, explaining that after his recent landslide victory in 1972, the party needed a strong man to build a new coalition. Bush accepted the challenge, but no one knew at the time what a tough assignment it would be. The Watergate scandal broke a few months later, and the challenge for the committee members was less to build a new coalition than to keep the old one from crashing around their heads.

During the Ford Administration, Bush was offered his choice of posts as Ambassador to Great Britain or France, but

Bush family parties usually spilled out into the stair hall (above), and Mrs. Bush often had musicians entertaining from the landing.

held out instead for the job of head of the U.S. Liason Office in China. As though he hadn't been challenged enough in recent months, he said he and Barbara wanted "a challenge, a journey into the unknown," as they had all those years before when they headed for Texas in an old Studebaker.

In 1974, George, Barbara and the family dog set off on their journey into the unknown. They lived and worked in Beijing for fifteen months, during which time "the Bushers," as the Chinese called them, became part of the local scene, riding around the city on bicycles, as the natives do, even though they had a car and driver at their disposal. As the unknown became familiar, they were reluctant to leave, but in December, 1975, President Ford designated George Bush the new head of the Central Intelligence Agency.

As the CIA was under investigation at the time by two Congressional committees for alleged abuse of power, the job of restoring its image seemed to Bush to be as thankless as his chairmanship of the Republican National Committee had been. But he rose to the occasion, and by the time Jimmy Carter was elected president, agency personnel had regained their self-respect and the image of the CIA itself had been restored. On the other hand, George Bush was out of a job. But he had his sights on a better one. On May 1, 1979, he announced he was running for president.

He lost his bid, but made a strong enough impression on his opponent in the primaries, Ronald Reagan, to become the winning candidate for vice president. His duties in the first Reagan Administration went well beyond those normally assigned to a vice president. His first assignment was to head the Presidential Task Force on Regulatory Relief, a key agency in Reagan's economic recovery program, and he was made the Aministration's chief spokesman on the entire economic program. His service was rewarded with the vice presidential nomination again in 1984, and finally with the presidential nomination and his election to the highest office itself in 1988.

When they moved into the White House, George and Barbara Bush noted that it was the twenty-ninth time they had moved from one house to another in four decades. Over those years, from his days of building a business to serving in Congress, at the U.N., in China, at the CIA, in the Reagan Administration, and finally in his own presidency, he had done enough to make any man proud. But when he was asked what single accomplishment he was proudest of, George Bush answered, without the blink of an eye, "the fact that our children still come home."

42

BILL CLINTON

(b. 1946)

To most Americans he is just plain Bill, but President Clinton's more formal name is William Jefferson Blythe Clinton. However, like Gerald Ford, the president's name on official documents isn't quite the same as the one on his birth certificate. Three months before he was born William Jefferson Blythe VI on August 19, 1946, the future president's father, a traveling salesman, was killed when his car went out of control on a rain-slicked highway. When the boy was four years old his mother married a car dealer named Roger Clinton, and young Billy Blythe became known as Billy Clinton.

Photo courtesy The White House

The change of name also brought a change of scene when the family moved from their home at Hope, Arkansas, up the road to Hot Springs. But although he grew up in the famous resort city, Bill Clinton always thought of Hope as his home town. When he was born there, it was well-known as the watermelon capital of the state and, with its record-holder weighing in at nearly two-hundred pounds, possibly the world. It eventually took on the aura of the birthplace of a president, but in his early years the man who would bring fame to Hope had his eye on a much different career. He had dreams of becoming a doctor until 1963, when he was chosen to go to Washington as part of the American Legion's Boys' Nation program, designed to give participants a chance to simulate a national government. It also gave him a chance to shake hands with President John F. Kennedy in the Rose

This house on South Hervey in Hope, belonging to Bill Clinton's grandparents Eldridge and Edith Cassidy, was his home until the age of four. The Cassidys ran a grocery store in the town.

Garden, and Bill Clinton's life was changed forever. His mother recalled that when he arrived home from the trip, "... the first thing he did was open his bag and present me with this photograph of himself with John Kennedy ... I could just read the expression on his face, and I never questioned what he was going to do."

He went back to Washington as a student at Georgetown University's School of Foreign Service and earned his way working in the office of Arkansas Senator J. William Fulbright, who was chairman of the Senate Foreign Relations Committee. As part of his job Clinton acquired the habit of reading six newspapers a day, and through his access to committee information began forming opinions, common among his peers, opposing the war in Vietnam. In 1969 he won a Rhodes scholarship to Oxford, and after returning from England he went on to Yale Law School.

It was at Yale that he first saw his future wife, Hillary Rodham, a Wellesley graduate from suburban Chicago. As she tells the story, she introduced herself to him after noticing that he was staring at her instead of the books in the law school library. "I decided this was ridiculous," she recalled, "so I got up and walked up to him ... and I said, 'You know, if you are going to keep looking at me and I'm going to keep looking back, we at least ought to get to know each other'." In 1972 they both went to Texas, where they worked on the campaign of the unsuccessful Democratic presidential candidate George McGovern, and then Clinton went on to Washington to take a job on the staff of the House Judiciary Committee. In 1974 he went back to Arkansas to teach at the University of Arkansas at Fayetteville, a post he held until 1976, when he was elected State Attorney General. In the meantime, he had made an unsuccessful bid for Congress, but a successful bid for Hillary Rodham's hand in marriage. The couple moved into a Fayetteville house that Hillary had characterized as her favorite in the entire city, and it was their home when their daughter, Chelsea, was born in 1980.

But for the previous two years they had lived in the Governor's Mansion at Little Rock, after Clinton was elected the nation's youngest governor at the age of 32 in 1978. Two years later he had become the country's youngest ex-Governor when voters denied him a second term in retaliation for a hike in automobile license fees as a means of financing education. At least, that is what the pundits said. The young governor had other strikes against him for his progressive social ideas in a basically conservative state and, to make matters worse, Bill Clinton was still very much a child of the 1960s. His long hair alone made some voters cringe. Added to that was the fact that his wife had not adopted his name, and it rankled

Photo: A.C. Haralson/Arkansas Dept. of Parks and Tourism

The Clintons moved north from Hope to Hot Springs in 1953, where the house pictured above became their first home. Although Bill Clinton grew up in the famous resort city, he always thought of Hope as his home town, and Hope still considers him as her own. The Hope Visitor Center, pictured right and facing page, is housed in the town's old railroad station and boasts displays of her famous son.

Photo: Sheila Yount

Photo: Sheila Yount

Photo: Sheila Yount

Photo: Arkansas Dept. of Parks and Tourism

Photo: A.C. Haralson/Arkansas Dept. of Parks and Tourism

Photo: A.C. Haralson/Arkansas Dept. of Parks and Tourism

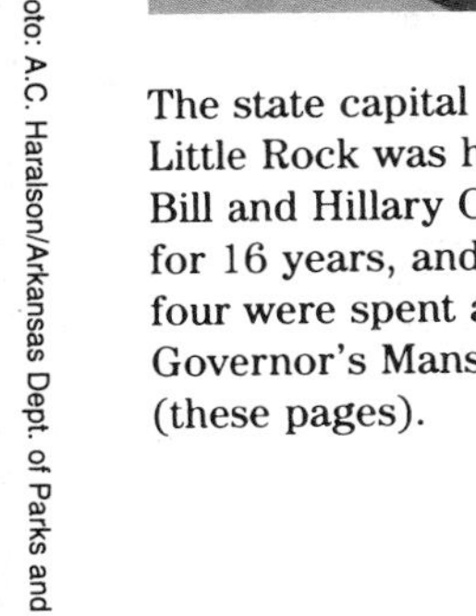

The state capital of Little Rock was home to Bill and Hillary Clinton for 16 years, and all but four were spent at the Governor's Mansion (these pages).

many Arkansans that their governor and their First Lady answered to different names. Clinton didn't alter his principles, but he cut his hair, his wife began calling herself Hillary Clinton, and by the 1982 election all was forgiven and they moved back to Little Rock, where he served as Governor of Arkansas until his election to the presidency ten years later.

Although the turning point in Bill Clinton's life was the photo opportunity in the Rose Garden during the Kennedy administration, friends and family agree that his life was filled with events, large and small, that not only shaped his character but honed the skills and instincts that define the art of politics. It began, they say, at the age of fourteen, when he stood up to his stepfather, an alcoholic who abused his mother, and managed to stop his abusive behavior without alienating him. Though an unpleasant confrontation, it is often cited as a classic example of Clinton's ability to understand another man's point of view and to blend opposites in the interest of finding a common ground; a key to success in life as well as in politics. As one of his oldest friends put it, "... He learned the fine art of compromise. And not compromise out of a sense of fear, but out of a sense of strength."

All presidents make changes in the White House to suit their own lifestyles, and the first one Clinton ordered was the addition of more bookshelves. He had done the same when he moved into the Governor's Mansion at Little Rock in 1979, and when he moved back in 1983 he added even more. It was estimated that when they moved to Washington the Clintons took along a personal library of some 4,500 volumes. It is an eclectic collection ranging from the Meditations of Marcus Aurelius to current mysteries and thrillers he characterizes as "grocery store trash." He also reads books and magazines in German, and has encouraged his daughter, Chelsea, to learn the language. After several summers at a German-speaking summer camp, Chelsea and her father often converse with each other in that language. It has been reported that Mr. Clinton regularly reads at least five books a week, an accomplishment not seen in the White House, with the possible exception of John F. Kennedy, since the days of Theodore Roosevelt. Like T.R., President Clinton also prefers to write his own speeches.

Photo: Arkansas Dept. of Parks and Tourism

Construction work on the Arkansas Governor's Mansion in Little Rock began in 1947, when Bill Clinton was barely a year old. He moved into the Colonial-style residence in 1979 as the nation's youngest governor.

President Clinton's talent in playing the saxophone once prompted an ambition to become a jazz musician, a dream professionals say could have come true. But close friends say that he really prefers classical to pop music, and the truth may be that his musical tastes may be as broad as his choice of reading material. He is also an accomplished singer and, in addition to singing Bach chorales, he mastered the technique of gospel singing as a member of the choir at the Immanuel Baptist Church in Little Rock. He routinely selects the music for ceremonial events, always including his favorite, Bach's Jesu, Joy of Man's Desiring, and liberally mixing jazz and rock with symphonic and operatic selections. Mr. and Mrs. Clinton are also avid collectors of Oriental porcelain, and the president himself is an accomplished student of fine art. On what may seem to be the opposite side of that coin, before moving into the White House Mr. Clinton took a walking tour of the neighborhood to see if there might be a McDonald's nearby. There was, but the president never indicated that he might not make the move if it placed him out of jogging distance of a Big Mac and fries.

Hollywood Portraits

HUMPHREY BOGART

Hollywood Portraits

HUMPHREY BOGART

Marie Cahill

BISON GROUP

First published in 1992 by
Bison Books Ltd.

Kimbolton House
117 A Fulham Rd.
London SW3 6RL

ISBN 0 86124 965 8

Printed in Hong Kong

All photos courtesy American Graphic Systems except:
Brompton Books Archives 25 (bottom), 40, 62 (bottom), 63, 64, 71 (bottom), 85 (top), 102 (bottom)
The Paul Ballard Collection, Wagner Library, Rancho Palos Verde Art Center 8
RE DeJauregui 76 (bottom), 109
Marc Wanamaker/Brompton Archives 6

Page 1: Humphrey Bogart in one of his greatest roles – Rick in **Casablanca** (1942).
Page 2: This still of Bogey catches something of the intensity that he brought to every part he played.
Facing page: Bogey as Sam Spade, the ruthless and cynical private eye in **The Maltese Falcon** (1941).

INTRODUCTION

Humphrey Bogart was born in New York City in 1899, the son of a prominent surgeon and a successful magazine illustrator. Bogart's father had plans for his son to follow in his footsteps and sent him to the prestigious Phillips Academy in Andover, Massachusetts in preparation for medical studies at Yale. As if foreshadowing the Bogey legend that was to come, young Bogart was expelled for disciplinary problems and later joined the Navy when the United States entered World War I. While on duty on the USS *Leviathan*, Bogart was injured during a shelling and was left with a partially paralyzed upper lip—the source of his characteristic tight-set mouth and lisp.

After Bogart's discharge from the service, with the help of a family friend, he found a job in the theater as an office boy and worked his way up to road company manager and stage manager. About 1920 he decided to try his hand at acting, and although his performance in the play *Swiftly* (1922) was characterized by Alexander Woollcott as 'what is usually and mercifully described as inadequate,' Bogart was not deterred and went on to play numerous, albeit

Facing page: Quintessential Bogart.

Below: There is no truth to the rumor that Bogey began his acting career with the words 'Tennis anyone?'

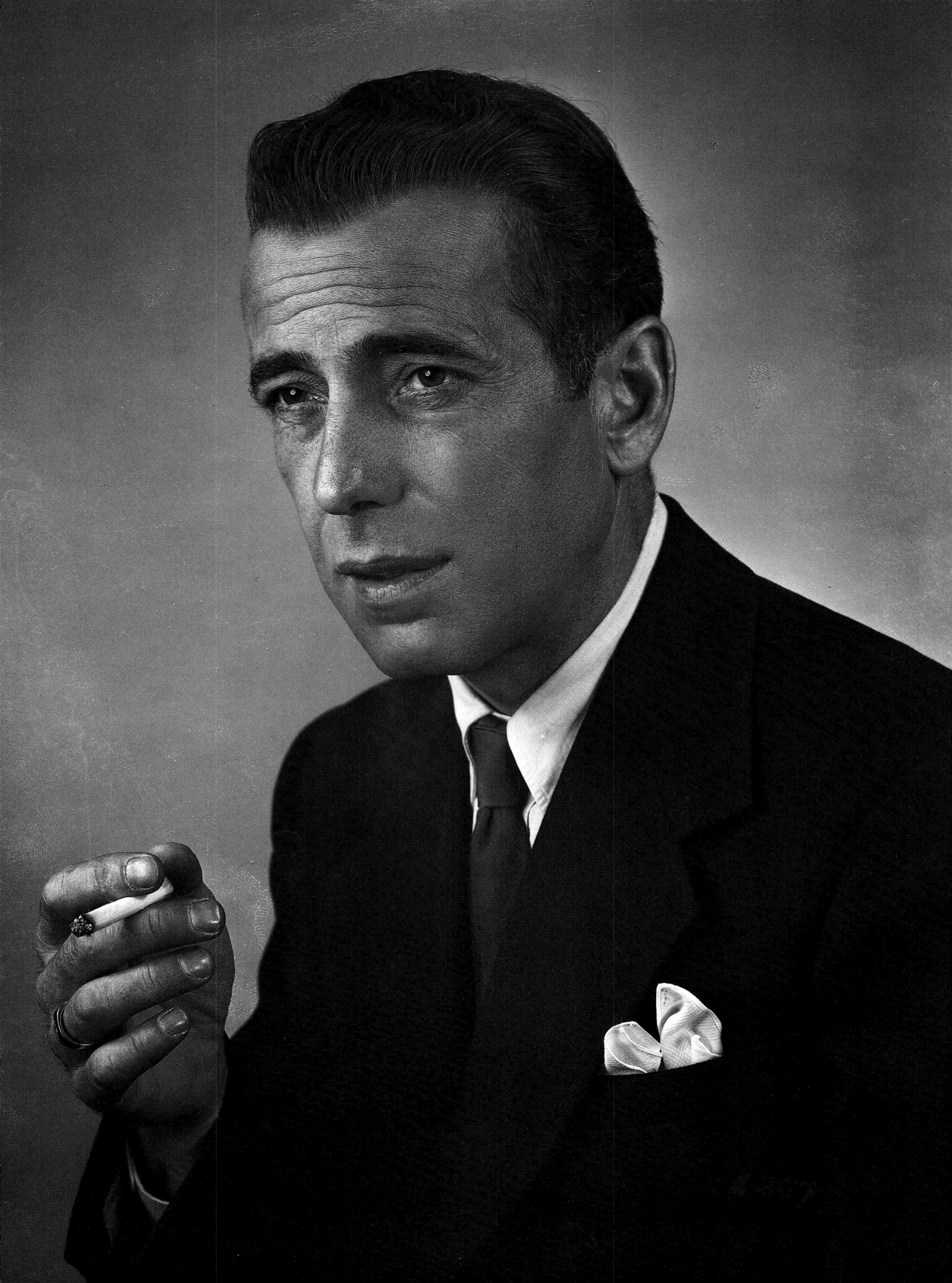

indifferent, stage roles throughout the 1920s.

He turned to film, but, frustrated by the succession of second-lead roles, he divided his time between Hollywood and Broadway. His luck finally changed in 1935, when he landed the part of the gangster Duke Mantee in the Broadway production of Robert E Sherwood's *The Petrified Forest*. Warner Bros acquired the film rights to the play, intending to cast Edward G Robinson in the Bogart part, but Leslie Howard, who had played the leading role on Broadway, threatened to quit unless the part of Duke Mantee went to Bogey. Warners acceded to Howard's demands, **The Petrified Forest** (1936) was a great success, and Humphrey Bogart was finally on the path to stardom.

The path, however, was somewhat rocky. Between 1936 and 1940, Bogart appeared in 28 films, usually playing a gangster. The turning point came in 1941 with **High Sierra**. Though cast again as a villain, Bogart's part—with thanks to screenwriter John Huston—was a step above the others.

Later in the year, when Huston was given the opportunity to direct his first film, he found himself working once again with Bogart as Sam Spade, the archetypal tough guy, in

Above: Bogart converses with Dooley Wilson, as Sydney Greenstreet looks on, in **Casablanca** (1942).

Facing page: After starring in nearly three dozen films, Bogart finally broke out of the gangster mold when he landed the leading role in **The Maltese Falcon** (1941).

The Maltese Falcon (1941). The role had been offered to George Raft, but he turned it down, probably because he didn't want to work with an inexperienced director. Raft's loss was Bogart's gain, for Sam Spade was the best role Bogart had had the opportunity to play. It proved that Bogart could play the hero and romantic lead—and thus was born the Bogey legend. Though he wasn't the typical handsome leading man, Bogart played the romantic lead with aplomb. In subsequent roles, Bogart's characters would capture the hearts of Hollywood's most alluring leading ladies, from Ingrid Bergman to Lauren Bacall, whose heart he captured off-screen as well. After starring with Bogart in **To Have and Have Not** (1945), Lauren Bacall became Bogart's fourth and last wife.

After **The Maltese Falcon**, Bogart successfully reprised his tough guy image in various films, most notably in **Casablanca** (1942), **To Have and Have Not** (1945), **The Big Sleep** (1946) and **Key Largo** (1948). In 1948, Bogart again worked under the direction of John Huston in **The Treasure of the Sierra Madre**, in which he played the part of the greedy and paranoid prospector, one of his most acclaimed roles. In the 1950s, Bogart demonstrated the range of his skill with widely diverse roles in such films as **The African Queen** (1951), **The Caine Mutiny** (1954), **Sabrina** (1954) and **The Barefoot Contessa** (1954).

Humphrey Bogart died in 1957, but the Bogey legend lives on. Remembered for his effective portrayals of the brooding, self-reliant cynic, Humphrey Bogart is the subject of numerous film festivals. Though he may have seemed an unlikely movie star, Humphrey Bogart made a lasting mark in the history of cinema.

Above: Bogart with Ida Lupino in **High Sierra** (1941).

Facing page: A publicity still from the early years at Warner Bros.

HUMPHREY BOGART

Facing page: Bogey didn't mind posing for portraits like these, but he refused to do the image-making 'at home shots' of actors with their dogs, horses, cars, guns or whatever.

Above: After Bogart received rave reviews for his performance as Duke Mantee in the Broadway production of *The Petrified Forest*, Warner Bros optioned him for the film version, but then decided to give the role to Edward G Robinson. When Leslie Howard, who was reprising his stage role, learned this, he issued an ultimatum to the studio: If Bogart didn't get the part, Howard wouldn't make the film.

The studio reconsidered their position, and Bogart got the part. It was a turning point in his career, and years later Bogart would name his daughter Leslie after the actor who helped launched his career.

Bogart's Duke Mantee set the standard for Hollywood's portrayal of gangsters. This still shows Bogart with Leslie Howard and Bette Davis, the waitress who finds a kindred soul in Alan Squier, the poet portrayed by Leslie Howard.

Above: Not wanting to tamper with success, Warner Bros immediately cast Bogart in another gangster film, **Bullets and Ballots** (1936), with Edward G Robinson as Johnny Blake, a cop out to smash the mob. Bogart played Nick 'Bugs' Fenner, the mobster's lieutenant.

In a pattern that would be repeated again and again over the next few years, Bogart's character would always be the heavy who was killed or wounded, never the hero who gets the girl.

Above: Bogart with Bette Davis in **Marked Woman** (1937). The woman in the center of the photo is Mayo Methot, who later became the third Mrs Humphrey Bogart.

The daughter of a sea captain, Mayo had been an actress since childhood. Like Bogart, Mayo loved the sea. She also loved a good fight, and the couple became known as 'The Battling Bogarts.' Their free-for-alls were legendary: Mayo once stabbed Bogart with a butcher knife and on another occasion she set the house on fire. They freely acknowledged their volatile relationship. Their home was dubbed Sluggy Hollow, Bogart's pet name for Mayo was Sluggy, and their boat, in honor of Mayo, also wore the epithet, *Sluggy*.

Above: A publicity still for **Kid Galahad** (1937), in which Bogey played Turkey Morgan, the gangster-manager of a prize fighter.

Facing page: As Baby Face Martin in **Dead End** (1937), Bogart played an infamous gangster who returns to the streets of his youth to visit his mother and his childhood sweetheart.

Based on the play by Sidney Kingley, the film was directed by William Wyler, with photography by Gregg Toland. Though dated today, it was a well-done film for the era, inspiring Hollywood to make more social dramas.

Overleaf: Bogey and the Dead End Kids. This group of young actors would recreate their roles as juvenile delinquents in various films, eventually turning from crime to comedy as the Bowery Boys.

PLACE

These pages: **Stand-In** (1937) was a comedy that tried to establish Bogey as a romantic charmer. His next few films would also attempt to move him away from the gangster image. Audiences, however, preferred Bogey as the heavy, and he was soon back in gangland.

Above: **Men Are Such Fools** (1938) was one of the early attempts to break out of the gangster mold, but the film didn't have much going for it. Bogart played a radio executive who pursues Priscilla Lane.

Right: In **Crime School** (1938), Bogart played the Deputy Commissioner of Correction who assumes control of a reform school when he discovers the superintendent has beaten his young charges. The juvenile delinquents were played by the Dead End Kids.

Above: For **Angels With Dirty Faces** (1938), Bogart was teamed with another of Warners' famous actors of the gangster film era—James Cagney. The film also featured the Dead End Kids.

Angels With Dirty Faces was directed by Michael Curtiz, who would later direct Bogey in one of his most unforgettable roles—Rick in **Casablanca** (1942).

Facing page, above: **Angels With Dirty Faces** (1938) typifies the successful gangster films produced by Warner Bros during the 1930s. Finding their inspiration from the exploits of real-life gangsters John Dillinger, Al Capone, Bonnie and Clyde and so on, these films offered action, excitement and, most of all, an escape from the gloom of the Great Depression.

Facing page, below: Still the bad guys, Bogart and Cagney played outlaws in **The Oklahoma Kid** (1939).

H.B.

Facing page: A publicity still for **Dark Victory** (1939), a melodrama that cast Bogey as a horse trainer and Bette Davis as a fast-living young heiress. His next role as a petty crook (*above*) in **You Can't Get Away With Murder** (1939) was a return to the old, familiar image.

These pages: Set against the backdrop of Prohibition, **The Roaring Twenties** (1939) was among the best of the gangster films. It was also one of the most violent gangster movies ever made. The film traces the intertwined lives of three Army buddies who go their separate ways at the end of World War I, but whose paths cross again as the mobs battle for control of the underworld.

Bogart played a saloon keeper turned bootlegger who is eventually gunned down by his old Army pal and former bootlegging partner, Eddie (James Cagney). Priscilla Lane (*above*) played Cagney's wartime sweetheart who rejects him in favor of Lloyd, the third Army pal.

RT- 72

Right: Perhaps the most unusual film in the Bogart catalogue is **The Return of Dr X** (1939), in which Bogart played the mysterious Doctor Xavier. Also known as Marshall Quesne, Doctor X had been executed and was brought back to life through injections of a rare blood type. The movie revolves around a series of murders that Dr X commits so that he may obtain the blood he needs to sustain his life.

Fortunately, Bogey's career did not include any more forays into the world of science fiction.

RD- 42

Above: **Invisible Stripes** (1939) is yet another film in which Bogey is gunned down in the end. From 1938 through 1940, Bogey starred in 17 films. Out of those 17 films, he was a gangster or a criminal in 11 and was killed in 9. Bogart argued with Jack Warner about continually playing the heavy, but Warner listened to box office returns, not to Bogey, and the gangster image remained firmly fixed.

Facing page: Humphrey Bogart as the sinister Marshall Quesne in **The Return of Dr X** (1939).

Overleaf: Bogey, as a gangster on the lam, hides out in a boarding house run by Jesse Busley in **It All Came True** (1940). The film, which also starred Ann Sheridan and Jeffrey Lynn, is an interesting mix of drama, comedy and music.

REMINGTON
.45 AUTO COLT
Remington
AMMUNITION AND FIREARMS
.38 S. & W. SPECIAL
GUARANTEE
GARANTIA
REMINGTON

CT-25

These pages: In **They Drive By Night** (1940), Bogart and George Raft starred as two brothers in the trucking business.

Overleaf: Bogart's next film was **High Sierra** (1941). Bogey got the part by default, after both George Raft and Paul Muni turned it down. Rumor has it that James Cagney and Edward G Robinson also turned down the part. Though he was tired of playing gangsters, Bogey took the part because he believed an actor should always be acting. As it turned out, the film marked a turning point in his career. Just as **The Petrified Forest** had established the gangster image, **High Sierra** refined it. By giving the part of Roy Earle a sensitive side, Bogart made audiences feel sympathy for a man who would otherwise be regarded as a ruthless killer. Above all, it made Hollywood look at Bogart as a serious actor.

Bogey's effective portrayal of Roy Earle (*above*) in **High Sierra** (1941) was aided by an excellent screenplay by John Huston and WR Burnett. Pleased with Huston's work as a screenwriter, Jack Warner of Warner Bros had promised Huston that he could direct **The Maltese Falcon** (1941) if he could produce a workable script. The leading role of Sam Spade, the cynical private eye, was offered to George Raft. Not wanting to put his career in the hands of a novice director, Raft turned down the part.

Once again Bogart accepted what Raft had rejected. As Sam Spade (*facing page*), Bogey laid the gangster image to rest and in its place a new one was born—Bogey the leading man.

SPADE
AND
CHER

Left: **The Maltese Falcon** (1941) begins with a Miss Wonderley (Mary Astor) seeking the services of Spade and Archer (Jerome Cowan), a detective firm, to help her find her missing sister. Her story is as false as her name, but that doesn't deter the two detectives from taking the case.

Miles Archer is killed almost immediately, leaving Spade to handle the case and his partner's widow (*above*), Iva (Gladys George). Though he didn't like Miles, Spade's code of ethics will compel him to find his partner's killer, as he explains later: 'When a man's partner is killed he's supposed to do something about it. It doesn't make any difference what you thought of him. He was your partner and you're supposed to do something about it.'

Warner Bros had previously released two other versions of Dashiell Hammett's riveting novel, *The Maltese Falcon*. The first version was directed by Roy del Ruth and featured Bebe Daniels and Ricardo Cortez. In 1936, a second film made its way to the silver screen starring Bette Davis and Warren William under the direction of William Dieterle. The title was changed to **Satan Met a Lady**, a reference to Hammett's description of Sam Spade as a 'blond Satan.' These two films are all but forgotten. The John Huston-Humphrey Bogart version lives on – a Hollywood classic and one of the best detective movies ever made.

The gritty realism depicted in **The Maltese Falcon** (1941) set the tone for the urban crime thrillers that came to be known as film noir, which translates as dark film. The term was first used by a French film critic to describe the moody, downbeat character melodramas of the late 1930s, such as **Quai des Brumes** and **Le Jour se Leve**, but it soon was applied to American urban crime thrillers of the 1940s and 1950s, of which **The Maltese Falcon** was one of the first and the best.

The scenes on *these pages* are rich in the atmospheric details that define film noir. In the scene *above*, the two actors stand in the light of a lone street lamp, a dark shadow cast against the nearby brick wall, as unidentified faces stare down at them. The grim and dreary locale of a deserted alley provides a realistic setting for a murder. The characters, especially Spade, are typical of the genre: loners disillusioned by life's ugly realities.

Though the scene *on the left* is an interior shot, it is as shadow-laden as the exterior shot *above*. The two policemen are in the dark (literally as well as figuratively), and Spade sits half in, half out of a shadow.

Overleaf: Sam Spade confronts Brigid O'Shaughnessy (Mary Astor).

Above: As **The Maltese Falcon** races to a conclusion, Sam Spade (Humphrey Bogart), Joel Cairo (Peter Lorre), Brigid O'Shaughnessy (Mary Astor) and Kasper Gutman (Sydney Greenstreet) gather round the object they have been searching for—the black bird. Their eyes revealing their greed, Brigid O'Shaughnessy's and Joel Cairo's attention is riveted to the black bird and to Gutman, who gently caresses the falcon. In a moment, though, his penknife will scar its surface, revealing that the bird is a fake and that his long search is not yet over.

Facing page: Bogey and Mary Astor. A ruthless character, outside of the law, Brigid (Mary Astor) has counted on Spade to protect her. But things will not turn out as she planned: 'I won't play the sap for you,' he tells her. 'I won't walk in Thursby's and who knows who else's footsteps. You killed Miles and you're going over for it.'

Overleaf: After **The Maltese Falcon** (1941), Bogart played Gloves Donahue in **All Through the Night** (1942), in which he thwarts a Nazi plot to blow up a battleship in New York Harbor. His leading lady was played by Karen Verne.

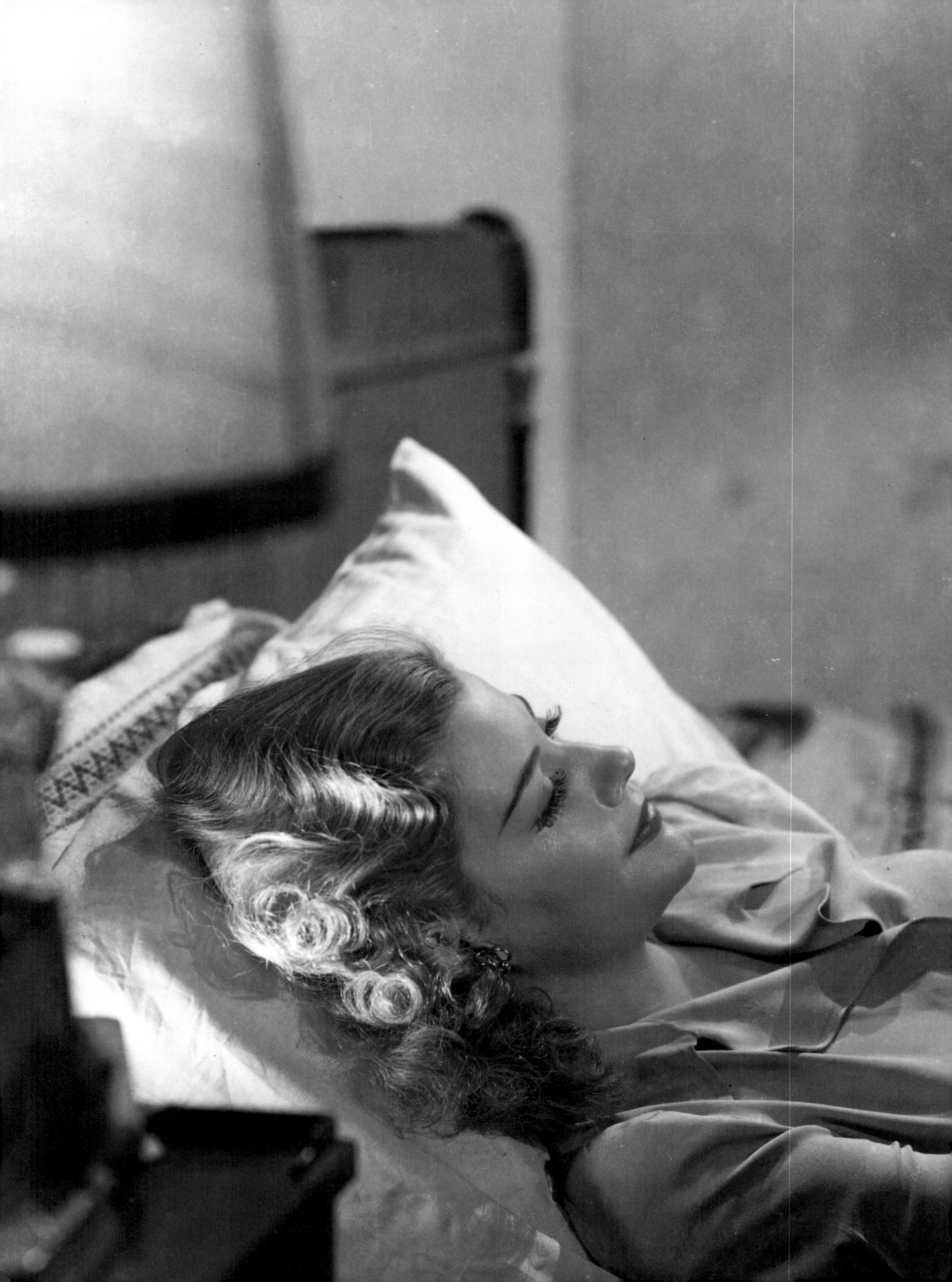

These pages: With the advent of World War II, gangster films suddenly seemed trivial, and films began to focus on the dramatic events that were unfolding around the world. In John Huston's **Across the Pacific** (1942), Bogey was again teamed with Mary Astor and Sydney Greenstreet in a war drama about Japanese sympathizers on the eve of Pearl Harbor. **Across the Pacific** was well-received in its day, but today it is overshadowed by Bogey's next film—**Casablanca.**

GENOA
No.1

Above: The role that most people associate with Humphrey Bogart is Rick in **Casablanca** (1942). With his performance a year earlier in **The Maltese Falcon** (1941) Bogart had shown that he was more than capable of playing a romantic lead. **Casablanca** smoothed out the remaining rough edges and refined the Bogey screen persona – the worldly-wise and weary tough guy who plays by his own set of rules. Underneath the seemingly impenetrable surface he is susceptible to a vulnerable romanticism.

Set against the backdrop of World War II, **Casablanca** focuses on the romantic torment of Rick Blaine (Bogart), owner of Rick's Café Américain. Unable to forget the past, Rick is cynical and disillusioned, unmoved by the political drama unfolding before him. But Rick wasn't always like this, as the flashback (*facing page*) to Paris reveals. While in Paris, Rick had a brief but torrid love affair with the beautiful Ilsa Lund (Ingrid Bergman). Unbeknownst to Rick, Ilsa was married to Victor Laszlo (Paul Henreid), a leader of the Resistance Movement. She believed that he was dead, and when she learns otherwise, she leaves Paris and Rick without explanation. Jilted by the woman he loves, a stunned Rick (*overleaf*) is left standing in the rain at the train station. Were it not for his loyal friend Sam (Dooley Wilson), who pulls him aboard, he would have missed the last train fleeing Paris before the Nazis occupied the city.

Left: The screenplay for **Casablanca** was being written even as the movie was being filmed, which meant that no one knew which leading man would 'get the girl,' a source of considerable frustration for the actors involved. Director Michael Curtiz planned to film it both ways, but as soon as everyone saw it, they knew that the only possible conclusion was to have Ilsa board the plane with Victor Laszlo.

Moments after Ilsa and Victor have boarded their plane, the head Nazi—Major Strasser—arrives. When he attempts to stop the plane, Rick shoots him (*above*). Fortunately for Rick, Captain Louis Renault (Claude Rains), the chief of police, is on his side and gives the order to 'Round up the usual suspects.' In a conclusion guaranteed to encourage cheers from the audience, Rick and Louis walk off in the fog together, united in purpose, as the movie ends with one of the finest closing lines ever written—'Louis, I think this is the start of a beautiful friendship.'

Above: The stars of **Casablanca**—Claude Rains, Paul Henreid, Ingrid Bergman and Humphrey Bogart.

In the hands of a less skillful director and cast, **Casablanca** would have been vapid melodrama. Instead, the film earned three Academy Awards for Best Picture, Best Director and Best Screenplay, as well as a place in the hearts of moviegoers for the last 50 years.

Facing page: Paul Henreid, Ingrid Bergman and Humphrey Bogart—the stars of one of Hollywood's finest movies—gather in front of Rick's Café Américain, the most famous saloon in the world.

Rick's
Café Américain

Action in the North Atlantic (1943) is a World War II action adventure film about an American tanker torpedoed by a German submarine. Bogey played the first mate, who is then reassigned to the *Sea Witch*, a new Liberty ship. The still *above* shows Bogey with Julie Bishop, while the one *below* shows Bogey with Sam Levene, Alan Hale and Raymond Massey.

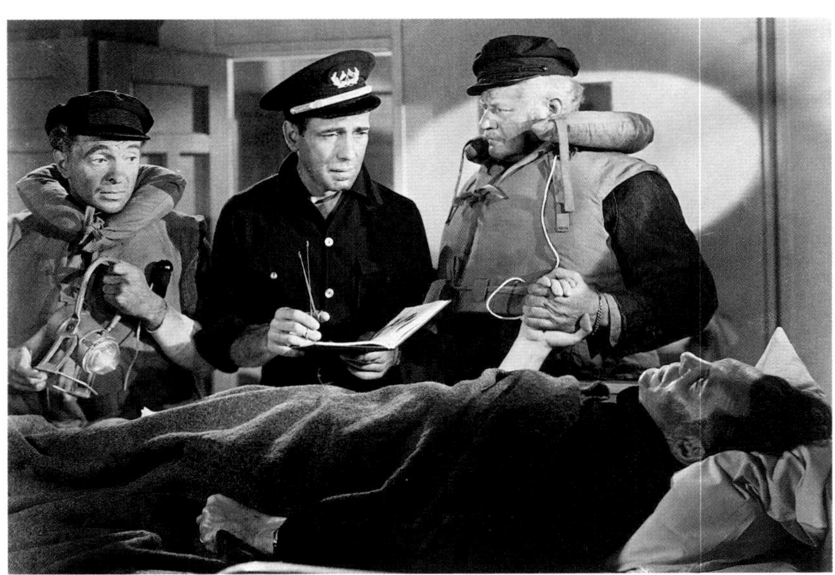

Above: As World War II raged on, movies about the war continued to pour out of Hollywood. For his last film in 1943, Bogey was loaned out to Columbia for **Sahara**, in which he played a tank commander in the Libyan desert. The image of Bogey at war filled American audiences with confidence. With men like him leading the troops, victory was assured.

While the Bogey persona was waging war in **Sahara** (*above*), Bogey and his wife, Mayo, were doing their part for the war effort by entertaining the troops in North Africa and Italy. They left the States in December 1943 and were gone for three months. Film clips of their trip, along with combat shots with Bogart doing the voiceover, were compiled into a Red Cross short called **Report From the Front**.

Facing page: Hoping to recreate the magic of **Casablanca**, Warner Bros adapted Ernest Hemingway's *To Have and Have Not* for the screen. Bogey was again a cynic claiming neutrality, Dooley Wilson was replaced by Hoagy Carmichael, and this time the love interest was played by Lauren Bacall—who would soon become the fourth and last Mrs Humphrey Bogart.

Right: **To Have and Have Not** (1945) bore very little resemblance to Hemingway's novel, but that hardly mattered. In fact, with the dynamic combination of Bogart and Bacall, the film really didn't need much of a plot to carry it.

It was Lauren Bacall's film debut, and she was hailed as an up-and-coming star. Though an inexperienced actress, she managed to deliver one of filmdom's most memorable lines: 'If you want anything, just whistle. You know how to whistle, don't you, Steve? Just put your lips together and blow.'

Overleaf: Bogey and Bacall in a scene from **To Have and Have Not** (1945). Lauren Bacall began her career as a model for *Harper's Bazaar*. She was bestowed with the name Lauren because it fit her slim and sultry image better than her own name of Betty. She hated the name Lauren, and Bogey, as did all her friends, always called her Betty.

She was 19 when she first met Humphrey Bogart; he was 45. He had also been married three times before. None of that mattered. He had finally found the right woman.

These pages: Bogey and Bacall together again in **The Big Sleep** (1946). Based on Raymond Chandler's thriller, **The Big Sleep** featured Humphrey Bogart as hard-boiled detective Philip Marlowe and Lauren Bacall as Vivien Rutledge, the daughter of General Sternwood, who has hired Marlowe to handle a blackmail case.

The story involves nymphomania, pornography, drug addiction and insanity, and if that wasn't enough to confuse anybody, the plot was made even more convoluted because the Hays Production Code prohibited more than just a suggestion of the seamier side of life. Despite the shortcomings of the script (which William Faulkner co-wrote) Bogart and Bacall never fail to ignite the screen.

Overleaf: Bogart and Bacall in the restaurant scene from **The Big Sleep**.

Rex
MATCHES

On the set of Columbia's **Dead Reckoning** (1947), Humphrey Bogart (*facing page*) takes a break between scenes. During another lull in the action (*above*), Bogart is paid a visit by young Jeanie Morelli, the daughter of his stand-in, Mike Morelli.

These pages: The era of gangster films long behind him, Bogey was a well-established leading man by the time of **Dead Reckoning** (1947), and it was hard to imagine him as anything else. In this film, he romanced Lizabeth Scott, who was touted as a Lauren Bacall type.

These pages: With a little assistance from his wife, Lauren Bacall, Humphrey Bogart leaves his hand and footprints at Grauman's Chinese Theater, as proprietor Sid Grauman looks on. The date is 21 August 1946. In typical Bogey fashion, he has written a 'tough guy' message to Sid.

Today, Grauman's is known as Mann's Chinese Theater, and Bogey and Sid are both dead, but the Bogey legend lives on in his films and in this tribute for all his fans to see.

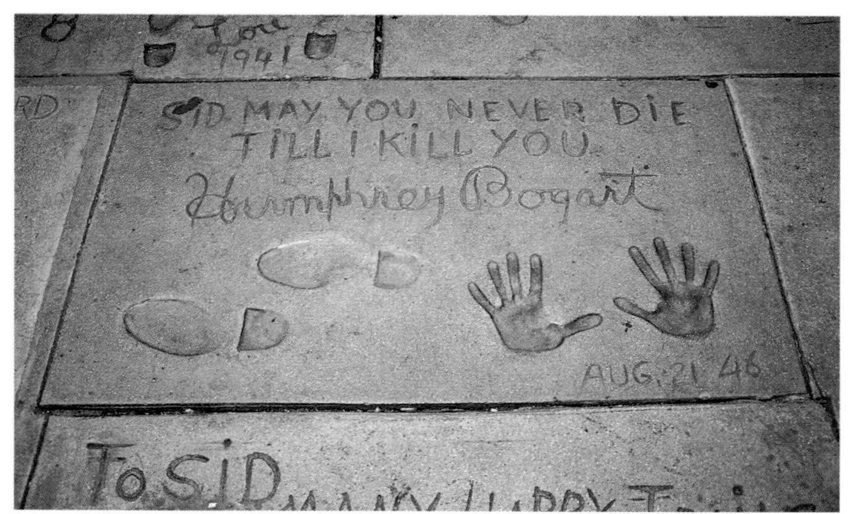

SID MAY YOU NEVER DIE
TILL I KILL YOU.
Humphrey Bogart
AUG. 21 46
TO SID

Above: Bogey, with Walter Huston, in what many people consider to be Bogey's finest film—**The Treasure of the Sierra Madre** (1948). Bogey played Dobbs, whose quest for gold leads to his death. The film marked another new stage in his career—from this point on, Bogart would play a range of diverse roles.

A tale of greed and paranoia, **The Treasure of the Sierra Madre** was directed by John Huston, who won two Academy Awards for the film—Best Director and Best Screenplay. His father, Walter Huston, who played Howard, the old prospector, also won an Oscar for Best Supporting Actor.

Facing page: Once again, Warner Bros paired Bogey and Bacall in **Dark Passage** (1947). Bogey played a man wrongly imprisoned for the murder of his wife. He escapes from prison but eventually must flee the country, with Lauren Bacall by his side.

These pages: **Key Largo** (1948) was the fourth and final film that Bogey and Bacall did together. Bogart played Frank McCloud, a former Army officer, who goes to Key Largo to visit James and Nora (Lauren Bacall) Temple, the father and widow of a friend killed in the war.

The hotel run by the Temples has been taken over by a notorious gangster, Johnny Rocco. Disillusioned by the war, McCloud is unwilling to fight for any cause and makes no attempt to stop Rocco. Eventually, however, he realizes that the forces of evil cannot be ignored and he kills Rocco as they head to Cuba. Frank then returns to Key Largo and the waiting Nora, who has fallen in love with him.

1816-EX-5

Above: Frank McCloud (Humphrey Bogart) offers a cigarette to Gaye Dawn (Claire Trevor). Trevor won an Academy Award for Best Supporting Actress for her portrayal of Johnny Rocco's alcoholic girl friend.

Facing page: Humphrey Bogart, Lauren Bacall and Edward G Robinson, who played the gangster Johnny Rocco, rehearse their lines. Once again Bogey found himself guided by the skillful direction of John Huston. All told, Huston directed Bogey in half a dozen films: **The Maltese Falcon** (1941), **Across the Pacific** (1942), **The Treasure of the Sierra Madre** (1948), **Key Largo** (1948), **The African Queen** (1951) and **Beat the Devil** (1954).

Above and below: Rehearsals for **Key Largo**. Bogart once said that the key to acting was concentration. When he worked, Bogey was all business, but when he left the set, he left his work behind him.

Above: **Key Largo** cast members review their lines.

Below: John Huston presides over a reading of the script.

In 1947, Humphrey Bogart formed his own production company, Santana Pictures Corporation (named after his boat), and appointed himself president, and producer Robert Lord (*above*) vice-president. Santana made four films starring Bogart for Columbia Pictures: **Knock on Any Door** (1949), **Tokyo Joe** (1949), **In a Lonely Place** (1950) and **Sirocco** (1951).

Bogey created Santana because he was dissatisfied with the quality of the films from Warner Bros. Unfortunately, none of the Santana films lived up to his expectations.

Facing page: The first Santana Production was **Knock on Any Door** (1949), with Bogey as the defense attorney for a young hoodlum accused of killing a policeman.

As an interesting aside, the part of the young criminal was played by John Derek, who would later achieve somewhat dubious fame directing his sex symbol wives, first Ursala Andress and then Bo Derek, in various films.

Above: Bogey's costar in **Tokyo Joe** (1949) was Florence Marly. The film was about a pilot who returns to Tokyo and the wife he deserted in 1941. In his absence, she divorced him and is now remarried with a seven-year-old daughter. Reflecting post-war sensibilities, the film was sharply divided between the good guys and the bad, with the Japanese as the bad.

Facing page: Bogey and Betty with their son, Steve. They chose the name Steve because that was what Betty's character called the Bogey character (who was really named Harry) in **To Have and Have Not**, their first film together.

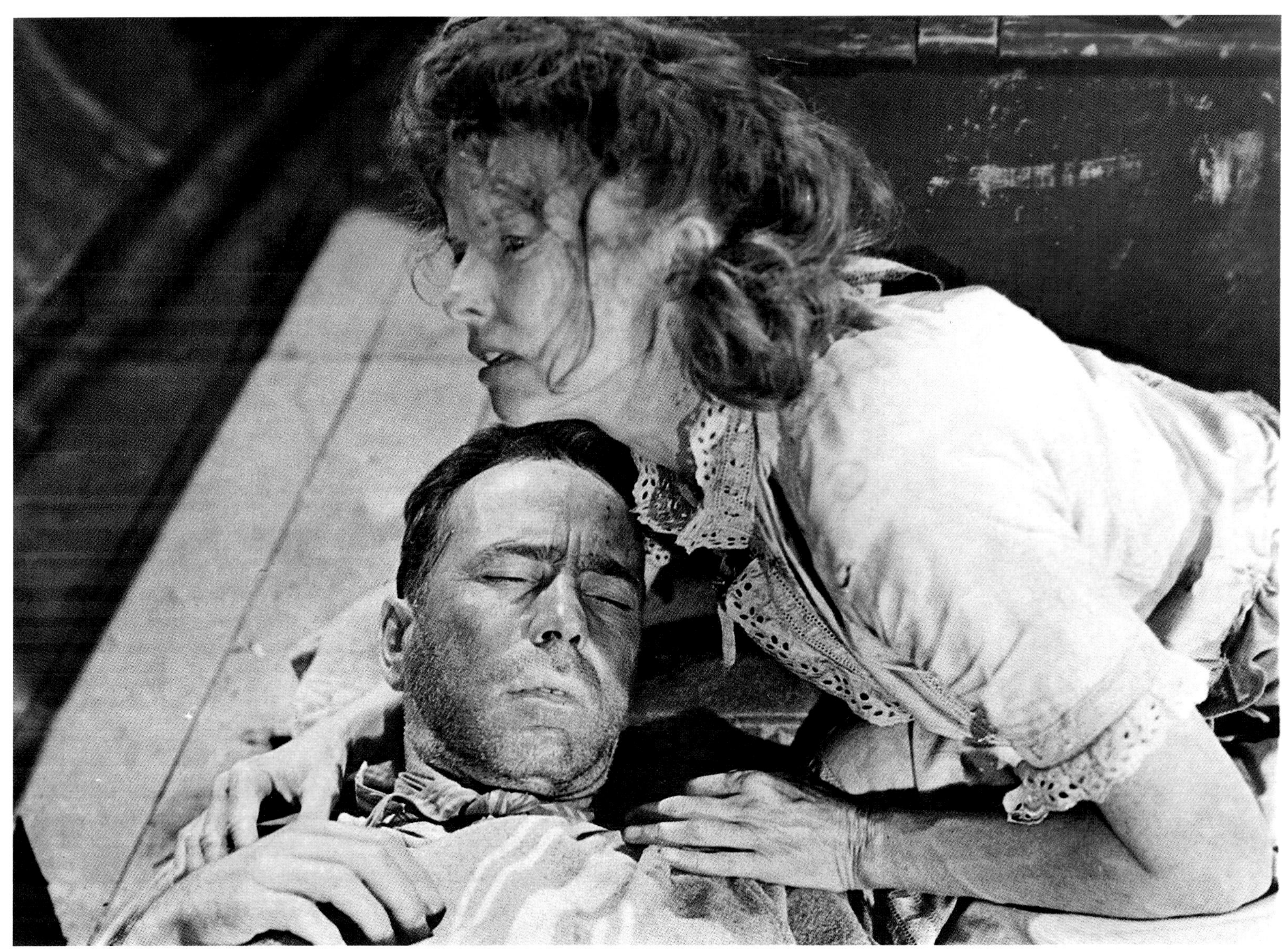

Above: Set in German East Africa at the outset of World War I, **The African Queen** (1951) tells the story of the unlikely romance between Charlie Allnut (Bogey), a hard-drinking skipper, and Rose Sayer (Katherine Hepburn), a teetotaling spinster. The two battle malaria, insects, leeches and rapids before taking on a German gunboat in a rickety old mailboat, the *African Queen*.

The cast endured similar hardships (minus the Germans), but their efforts were well rewarded. **The African Queen** was one of the top grossing movies of the year.

Above: The climax of the movie—Charlie and Rose are about to be executed.

Bogart was nominated for an Academy Award for his performance as Charlie Allnut, but everyone expected the Oscar to go to Marlon Brando for **A Streetcar Named Desire**. In fact, the night of the awards ceremony, it seemed that **Streetcar** would sweep the Oscars. Vivien Leigh won Best Actress, Karl Malden won Best Supporting Actor and Kim Hunter won Best Supporting Actress. Cheers erupted when Greer Garson announced that Bogart had won Best Actor. A stunned Humphrey Bogart trotted to the stage, gingerly took Oscar in his arms and said: 'It's a long way from the Belgian Congo to the stage of the Pantages, but it's a lot nicer here. I want to pay tribute to John Huston and Katherine Hepburn, who helped me to be where I am now.' Once backstage he recovered from his surprise and was able to serve up a few Bogey-like quips.

Nominations for Academy Awards also went to John Huston for Best Director and to James Agee (along with Huston) for Best Screenplay.

These pages: Bogey, Betty and two-year-old Steve at home. Fatherhood came late in life to Bogey, and he was apprehensive when he first heard the news, but once Stephen, and later Leslie, arrived, he took to the role with relish.

Dogs were also an important part of the Bogart household, but legend has it that the neighbors didn't share Bogey's enthusiasm for his beloved boxers.

Above: Young Stevie Bogart visits his dad on the set.

Facing page: In perhaps what was an attempt to evoke the atmosphere of **Casablanca** (1942), Bogey donned a trench coat for **Sirocco** (1951). The setting is French-occupied Damascus in 1925, with Bogey cast as a gunrunner.

Based on James Helvick's crime novel, **Beat the Devil** (1954) was intended to be another **Maltese Falcon** (1941), but somehow things didn't quite work out that way. Truman Capote, who was brought in to help salvage the script, added a dose of satire, but that didn't work either. The still *above* shows Humphrey Bogart with Jennifer Jones.

Facing page: Bogart as Captain Queeg in **The Caine Mutiny** (1954). The part of Queeg, a strict disciplinarian who cannot handle the stress of war, highlighted Bogart's skill as an actor and earned Bogey his third nomination for an Academy Award. Marlon Brando, who had lost to Bogart in the 1951 Academy Awards, won the Oscar for **On the Waterfront**.

Overleaf: Bogart in **The Caine Mutiny**. The film was based on Herman Wouk's best-selling novel.

Above and below: In a twist on the old gangster theme, Bogey played an escaped convict in **We're No Angels** (1955), a comedy.

Facing page: Bogey's next role was a downed pilot who disguises himself as a priest in **The Left Hand of God** (1955).

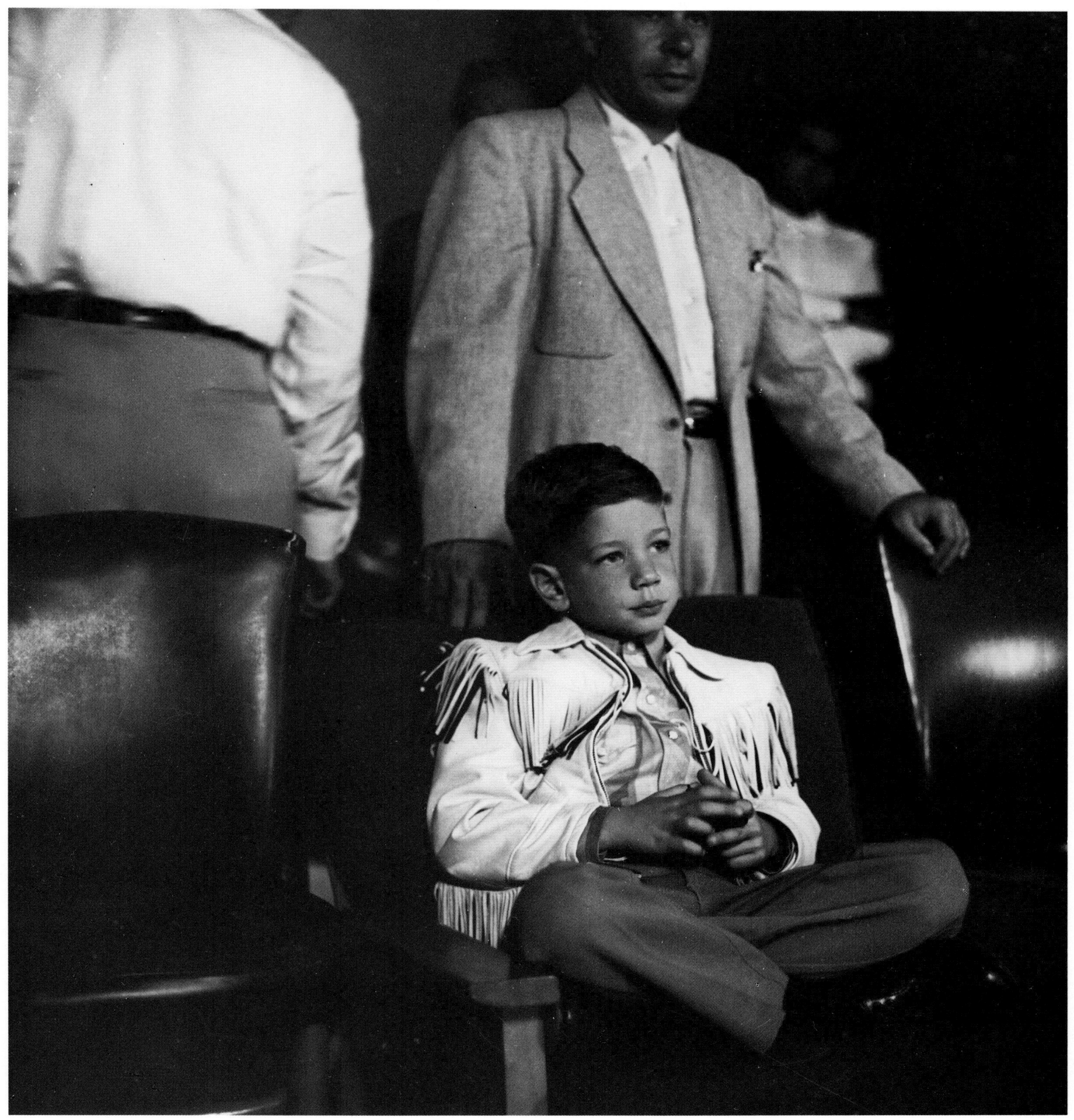

Facing page: **The Desperate Hours** (1955) gave Bogey the chance to revive the Duke Mantee image, and he proved that he still had the right touch. Indeed, the film was compared to **The Petrified Forest** (1936), and one critic described Bogart's performance as 'a fearful symbol of brute force.' In 1955, Bogart was once again among the top ten box office draws.

Above: Stephen Bogart, age six, watches his famous father film a scene from **The Harder They Fall** (1956), Bogey's final movie.

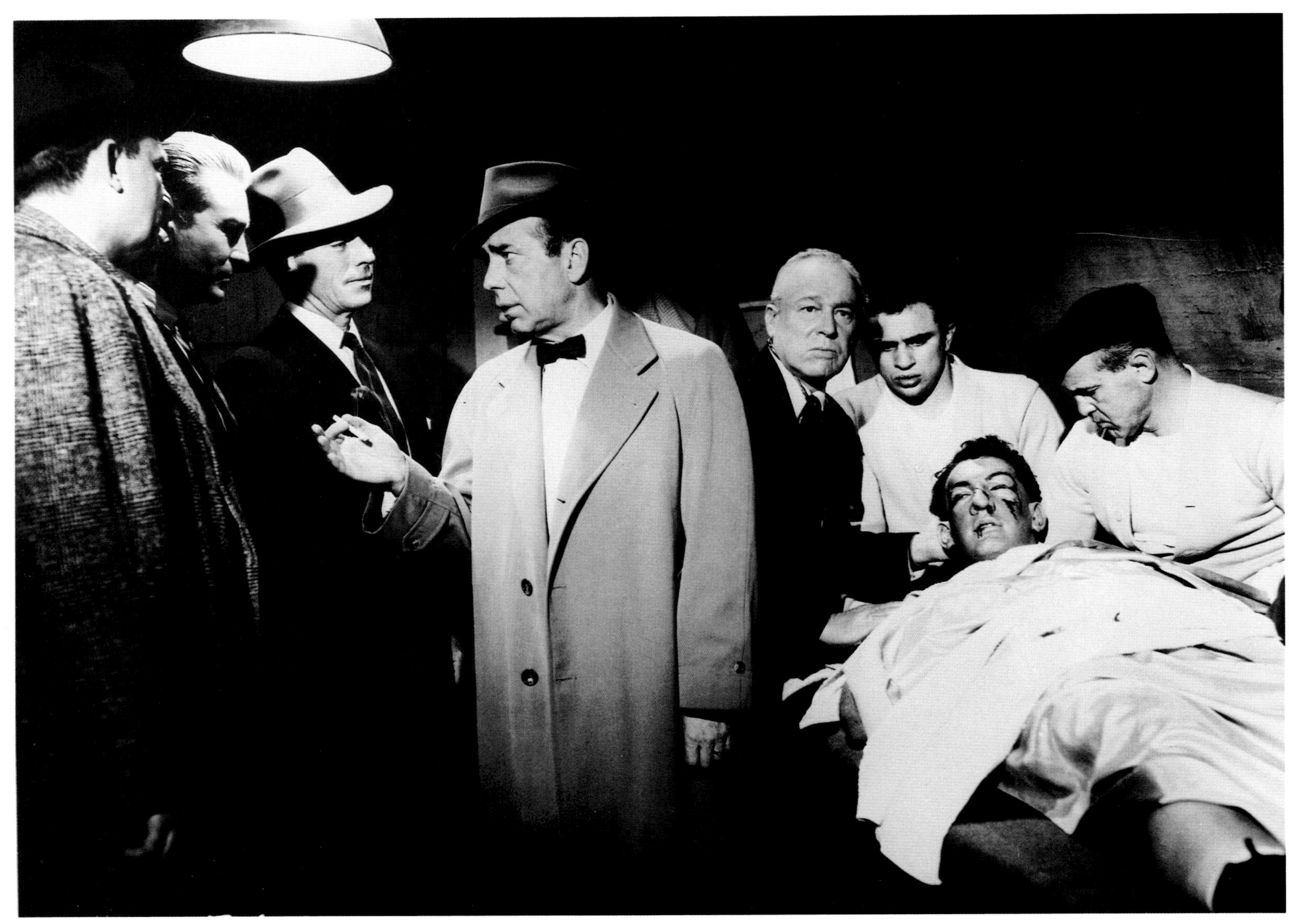

Above: In **The Harder They Fall** (1956), Bogart played an ex-sportswriter hired to promote Toro Moreno, a seven-foot tall boxer from Argentina. Despite Toro's formidable appearance, he lacks any real talent and is merely a pawn of the syndicate. The film concludes with Bogey's character vowing to write a series of articles to expose the syndicate.

Facing page: A publicity still of Bogey with Jan Sterling and Mike Lane, who played the boxer Toro Moreno.

Above: On 9 February 1960, three years after his death from cancer, Humphrey Bogart was honored with a star on Hollywood Boulevard.

Facing page: Over the course of his career, Humphrey Bogart made 75 feature films. Not all of them were good, and Bogey himself once remarked 'I made more lousy pictures than any actor in history.' But Bogey had that unnameable quality that makes one a star, and even a dozen mediocre films couldn't stop him from becoming a Hollywood legend.

Filmography

Broadway's Like That (1930)
A Devil With Women (1930)
Up the River (1930)
Body and Soul (1931)
Bad Sister (1931)
Women of All Nations (1931)
A Holy Terror (1931)
Love Affair (1932)
Big City Blues (1932)
Three on a Match (1932)
Midnight (1934)
The Petrified Forest (1936)
Bullets or Ballots (1936)
Two Against the World (1936)
China Clipper (1936)
Isle of Fury (1936)
Black Legion (1937)
The Great O'Malley (1937)
Marked Woman (1937)
Kid Galahad (1937)
San Quentin (1937)
Dead End (1937)
Stand-In (1937)
Swing Your Lady (1938)
Crime School (1938)
Men Are Such Fools (1938)
The Amazing Dr Clitterhouse (1938)
Racket Busters (1938)
Angels with Dirty Faces (1938)
King of the Underworld (1939)
The Oklahoma Kid (1939)
Dark Victory (1939)
You Can't Get Away with Murder (1939)
The Roaring Twenties (1939)
The Return of Doctor X (1939)
Invisible Stripes (1939)
Virginia City (1940)
It All Came True (1940)
Brother Orchid (1940)
They Drive by Night (1940)
High Sierra (1941)
The Wagons Roll at Night (1941)
The Maltese Falcon (1941)
All Through the Night (1942)
The Big Shot (1942)
Across the Pacific (1942)
Casablanca (1942)
Action in the North Pacific (1943)
Thank Your Lucky Stars (1943)
Sahara (1943)
Passage to Marseille (1944)
Report from the Front (1944, short)
To Have and Have Not (1945)
Conflict (1945)
Hollywood Victory Caravan (1945)
Two Guys from Milwaukee (1946)
The Big Sleep (1946)
Dead Reckoning (1947)
The Two Mrs Carrolls (1947)
Dark Passage (1947)
Always Together (1948)
The Treasure of the Sierra Madre (1948)
Key Largo (1948)
Knock on Any Door (1949)
Tokyo Joe (1949)
Chain Lightning (1950)
In a Lonely Place (1950)
The Enforcer (1951)
Sirocco (1951)
The African Queen (1951)
Deadline—USA (1952)
Battle Circus (1953)
Beat the Devil (1954)
The Caine Mutiny (1954)
Sabrina (1954)
The Barefoot Contessa (1954)
We're No Angels (1955)
The Left Hand of God (1955)
The Desperate Hours (1955)
The Harder They Fall (1956)

Index

Page 112: Humphrey Bogart as Sam Spade, the archetypal hard-boiled detective, in **The Maltese Falcon** (1941).